C# DESIGN PATTERNS

C# DESIGN PATTERNS

A Tutorial

James W. Cooper

Addison-Wesley

Boston • San Francisco • New York • Toronto • Montreal
London • Munich • Paris • Madrid
Capetown • Sydney • Tokyo • Singapore • Mexico City

The publisher offers discounts on this book when ordered in quantity for special sales. For more information, please contact:

U.S. Corporate and Government Sales
(800) 382-3419
corpsales@pearsontechgroup.com

For sales outside of the U.S., please contact:

International Sales
(317) 581-3793
international@pearsontechgroup.com

Visit Addison-Wesley on the Web: www.awprofessional.com

Library of Congress Cataloging-in-Publication Data

Cooper, James William, 1943–
    C# design patterns : a tutorial / James W. Cooper.
      p. cm.
    Includes bibliographical references and index.
    ISBN 0-201-84453-2 (alk. paper)
     1. C# (Computer program language) 2. Software patterns. I. Title.

    QA76.73.C154 C664 2003
    005.13'3—dc21   2002074380

Text printed on recycled and acid-free paper.

ISBN 0201844532

3 4 5 6 7 8   CRS   06 05 04 03

3rd Printing   August 2003

CONTENTS

PREFACE

This is a practical book that tells you how to write C# programs using some of the most common design patterns. It also serves as a quick introduction to programming in the new C# language. The pattern discussions are structured as a series of short chapters, each describing a design pattern and giving one or more complete working, visual example programs that use that pattern. Each chapter also includes UML diagrams illustrating how the classes interact.

This book is not a "companion" book to the well-known *Design Patterns* text by the "Gang of Four." Instead, it is a tutorial for people who want to learn what design patterns are about and how to use them in their work. You do not have to have read *Design Patterns* to read this book, but when you are done here, you may well want to read or reread it to gain additional insights.

In this book, you will learn that design patterns are frequently used ways of organizing objects in your programs to make them easier to write and modify. You'll also see that by familiarizing yourself with them, you've gained some valuable vocabulary for discussing how your programs are constructed.

People come to appreciate design patterns in different ways—from the highly theoretical to the intensely practical—and when they finally see the great power of these patterns, an "Aha!" moment occurs. Usually this is the moment when you discover how that pattern can help you in *your* work.

In this book, we try to help you form that conceptual idea, or *gestalt,* by describing the pattern in as many ways as possible. The book is organized into six main sections: an introductory description, an introduction to C#, and descriptions of patterns that are grouped as creational, structural, and behavioral.

For each pattern, we start with a brief verbal description and then build simple example programs. Each of these examples is a visual program that you can run and examine to make the pattern as concrete a concept as possible. All of the example programs and their variations are on the companion CD-ROM, where you run them, change them, and see how the variations you create work.

Since each of the examples consists of a number of C# files for each of the classes we use in that example, we provide a C# project file for each example and place each example in a separate subdirectory to prevent any confusion. This book assumes you have and will be using a copy of Visual Studio.NET, which comes in several versions. We used the Professional Edition in developing the code samples.

If you leaf through the book, you'll see screenshots of the programs we developed to illustrate the design patterns, providing yet another way to reinforce your learning of these patterns. In addition, you'll see UML diagrams of these programs, illustrating the interactions between classes in yet another way. UML diagrams are just simple box-and-arrow illustrations of classes and their inheritance structure, where arrows point to parent classes, and dotted arrows point to interfaces. And if you're not yet familiar with UML, we provide a simple introduction in the second chapter. All of the diagrams were produced using WithClass 2000, and a demonstration version of that program is included on the CD-ROM.

When you finish this book, you'll be comfortable with the basics of design patterns and will be able to start using them in your day-to-day C# programming work.

James W. Cooper
Nantucket, MA
Wilton, CT
Kona, HI

ACKNOWLEDGMENTS

I'd like to thank Bob Mack and Alan Marwick for their support of my study of Design Patterns, and Java and .NET in general, and John Vlissides for suggesting that I write these books in the first place. I also want to acknowledge helpful suggestions from any number of people who read the manuscript, including V. S. Rajesh, Howard Harkness, Zane Thomas, Jay Harlow, Mike McCann, Devin Jensen, Cleveland Gibbon, Fred Mellender, Gerald Aden, and Yazid Areki. Finally, I could never have written these books without the continuing support of my wife, Vicki.

PART I

Object-Oriented Programming in C#

The first section of this book introduces the C# language and the principles of object-oriented programming in general. We cover the syntax of C# and how to create simple programs. Then we discuss classes, objects, inheritance, and interfaces and explain the fundamentals of UML diagrams. By the time you've finished this introductory section, you should feel quite at home in C# and OO programming and ready to learn how to use Design Patterns in your programming.

CHAPTER 1

What Are Design Patterns?

Sitting at your desk in front of your workstation, you stare into space, trying to figure out how to write a new program feature. You know intuitively what must be done, what data and what objects come into play, but you have this underlying feeling that there is a more elegant and general way to write this program.

In fact, you probably don't write any code until you can build a picture in your mind of what the code does and how the pieces of the code interact. The more that you can picture this "organic whole," or *gestalt,* the more likely you are to feel comfortable that you have developed the best solution to the problem. If you don't grasp this whole right away, you may keep staring out the window for a time, even though the basic solution to the problem is quite obvious.

In one sense you feel that the more elegant solution will be more reusable and more maintainable, but even if you are the sole likely programmer, you feel reassured once you have designed a solution that is relatively elegant and that doesn't expose too many internal inelegancies.

One of the main reasons that computer science researchers began to recognize design patterns is to satisfy this need for elegant, but simple, reusable solutions. The term *design patterns* sounds a bit formal to the uninitiated and can be somewhat offputting when you first encounter it. But, in fact, design patterns are just convenient ways of reusing object-oriented code between projects and between programmers. The idea behind design patterns is simple: write down and catalog common interactions between objects that programmers have frequently found useful.

One of the frequently cited patterns from early literature on programming frameworks is the Model-View-Controller framework for Smalltalk (Krasner and Pope 1988), which divided the user interface problem into three parts, as shown in Figure 1-1. The parts were referred to as a *data model,* which contains the computational parts of the program; the *view,* which presented the user interface; and the *controller,* which interacted between the user and the view.

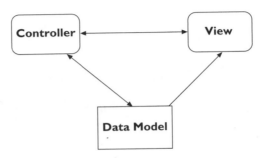

Figure 1-1   The Model-View-Controller framework

Each of these aspects of the problem is a separate object, and each has its own rules for managing its data. Communication among the user, the GUI, and the data should be carefully controlled, and this separation of functions accomplished that very nicely. Three objects talking to each other using this restrained set of connections is an example of a powerful design pattern.

In other words, design patterns describe how objects communicate without become entangled in each other's data models and methods. Keeping this separation has always been an objective of good OO programming, and if you have been trying to keep objects minding their own business, you are probably using some of the common design patterns already.

Design patterns began to be recognized more formally in the early 1990s by Eric Gamma (1992), who described patterns incorporated in the GUI application framework, ET++. The culmination of these discussions and a number of technical meetings was the publication of the parent book in this series, *Design Patterns: Elements of Reusable Software,* by Gamma et al. (1995). This book, commonly referred to as the "Gang of Four," or "GoF," book, has had a powerful impact on those seeking to understand how to use design patterns and has become an all-time bestseller. It describes 23 commonly occurring and generally useful patterns and comments on how and when you might apply them. We will refer to this groundbreaking book as *Design Patterns* throughout this book.

Since the publication of the original *Design Patterns* text, there have been a number of other useful books published. One closely related book is *The Design Patterns Smalltalk Companion* (Alpert, Brown, and Woolf 1998), which covers the same 23 patterns from the Smalltalk point of view. We'll refer to this book throughout as the *Smalltalk Companion.* Finally, we recently published *Java Design Patterns: A Tutorial* and *Visual Basic Design Patterns: VB6 and VB.NET,* which illustrate all of these patterns in those languages (Cooper 2000, 2002).

Defining Design Patterns

We all talk about the way we do things in our jobs, hobbies, and home life, and we recognize repeating patterns all the time.

- Sticky buns are like dinner rolls, but I add brown sugar and nut filling to them.
- Her front garden is like mine, but I grow astilbe in my garden.
- This end table is constructed like that one, but in this one, there are doors instead of drawers.

We see the same thing in programming when we tell a colleague how we accomplished a tricky bit of programming so he doesn't have to recreate it from scratch. We simply recognize effective ways for objects to communicate while maintaining their own separate existences.

Some useful definitions of design patterns have emerged as the literature in this field has expanded.

- Design patterns are recurring solutions to design problems you see over and over. *(The Smalltalk Companion)*
- Design patterns constitute a set of rules describing how to accomplish certain tasks in the realm of software development. (Pree 1995)
- Design patterns focus more on reuse of recurring architectural design themes, while frameworks focus on detailed design and implementation. (Coplien and Schmidt 1995)
- A pattern addresses a recurring design problem that arises in specific design situations and presents a solution to it. (Buschmann et al. 1996)
- Patterns identify and specify abstractions that are above the level of single classes and instances or of components. (Gamma, Johnson, and Vlissides, 1993)

But while it is helpful to draw analogies to architecture, cabinetmaking, and logic, design patterns are not just about the design of objects but about the *interaction* between objects. One possible view of some of these patterns is to consider them as *communication patterns*.

Some other patterns deal not just with object communication but with strategies for object inheritance and containment. It is the design of simple, but elegant, methods of interaction that makes many design patterns so important.

Design patterns can exist at many levels from very low-level, specific solutions to broadly generalized system issues. There are now hundreds of patterns in the literature. They have been discussed in articles and at conferences of all levels of granularity. Some are examples that apply widely, and a few writers have ascribed pattern behavior to class groupings that apply to just a single problem (Kurata 1998).

It has become apparent that you don't just *write* a design pattern off the top of your head. In fact, most such patterns are *discovered* rather than written. The process of looking for these patterns is called "pattern mining," and it is worthy of a book of its own.

The 23 design patterns covered in the original *Design Patterns* book had several known applications and were on a middle level of generality, where they could easily cross application areas and encompass several objects.

The authors divided these patterns into three types: creational, structural, and behavioral.

- *Creational patterns* create objects for you rather than having you instantiate objects directly. This gives your program more flexibility in deciding which objects need to be created for a given case.
- *Structural patterns* help you compose groups of objects into larger structures, such as complex user interfaces or accounting data.
- *Behavioral patterns* help you define the communication between objects in your system and how the flow is controlled in a complex program.

We'll be looking at C# versions of these patterns in the chapters that follow, and we will provide at least one complete C# program for each of the 23 patterns. This way you can examine the code snippets provided and also run, edit, and modify the complete working programs on the accompanying CD-ROM. You'll find a list of all the programs on the CD-ROM at the end of each pattern description.

The Learning Process

We have found that, regardless of the language, learning design patterns is a three-step process.

1. Acceptance

2. Recognition

3. Internalization

First, you accept the premise that design patterns are important in your work. Then, you recognize that you need to read about design patterns so you will know when you need them. Finally, you internalize the patterns in sufficient detail that you know which ones might help you solve a given design problem.

For some lucky people, design patterns are obvious tools, and these people can grasp their essential utility just by reading summaries of the patterns. For many of the rest of us, there is a slow induction period after we've read about a pattern followed by the proverbial "Aha!" when we see how we can apply them in our work. This book takes you to that final stage of internalization by providing complete, working programs that you can try out yourself.

The examples in *Design Patterns* are brief and are in C++ or, in some cases, Smalltalk. If you are working in another language, it is helpful to have the pattern examples in your language of choice. This book attempts to fill that need for C# programmers.

Studying Design Patterns

There are several alternate ways to become familiar with these patterns. In each approach, you should read this book and the parent *Design Patterns* book in one order or the other. We also strongly urge you to read the *Smalltalk Companion* for completeness, since it provides alternative descriptions of each of the patterns. Finally, there are a number of Web sites for you to peruse on learning and discussing design patterns.

Notes on Object-Oriented Approaches

The fundamental reason for using design patterns is to keep classes separated and prevent them from having to know too much about one another. Equally important, using these patterns helps you avoid reinventing the wheel and allows you to describe your programming approach succinctly in terms other programmers can easily understand.

There are a number of strategies that OO programmers use to achieve this separation, among them encapsulation and inheritance. Nearly all languages that have OO capabilities support inheritance. A class that inherits from a parent class has access to all of the methods of that parent class and to all of its nonprivate variables. However, by starting your inheritance hierarchy with a complete, working class, you may be unduly restricting yourself as well as carrying along specific method implementation baggage. Instead, *Design Patterns* suggests that you always do the following.

Program to an interface and not to an implementation.

Putting this more succinctly, you should define the top of any class hierarchy with an *abstract* class or an *interface,* which implements no methods but simply defines the methods that class will support. Then in all of your derived classes you have more freedom to implement these methods as most suits your purposes.

The other major concept you should recognize is that of *object composition*. This is simply the construction of objects that contain others: encapsulation of several objects inside another one. While many beginning OO programmers use inheritance to solve every problem, as you begin to write more elaborate programs, you will begin to appreciate the merits of object composition. Your new object can have the interface that is best for what you want to accomplish without having all the methods of the parent classes. Thus, this is the second major precept suggested by *Design Patterns*.

Favor object composition over inheritance.

C# Design Patterns

This book discusses each of the 23 patterns presented in *Design Patterns* and provides at least one working program example for that pattern. All of the programs have some sort of visual interface to make them that much more immediate to you. All of them also use class, interfaces, and object composition, but the programs themselves are of necessity quite simple so that the coding doesn't obscure the fundamental elegance of the patterns described.

However, even though C# is our target language, this isn't specifically a book on the C# language. There are a few features of C# that we don't cover, but we do cover most of what is central to C#. You will find, however, that this is a fairly useful tutorial in object-oriented programming in C# and provides a good overview of how to program in C#.

How This Book Is Organized

Chapters 1 through 7 introduce the fundamentals of the C# language and the whole concept of object-oriented (OO) programming and inheritance. We also show you how objects are represented in UML class diagrams.

Then we examine each of the 23 patterns, which are grouped into the general categories of creational, structural, and behavioral patterns. Many of the patterns stand more or less independently, but we do take advantage of already discussed patterns from time to time. For example, we use the Factory and Command patterns extensively after introducing them, and we use the Mediator pattern several times after we introduce it. We use the Memento again in the State pattern, the Chain of Responsibility in the Interpreter pattern discussion, and the Singleton pattern in the Flyweight pattern discussion. In no case do we use a pattern before we have introduced it formally.

We also take some advantage of the sophistication of later patterns to introduce new features of C#. For example, the Listbox, DataGrid, and TreeView are introduced in the Adapter and Bridge patterns. We show how to paint graphics objects in the Abstract Factory. We introduce the Enumeration interface in the Iterator and in the Composite, where we also take up formatting. We use exceptions in the Singleton pattern and discuss ADO.NET database connections in the Façade pattern. And we show you how to use C# timers in the Proxy pattern.

The overall .NET system is designed for fairly elaborate Web-based client-server interactions, but this book concentrates on object-oriented programming issues in general rather than how to write Web-based systems. We cover the core issues of C# programming and show simple examples of how Design Patterns can help write better programs.

CHAPTER 2

Syntax of the C# Language

C# has all the features of any powerful, modern language. If you are familiar with Java, C, or C++, you'll find most of C#'s syntax very familiar. If you have been working in Visual Basic or related areas, you should read this chapter to see how C# differs from VB. You'll quickly see that every major operation you can carry out in Visual Basic.NET has a similar operation in C#.

The two major differences between C# and Visual Basic are (1) C# is *case sensitive* (most of its syntax is written in *lowercase*), and (2) every statement in C# is terminated with a semicolon (;). Thus, C# statements are not constrained to a single line, and there is no line continuation character.

In Visual Basic, we could write the following.

```
y = m * x + b        'compute y for given x
```

Or we could write this.

```
Y = M * X + b        'compute y for given x
```

Both would be treated as the same. The variables *Y*, *M*, and *X* are the same whether written in upper- or lowercase. In C#, however, case is significant, and if we write this

```
y = m * x + b;          //all lowercase
```

or this

```
Y = m * x + b;          //Y differs from y
```

we mean two different variables: *Y* and *y*. While this may seem awkward at first, you should find that it is helpful to be able to use case to make distinctions. For example, programmers often capitalize symbols that refer to constants.

```
Const PI = 3.1416 As Single in VB
const float PI = 3.1416;    // in C#
```

The *const* modifier in C# means that the named value is a constant and cannot be modified.

Programmers also sometimes define data types with mixed case and variables of that data type with lowercase.

```
class Temperature {        //begin definition of
                           //new data type
Temperature temp;          //temp is of this new type
```

We'll cover classes in much more detail in the chapters that follow.

Data Types

The major data types in C# are shown in Table 2-1. Note that the lengths of these basic types are not related to the computer type or operating system. Characters and strings in C# are always 16 bits wide to allow for representation of characters in non-Latin languages. It uses a character coding system called Unicode, in which thousands of characters for most major written languages have been defined. You can convert between variable types in the usual ways.

Table 2-1   Data Types in C#

bool	true or false
byte	unsigned 8-bit value
short	16-bit integer
int	32-bit integer
long	64-bit integer
float	32-bit floating point
double	64-bit floating point
char	16-bit character
string	16-bit characters

- Any wider data type can have a narrower data type (having fewer bytes) assigned directly to it, and the promotion to the new type will occur automatically. If *y* is of type float and *j* is of type int, then you can promote an integer to a float in the following way.

```
float y = 7.0f;        //y is of type float
int j = 5;             //j is of type int
y = j;                 //convert int to float
```

- You can reduce a wider type (more bytes) to a narrower type by *casting* it. You do this by enclosing the data type name in parentheses and putting it in front of the value you wish to convert.

```
j = (int)y;            //convert float to integer
```

You can also write legal statements that contain casts that might fail.

```
float x = 1.0E45;
int k = (int) x;
```

If the cast fails, an exception error will occur when the program is executed.

Boolean variables can only take on the values represented by the reserved words *true* and *false*. Boolean variables also commonly receive values as a result of comparisons and other logical operations.

```
int k;
boolean gtnum;

gtnum = (k > 6);       //true if k is greater than 6
```

Unlike C or C++, you cannot assign numeric values to a Boolean variable and you cannot convert between Boolean and any other type.

Converting between Numbers and Strings

To make a string from a number or a number from a string, you can use the Convert methods. You can usually find the right one by simply typing "Convert" and a dot in the development environment, and the system will provide you with a list of likely methods.

```
string s = Convert.ToString (x);
float y = Convert.ToSingle (s);
```

Note that "Single" means a single-precision floating point number.

Numeric objects also provide various kinds of formatting options to specify the number of decimal places.

```
float x = 12.341514325f;
string s = x.ToString ("###.###");           //gives 12.342
```

Declaring Multiple Variables

You should note that in C# you can declare a number of variables of the same type in a single statement.

```
int i, j;
float x, y, z;
```

This is unlike VB6, where you had to specify the type of each variable as you declare it.

```
Dim i As Integer, j As Integer
Dim x As Single, y As Single, z As Single
```

Many programmers find, however, that it is clearer to declare each variable on a single line so they can comment on each one specifically.

```
int i;          //used as an outer loop index
int j;          //the index for the y variables
float x;        //the ordinate variable
```

Numeric Constants

Any number you type into your program is automatically of type int if it has no fractional part or type *double* if it does. If you want to indicate that it is a different type, you can use various suffix and prefix characters.

```
float loan = 1.23f;     //float
long pig   = 45L;       //long
int color = 0x12345;    //hexadecimal
```

C# also has three reserved word constants: *true*, *false*, and *null*, where *null* means an object variable that does not yet refer to any object. We'll learn more about objects in the following chapters.

Character Constants

You can represent individual characters by enclosing them in single quotes.

```
char c = 'q';
```

C# follows the C convention that *white space characters* (nonprinting characters that cause the printing position to change) can be represented by preceding special characters with a backslash, as shown in Table 2-2. Since in this case the backslash itself is a special character, it can be represented by using a double backslash.

Table 2-2   Representations of White Space and Special Characters

\n	newline (line feed)
\r	carriage return
\t	tab character
\b	backspace
\f	form feed
\0	null character
\"	double quote
\'	single quote
\\	backslash

Variables

Variable names in C# can be of any length and can be of any combination of upper- and lowercase letters and numbers, but, like VB, the first character must be a letter. Note that since case is significant in C#, the following variable names all refer to different variables.

```
temperature
Temperature
TEMPERATURE
```

You must declare all C# variables that you use in a program before you use them.

```
int j;
float temperature;
boolean quit;
```

Declaring Variables as You Use Them

C# also allows you to declare variables just as you need them, rather than requiring that they be declared at the top of a procedure.

```
int k = 5;
float x = k + 3 * y;
```

This is very common in the object-oriented programming style, where we might declare a variable inside a loop that has no existence or *scope* outside that local spot in the program.

Multiple Equal Signs for Initialization

C#, like C, allows you to initialize a series of variables to the same value in a single statement.

```
i = j = k = 0;
```

This can be confusing, so don't overuse this feature. The compiler will generate the same code for

```
i = 0; j = 0; k = 0;
```

whether the statements are on the same or successive lines.

A Simple C# Program

Now let's look at a very simple C# program for adding two numbers together. This program is a stand-alone program, or application.

```
using System;
class add2
    {
        static void Main(string[] args)
        {
            double a, b, c;  //declare variables
            a = 1.75;        //assign values
            b = 3.46;
            c = a + b;       //add together
            //print out sum
            Console.WriteLine ("sum = " + c);
        }
    }
```

This is a complete program as it stands, and if you compile it with the C# compiler and run it, it will print out the result.

```
sum = 5.21
```

Let's see what observations we can make about this simple program.

1. You must use the *using* statement to define libraries of C# code that you want to use in your program. This is similar to the imports statement in VB and the import statement in Java. It is also similar to the C and C++ #include directive.

2. The program starts from a function called Main, and it must have *exactly* the following form.

```
static void Main(string[] args)
```

3. Every program module must contain one or more classes.

4. The class and each function within the class is surrounded by *braces* { }.

5. Every variable must be declared by type before or by the time it is used. You could just as well have written the following.

```
double a = 1.75;
double b = 3.46;
double c = a + b;
```

6. Every statement must terminate with a semicolon. Statements can go on for several lines, but they must terminate with the semicolon.

7. Comments start with // and terminate at the end of the line.

8. Like most other languages (except Pascal), the equal sign is used to represent assignment of data.

9. You can use the + sign to combine two strings. The string "sum =" is concatenated, with the string automatically converted from the double precision variable c.

10. The writeLine function, which is a member of the Console class in the System namespace, can be used to print values on the screen.

This simple program is called add2.cs. You can compile and execute it in the development environment by just pressing F5.

Arithmetic Operators

The fundamental operators in C# are much the same as they are in most other modern languages. Table 2-3 lists the fundamental operators in C#.

The bitwise and logical operators are derived from C (see Table 2-4). *Bitwise operators* operate on individual bits of two words, producing a result based on an AND, OR or NOT operation. These are distinct from the Boolean operators because they operate on a logical condition that evaluates to *true* or *false*.

Table 2-3   C# Arithmetic Operators

+	addition
–	subtraction, unary minus
*	multiplication
/	division
%	modulo (remainder after integer division)

Table 2-4   Logical Operators in C#

&	bitwise And
|	bitwise Or
^	bitwise exclusive Or
~	one's complement
>> *n*	right shift *n* places
<< *n*	left shift *n* places

Increment and Decrement Operators

Like Java and C/C++ , C# allows you to express incrementing and decrementing of integer variables using the ++ and –– operators. You can apply these to the variable before or after you use it.

```
i = 5;
j = 10;
x = i++;        //x = 5, then i = 6
y = --j;        //y = 9 and j = 9
z = ++i;        //z = 7 and i = 7
```

Combining Arithmetic and Assignment Statements

C# allows you to combine addition, subtraction, multiplication, and division with the assignment of the result to a new variable.

```
x = x + 3;              //can also be written as:
x += 3;                 //add 3 to x; store result in x
```

```
//also with the other basic operations:
temp *= 1.80;        //mult temp by 1.80
z -= 7;              //subtract 7 from z
y /= 1.3;            //divide y by 1.3
```

This is used primarily to save typing; it is unlikely to generate any different code. Of course, these compound operators (as well as the ++ and –– operators) cannot have spaces between them.

Making Decisions in C#

The familiar if-then-else of Visual Basic, Pascal, and Fortran has its analog in C#. Note that in C#, however, we do not use the *then* keyword.

```
if ( y > 0 )
  z = x / y;
```

Parentheses around the condition are *required* in C#. This format can be somewhat deceptive. As written, only the single statement following the if is operated on by the if statement. If you want to have several statements as part of the condition, you must enclose them in braces.

```
if ( y > 0 )
  {
  z = x / y;
  Console.writeLine("z =  " + z);
  }
```

By contrast, if you write

```
if ( y > 0 )
  z = x / y;
  Console.writeLine("z =  " + z);
```

the C# program will always print out z= and some number because the if clause only operates on the single statement that follows. As you can see, indenting does not affect the program; it does what you say, not what you mean.

For this reason, we generally advise enclosing *all* if statements in braces, even when they refer to only a single line.

```
if ( y > 0 )
{
  z = x / y;
}
```

If you want to carry out either one set of statements or another depending on a single condition, you should use the else clause along with the if statement.

```
if ( y > 0 )
{
  z = x / y;
}
else
{
  z = 0;
}
```

If the else clause contains multiple statements, they must be enclosed in braces, as in the preceding code.

There are two accepted indentation styles for braces in C# programs. This is one.

```
if (y >0 )
    {
    z = x / y;
    }
```

The other style, popular among C programmers, places the brace at the end of the if statement and the ending brace directly under the if.

```
if ( y > 0 ) {
  z = x / y;
  Console.writeLine("z=" + z);
}
```

You will see both styles widely used, and, of course, they compile to produce the same result.

You can set options in Visual Studio.NET to select which formatting method to use. In the Tools | Options menu, select the Text editor | C# folder and select formatting. Check the box marked "Leave open braces" on the same line as construct if you want the second style above, and leave it unchecked if you want the first style.

Comparison Operators

Previously, we used the > operator to mean "greater than." Most of these operators are the same in C# as they are in C and other languages. In Table 2-5, note particularly that "is equal to" requires *two* equal signs and that "is not equal to" is different from in FORTRAN or VB.

Table 2-5   Comparison Operators in C#

>	greater than
<	less than
==	is equal to
!=	is not equal to
>=	greater than or equal to
<=	less than or equal to

Combining Conditions

When you need to combine two or more conditions in a single if or other logical statement, you use the symbols for the logical and, or, and not operators (see Table 2-6). These are totally different from any other languages except C/C++ and are confusingly like the bitwise operators shown in Table 2-6.

So, while we would write the following in VB.Net

```
If ( 0 < x) And (x <= 24) Then
  Console.writeLine ("Time is up")
```

we would write this in C#

```
if ( (0 < x) && ( x <= 24) )
  Console.writeLine("Time is up");
```

The Most Common Mistake

Since the is equal to operator is == and the assignment operator is =, they can easily be used incorrectly. If you write

Table 2-6   Boolean Operators in C#

&&	logical And
||	logical Or
~	logical Not

```
if (x = 0)
  Console.writeLine("x is zero");
```

> instead of

```
if (x == 0)
  Console.writeLine("x is zero");
```

you will get the confusing compilation error "Cannot implicitly convert double to bool" because the result of the fragment

```
(x = 0)
```

is the double precision number 0 rather than a Boolean true or false. Of course, the result of the fragment

```
(x == 0)
```

is indeed a Boolean quantity, and the compiler does not print any error message.

The Switch Statement

The switch statement allows you to provide a list of possible values for a variable and code to execute if each is true. In C#, however, the variable you compare in a switch statement must be either an integer, a character, or a string type and must be enclosed in parentheses.

```
switch ( j ) {
  case 12:
    System.out.println("Noon");
    break;
  case 13:
    System.out.println("1 PM");      "
    break;
  default:
    System.out.println("some other time...");
}
```

Note particularly that a *break* statement *must* follow each case in the switch statement. This is very important, since it says "go to the end of the switch statement." If you leave out the break statement, a compilation error occurs.

If control can be transferred to the end of the switch statement without a match being found, an error occurs. You must provide a *default* case for all switch statements.

C# Comments

As you have already seen, comments in C# start with a double forward slash and continue to the end of the current line. C# also recognizes C-style comments, which begin with /* and continue through any number of lines until the */ symbols are found.

```
//C# single-line comment
/*other C# comment style*/
/* also can go on
for any number of lines*/
```

You cannot nest C# comments. Once a comment begins in one style, it continues until that style concludes.

When you are learning a new language, your initial reaction may be to ignore comments, but those at the beginning are just as important as later ones. A program never gets commented at all unless you do it as you write it, and if you ever want to use that code again, you'll be glad to have some comments that help you decipher what you meant for it to do. For this reason, many programming instructors refuse to accept programs that are not thoroughly commented.

The Ornery Ternary Operator

C# has unfortunately inherited one of C/C++'s and Java's most opaque constructions: the ternary operator. This statement

```
if ( a > b )
  z = a;
else
  z = b;
```

can be written extremely compactly as

```
z = (a > b) ? a : b;
```

Like the postincrement operators, this statement was originally introduced into the C language to give hints to the compiler so it would produce more efficient code and to reduce typing when terminals were very slow. Today, modern compilers produce identical code for both forms just shown, and the necessity for this turgidity is long gone. Some C programmers coming to C# consider this an "elegant" abbreviation, but we don't, and we do not use it in this book.

Looping Statements in C#

C# has four looping statements: while, do-while, for, and foreach. Each of them provides a way to specify that a group of statements should be executed until some condition is satisfied.

The While Loop

The while loop is easy to understand. All of the statements inside the braces are executed as long as the condition is true.

```
i = 0;
while ( i < 100)
   {
    x = x + i++;
   }
```

Since the loop is executed as long as the condition is true, it is possible that such a loop may never be executed at all, and, of course, if you are not careful, that such a while loop will never be completed.

The Do-While Statement

The C# do-while statement is quite analogous, except in this case the loop must always be executed at least once, since the test is at the bottom of the loop.

```
i = 0;
do  {
    x += i++;
}
while (i < 100);
```

The For Loop

The for loop is the most structured. It has three parts: an initializer, a condition, and an operation that takes place each time through the loop. Each of these sections are separated by semicolons.

```
for (i = 0; i< 100; i++)  {
   x += i;
  }
```

Let's take this statement apart.

```
for (i = 0;          //initialize i to 0
  i < 100 ;          //continue as long as i < 100
  i++)               //increment i after every pass
```

In the preceding loop, *i* starts the first pass through the loop set to zero. A test is made to make sure that *i* is less than 100, and then the loop is executed. After the execution of the loop, the program returns to the top, increments *i,* and again tests to see if it is less than 100. If it is, the loop is again executed.

Note that this for loop carries out exactly the same operations as the while loop illustrated previously. It may never be executed, and it is possible to write a for loop that never exits.

Declaring Variables as Needed in For Loops

One very common place to declare variables on the spot is when you need an iterator variable for a for loop. You can simply declare that variable right in the for statement, as in the following.

```
for (int i = 0; i < 100; i++)
```

Such a loop variable exists, or has *scope*, only within the loop. It vanishes once the loop is complete. This is important because any attempt to reference such a variable once the loop is complete will lead to a compiler error message. The following code is incorrect.

```
for (int i =0; i< 5; i++) {
   x[i] = i;
}

//the following statement is in error
//because i is now out of scope
System.out.println("i=" + i);
```

Commas in For Loop Statements

You can initialize more than one variable in the initializer section of the C# for statement, and you can carry out more than one operation in the operation section of the statement. You separate these statements with commas.

```
for (x=0, y= 0, i =0; i < 100; i++, y +=2)
  {
   x = i + y;
  }
```

It has no effect on the loop's efficiency, and it is far clearer to write.

```
x = 0;
y = 0;
for ( i = 0; i < 100; i++)
   {
   x = i + y;
   y += 2;
   }
```

It is possible to write entire programs inside an overstuffed for statement, using these comma operators, but this is only a way of obfuscating the intent of your program.

How C# Differs from C

If you have been exposed to C or if you are an experienced C programmer, you might be interested in the main differences between C# and C.

1. C# does not usually make use of pointers. You can only increment or decrement a variable as if it were an actual memory pointer inside a special *unsafe* block.

2. You can declare variables anywhere inside a method that you want. They don't have to be at the beginning of the method.

3. You don't have to declare an object before you use it. You can define it just as you need it.

4. C# has a somewhat different definition of the struct types, and it does not support the idea of a union at all.

5. C# has enumerated types that allow a series of named values, such as colors or days of the week, to be assigned sequential numbers, but the syntax is rather different.

6. C# does not have bitfields, that is, variables that take up less than a byte of storage.

7. C# does not allow variable-length argument lists. You have to define a method for each number and type of argument. However, C# allows for the last argument of a function to be a variable parameter array.

8. C# introduces the ideas of delegates and indexers that are not present in any of the other common languages.

How C# Differs from Java

C# and Java are clearly close cousins, and since C# was designed after Java, it uses most of its best ideas. There are a few subtle differences.

1. Many system object methods such as *string* have identical method names, differing only in capitalization.

2. C# does not provide the *throws* keyword that allows the compiler to detect that you must catch the exception that might be thrown by a method.

3. C# has a much more limited concept of layout managers. Since it is Windows-centric, it assumes absolute placement of graphical elements most of the time.

4. C# allows operator overloading.

5. C# introduces delegates and indexers.

6. C# has enumerated types.

7. C# has an *unsafe* mode, where it allows you to use pointers.

8. You must specifically declare that a method can be overridden and that a method overrides another one.

9. You cannot distinguish inheritance from implementing an interface from the declaration; they are both declared the same way.

10. The *switch* statement allows string variables. If there is no specific match, there *must* be a default case or an error will occur. The break statement is required.

11. The Boolean variable type is spelled "bool" in C# and "boolean" in Java.

Summary

In this brief chapter, we have seen the fundamental syntax elements of the C# language. Now that we understand the tools, we need to see how to use them. In the chapters that follow, we'll take up objects and show how to use them and how powerful they can be.

CHAPTER 3

Writing Windows C# Programs

The C# language has its roots in C++, Visual Basic, and Java. Both C# and VB.Net use the same libraries and compile to the same underlying code. Both are managed languages with garbage collection of unused variable space, and both can be used interchangeably. Both also use classes with method names that are very similar to those in Java, so if you are familiar with Java, you will have no trouble with C#.

Objects in C#

In C#, everything is treated as an object. Objects contain data and have methods that operate on them. For example, strings are now objects. They have methods such as these.

```
Substring
ToLowerCase
ToUpperCase
IndexOf
Insert
```

Integers, float, and double variables are also objects, and they have methods.

```
string s;
float x;
x = 12.3;
s = x.ToString();
```

Note that conversion from numerical types is done using these methods rather than external functions. If you want to format a number as a particular kind of string, each numeric type has a Format method.

Managed Languages and Garbage Collection

C# and VB.Net are both *managed* languages. This has two major implications. First, both are compiled to an intermediate low-level language, and a common language runtime (CLR) is used to execute this compiled code, perhaps compiling it further first. So, not only do C# and VB.Net share the same runtime libraries, they are to a large degree two sides of the same coin and two aspects of the same language system. The differences are that VB7 is more Visual Basic–like and a bit easier for VB programmers to learn and use. C# on the other hand is more C++- and Java-like and may appeal more to programmers already experienced in those languages.

The other major implication is that managed languages are *garbage-collected*. Garbage-collected languages take care of releasing unused memory. (You never have to be concerned with this.) As soon as the garbage-collection system detects that there are no more active references to a variable, array, or object, the memory is released back to the system. Of course, it is still possible to write memory-eating code, but for the most part, you do not have to worry about memory allocation and release problems.

Classes and Namespaces in C#

All C# programs are composed entirely of classes. Visual windows forms are a type of class. You will see that all the program features we'll be writing are composed of classes. Since everything is a class, the number of names of class objects can be overwhelming. They have therefore been grouped into various functional libraries that you must specifically mention in order to use the functions in these libraries.

Under the covers these libraries are each individual DLLs. However, you need only refer to them by their base names, using the using statement, and the functions in that library are available to you.

```
using System;
using System.Drawing;
using System.Collections;
```

Logically, each of these libraries represents a different *namespace*. Each namespace is a separate group of class and method names, which the compiler will recognize after you declare that namespace. You can use namespaces that contain identically named classes or methods, but you will only be notified of a conflict if you try to use a class or method that is duplicated in more than one namespace.

The most common namespace is the System namespace, and it is imported by default without your needing to declare it. It contains many of the most fundamental classes and methods that C# uses for access to basic classes such as Application, Array, Console, Exceptions, Objects, and standard objects such as byte, bool, and string. In the simplest C# program we can simply write out a message to the console without ever bringing up a window or form.

```
class Hello {
      static void Main(string[] args)   {
         Console.WriteLine ("Hello C# World");
      }
}
```

This program just writes the text "Hello C# World" to a command (DOS) window. The entry point of any program must be a Main method, and it must be declared as static.

Building a C# Application

Let's start by creating a simple console application—that is, one without any windows that just runs from the command line. Start the Visual Studio.NET program, and select File | New Project. From the selection box, choose C# Console application, as shown in Figure 3-1.

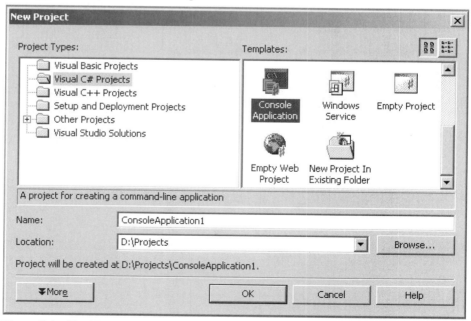

Figure 3-1   The New Project selection window: selecting a console application.

This will bring up a module with Main already filled in. You can type in the rest of the code as follows.

```
Console.WriteLine ("Hello C# World");
```

You can compile this and run it by pressing F5.

When you compile and run the program by pressing F5, a DOS window will appear and print out the message "Hello C# World" and then exit.

The Simplest Window Program in C#

C# makes it very easy to create Windows GUI programs. In fact, you can create most of it using the Windows Designer. To do this, start Visual Studio.NET, select File | New Project, and select C# Windows Application. The default name (and filename) is WindowsApplication1, but you can change this before you close the New dialog box. This brings up a single form project, initially called Form1.cs. You can then use the Toolbox to insert controls, just as you can in Visual Basic.

The Windows Designer for a simple form with one text field and one button is shown in Figure 3-2.

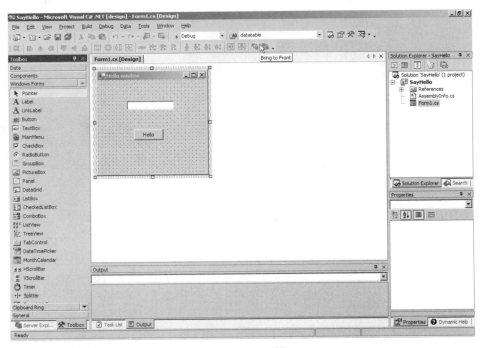

Figure 3-2   The Windows Designer in Visual Studio.NET

You can draw the controls on the form by selecting the TextBox from the Toolbox, dragging it onto the form, and then doing the same with the button. Then, to create program code, we need only double-click on the controls. In this simple form, we want to click on the "Hello" button, which copies the text from the text field to the textbox we called txHi and clears the text field. So in the designer, we double-click on that button, and this code is automatically generated.

```
private void btHello_Click(object sender, EventArgs e) {
txHi.Text ="Hello there";
}
```

Note that the Click routine passes in a sender object and an event object that you can query for further information. Under the covers, it also connects the event to this method. The running program is shown in Figure 3-3.

Figure 3-3　The SimpleHello form after clicking the Say Hello button

While we only had to write one line of code inside the previous subroutine, it is instructive to see how different the rest of the code is for this program. We first see that several libraries of classes are imported so the program can use them.

```
using System;
using System.Drawing;
using System.Collections;
using System.ComponentModel;
using System.Windows.Forms;
using System.Data;
```

Most significant is the Windows.Forms library, which is common to all the .NET languages.

The code the designer generates for the controls is illuminating—and it is right out there in the open for you to change if you want. Essentially, each control is declared as a variable and added to a container. Here are the control declarations. Note the event handler added to the btHello.Click event.

```
private System.Windows.Forms.TextBox txHi;
private System.Windows.Forms.Button btHello;

private void InitializeComponent()              {
      this.btHello = new System.Windows.Forms.Button();
      this.txHi = new System.Windows.Forms.TextBox();
      this.SuspendLayout();
      //
      // btHello
      //
      this.btHello.Location =
                 new System.Drawing.Point(80, 112);
      this.btHello.Name = "btHello";
      this.btHello.Size = new System.Drawing.Size(64, 24);
      this.btHello.TabIndex = 1;
      this.btHello.Text = "Hello";
      this.btHello.Click +=
           new EventHandler(this.btHello_Click);
      //
      // txHi
      //
      this.txHi.Location =
           new System.Drawing.Point(64, 48);
      this.txHi.Name = "txHi";
      this.txHi.Size = new System.Drawing.Size(104, 20);
      this.txHi.TabIndex = 0;
      this.txHi.Text = "";
      //
      // Form1
      //
      this.AutoScaleBaseSize =
           new System.Drawing.Size(5, 13);
      this.ClientSize = new System.Drawing.Size(240, 213);
      this.Controls.AddRange(
           new System.Windows.Forms.Control[] {
             this.btHello,
             this.txHi} );
             this.Name = "Form1";
             this.Text = "Hello window";
             this.ResumeLayout(false);

      }
```

If you change this code manually instead of using the property page, the window designer may not work anymore. We'll look more at the power of this system after we discuss objects and classes in the next chapter.

Windows Controls

All of the basic Windows controls work in much the same way as the TextBox and Button we have used so far. Many of the more common ones are shown in the Windows Controls program in Figure 3-4.

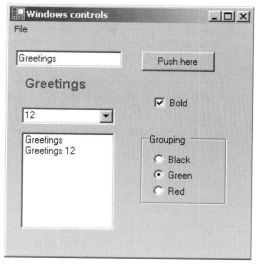

Figure 3-4 A selection of basic Windows controls

Each of these controls has properties such as Name, Text, Font, Forecolor, and Borderstyle that you can change most conveniently using the properties window shown at the right of Figure 3-2. You can also change these properties in your program code as well. The Windows Form class that the designer generates always creates a Form1 constructor that calls an InitializeComponent method like the preceding one. Once that method has been called, the rest of the controls have been created, and you can change their properties in code. Generally, we will create a private *init()* method that is called right after the Initialize-Component method, in which we add any such additional initialization code.

Labels

A label is a field on the window form that simply displays text. Usually programmers use this to label the purpose of text boxes next to them. You can't click on a label or tab to it so it obtains the focus. However, if you want, you can change the major properties in Table 3-1 either in the designer or at runtime.

Table 3-1   Properties for the Label Control

Property	Value
Name	At design time only
BackColor	A Color object
BorderStyle	None, FixedSingle, or Fixed3D
Enabled	True or false. If false, grayed out.
Font	Set to a new Font object
ForeColor	A Color object
Image	An image to be displayed within the label
ImageAlign	Where in the label to place the image
Text	Text of the label
Visible	True or false

TextBox

The TextBox is a single line or multiline editable control. You can set or get the contents of that box using its Text property.

```
TextBox tbox = new TextBox();
tbox.Text = "Hello there";
```

In addition to the properties in Table 3-1, the TextBox also supports the properties in Table 3-2.

CheckBox

A CheckBox can be either checked or not, depending on the value of the Checked property. You can set or interrogate this property in code as well as in the designer. You can create an event handler to catch the event when the box is checked or unchecked by double-clicking on the checkbox in the design mode.

CheckBoxes have an Appearance property that can be set to *Appearance. Normal* or *Appearance.Button*. When the appearance is set to the Button value,

Table 3-2   TextBox Properties

Property	Value
Lines	An array of strings, one per line
Locked	If true, you can't type into the text box
Multiline	True or false
ReadOnly	Same as locked. If true, you can still select the text and copy it, or set values from within code.
WordWrap	True or false

the control acts like a toggle button that stays depressed when you click on it and becomes raised when you click on it again. All the properties in Table 3-1 apply as well.

Buttons

A Button is usually used to send a command to a program. When you click on it, it causes an event that you usually catch with an event handler. Like the CheckBox, you create this event handler by double-clicking on the button in the designer. All of the properties in Table 3-1 can be used as well.

Buttons are also frequently shown with images on them. You can set the button image in the designer or at runtime. The images can be in bmp, gif, jpeg, or icon files.

Radio Buttons

Radio buttons or option buttons are round buttons that can be selected by clicking on them. Only one of a group of radio buttons can be selected at a time. If there is more than one group of radio buttons on a window form, you should put each set of buttons inside a Group box as we did in the program in Figure 3-4. As with checkboxes and buttons, you can attach events to clicking on these buttons by double-clicking on them in the designer. Radio buttons do not always have events associated with them. Instead, programmers check the Checked property of radio buttons when some other event, like an OK button click, occurs.

ListBoxes and ComboBoxes

Both ListBoxes and ComboBoxes contain an Items array of the elements in that list. A ComboBox is a single-line drop-down that programmers use to save space when selections are changed less frequently. ListBoxes allow you to set properties that allow multiple selections, but ComboBoxes do not. Some of their properties include those in Table 3-3.

Table 3-3   The ListBox and ComboBox Properties

Property	Value
Items	A collection of items in the list
MultiColumn	If true, the ColumnWidth property describes the width of each column. (Does not apply to ComboBox.)
SelectionMode	One, MultiSimple, or MultiExtended. If set to MultiSimple, you can select or deselect multiple items with a mouse click. If set to MultiExtended, you can select groups of adjacent items with a mouse. (Does not apply to ComboBox.)
SelectedIndex	Index of selected item
SelectedIndices	Returns collection of selections when ListBox selection mode is multiple.
SelectedItem	Returns the item selected

The Items Collection

You use the Items collection in the ListBox and ComboBox to add and remove elements in the displayed list. It is essentially an ArrayList, as we discuss in Chapter 7. The basic methods are shown in Table 3-4.

If you set a ListBox to a multiple selection mode, you can obtain a collection of the selected items or the selected indexes by

```
ListBox.SelectedIndexCollection it =
     new ListBox.SelectedIndexCollection (lsCommands);
ListBox.SelectedObjectCollection so =
     new ListBox.SelectedObjectCollection (lsCommands);
```

where *lsCommands* is the ListBox name.

Table 3-4   Methods for the Items Collection

Method	Value
Add	Add object to list
Count	Number in list
Item[i]	Element in collection
RemoveAt(i)	Remove element i

Menus

You add a menu to a window by adding a MainMenu control to the window form. Then you can select the menu control and edit its drop-down names and new main item entries, as shown in Figure 3-5.

Figure 3-5   Adding a menu to a form

As with other clickable controls, double-clicking on one in the designer creates an event whose code you can fill in.

ToolTips

A ToolTip is a box that appears when your mouse pointer hovers over a control in a window. This feature is activated by adding an (invisible) ToolTip control to the form and then adding specific ToolTip control and text combinations to the control. In our example in Figure 3-4, we add ToolTips text to the button and ListBox using the *tips* control we have added to the window.

```
tips.SetToolTip (btPush, "Press to add text to list box");
tips.SetToolTip (lsCommands, "Click to copy to text box");
```

This is illustrated in Figure 3-6.

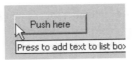

Figure 3-6   A ToolTip over a button

We discuss how to use the DataGrid and TreeList in Chapters 14 and 15, and Toolbar is discussed in Chapters 28 and 29.

The Windows Controls Program

The Windows Controls program, shown in Figure 3-4, controls changes in the text in the label.

- Font size is set from the combo box.
- Font color is set from the radio buttons.
- Boldface is set from the check box.

For the check box, we create a new font that is either lightface or boldface, depending on the state of the check box.

```
private void ckBold_CheckedChanged(object sender, EventArgs e) {
      if (ckBold.Checked ) {
            lbText.Font  =new Font ("Arial",
                        fontSize,FontStyle.Bold );
      }
      else {
            lbText.Font = new Font ("Arial", fontSize);
}
```

When we create the form, we add the list of font sizes to the combo box.

```
private void init() {
      fontSize = 12;
      cbFont.Items.Add ("8");
      cbFont.Items.Add ("10");
      cbFont.Items.Add ("12");
      cbFont.Items.Add ("14");
      cbFont.Items.Add ("18");
      lbText.Text ="Greetings";
      tips.SetToolTip (btPush, "Press to add text to list box");
      tips.SetToolTip (lsCommands, "Click to copy to text box");
}
```

When someone clicks on a font size in the combo box, we convert that text to a number and create a font of that size. Note that we just call the check box changing code so we don't have to duplicate anything.

```
private void cbFont_SelectedIndexChanged(
        object sender, EventArgs e) {
    fontSize= Convert.ToInt16 (cbFont.SelectedItem );
    ckBold_CheckedChanged(null, null);
}
```

For each radio button, we click on it and insert color-changing code.

```
private void opGreen_CheckedChanged(object sender, EventArgs e) {
    lbText.ForeColor =Color.Green;
}

private void opRed_CheckedChanged(object sender, EventArgs e) {
    lbText.ForeColor =Color.Red ;
}

private void opBlack_CheckedChanged(object sender, EventArgs e) {
    lbText.ForeColor =Color.Black ;
}
```

When you click on the ListBox, it copies that text into the text box by getting the selected item as an object and converting it to a string.

```
private void lsCommands_SelectedIndexChanged(
        object sender, EventArgs e) {
    txBox.Text = lsCommands.SelectedItem.ToString () ;
}
```

Finally, when you click on the File | Exit menu item, it closes the form and, hence, the program.

```
private void menuItem2_Click(object sender, EventArgs e) {
    this.Close ();
}
```

Summary

Now that we've seen the basics of how to write programs in C#, we are ready to talk more about objects and OO programming in the chapters that follow.

Programs on the CD-ROM

Console Hello	\IntroCSharp\Hello
Windows Hello	\IntroCSharp\SayHello
Windows Controls	\IntroCSharp\WinControls

CHAPTER 4

Using Classes and Objects in C#

What Do We Use Classes For?

All C# programs are composed of classes. The Windows forms we have just seen are classes, derived from the basic Form class, and all the other programs we will be writing are made up exclusively of classes. C# does not have the concept of global data modules or shared data that are not part of classes.

Simply put, a class is a set of public and private *methods* and private data grouped inside named logical units. Usually, we write each class in a separate file, although this is not a hard and fast rule. We have already seen that these Windows forms are classes, and in this chapter we will see how we can create other useful classes.

When you create a class, it is not a single entity but a master from which you can create copies, or *instances*, using the *new* keyword. When we create these instances, we pass some initializing data into the class using its *constructor*. A constructor is a method that has the same name as the class name, has no return type and can have zero or more parameters that get passed into each instance of the class. We call each of these instances an *object*. In the sections that follow we'll create some simple programs and use some instances of classes to simplify them.

A Simple Temperature Conversion Program

Suppose we wanted to write a visual program to convert temperatures between the Celsius and Fahrenheit temperature scales. You may remember that water freezes at 0° on the Celsius scale and boils at 100°C, whereas water freezes at 32° on the Fahrenheit scale and boils at 212°F. From these numbers you can quickly deduce the conversion formula that you may have forgotten.

43

The difference between freezing and boiling on one scale is 100 and 180 degrees on the other, or 100/180 or 5/9. The Fahrenheit scale is "offset" by 32, since water freezes at 32 on its scale. Thus,

$$C = (F - 32) * 5/9$$

and

$$F = 9/5 * C + 32$$

In our visual program, we'll allow the user to enter a temperature and select the scale on which to convert it, as in Figure 4-1.

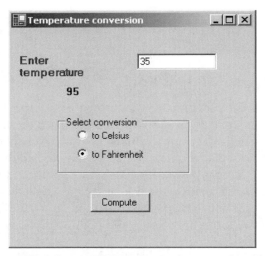

Figure 4-1   Converting 35° Celsius to 95° Fahrenheit with our visual interface

Using the visual builder provided in Visual Studio.NET, we can draw the user interface in a few seconds and simply implement routines to be called when the two buttons are pressed. If we double-click on the Compute button, the program generates the btConvert_Click method. You can fill it in to have it convert the values between temperature scales.

```
private void> btCompute_Click(object sender,
          System.EventArgs e) {
     float temp, newTemp;
     //convert string to input value
     temp = Convert.ToSingle (txEntry.Text );
     //see which scale to convert to
     if(opFahr.Checked)
          newTemp = 9*temp/5 + 32;
     else
          newTemp = 5*(temp-32)/9;
     //put result in label text
```

```
          lbResult.Text =newTemp.ToString ();
          txEntry.Text ="";   //clear entry field
}
```

The preceding program is extremely straightforward and easy to understand, and it is typical of how some simple C# programs operate. However, it has some disadvantages that we might want to improve on.

The most significant problem is that the user interface and the data handling are combined in a single program module rather than handled separately. It is usually a good idea to keep the data manipulation and the interface manipulation separate so that changing interface logic doesn't impact the computation logic and vice-versa.

Building a Temperature Class

A *class* in C# is a module that can contain both public and private functions and subroutines, and can hold private data values as well. These functions and subroutines in a class are frequently referred to collectively as *methods*.

Class modules allow you to keep a set of data values in a single named place and fetch those values using get and set functions, which we then refer to as *accessor methods*.

You create a class module from the C# integrated development environment (IDE) using the menu item Project | Add Class module. When you specify a filename for each new class, the IDE assigns this name as the class name as well and generates an empty class with an empty constructor. For example, if we wanted to create a Temperature class, the IDE would generate the following code for us.

```
namespace CalcTemp
{
      /// <summary>
      /// Summary description for Temperature
      /// </summary>
      public class Temperature
      {
            public Temperature()
            {
                  //
                  // TODO: Add constructor logic here
                  //
            }
      }
}
```

If you fill in the "summary description" special comment, that text will appear whenever your mouse hovers over an instance of that class. Note that the system generates the class and a blank constructor. If your class needs a constructor with parameters, you can just edit the code.

Next we want to move all of the computation and conversion between temperature scales into this new Temperature class. One way to design this class is to rewrite the calling programs that will use the class module first. In the code sample below, we create an instance of the Temperature class and use it to do whatever conversions are needed.

```csharp
private void btCompute_Click(object sender, System.EventArgs e) {
    string newTemp;
    //use input value to create instance of class
    Temperature temp = new Temperature (txEntry.Text );
    //use radio button to decide which conversion
    newTemp = temp.getConvTemp (opCels.Checked );

    //get result and put in label text
    lbResult.Text =newTemp.ToString ();
    txEntry.Text ="";    //clear entry field
}
```

The actual class is shown following. Note that we put the string value of the input temperature into the class in the constructor and that inside the class it gets converted to a float. We do not need to know how the data are represented internally, and we could change that internal representation at any time.

```csharp
public class Temperature   {
    private float temp, newTemp;
    //-------------
    //constructor for class
    public Temperature(string thisTemp)                {
        temp = Convert.ToSingle(thisTemp);
    }
    //-------------
    public string getConvTemp(bool celsius){
    if (celsius)
        return getCels();
    else
        return getFahr();
    }
    //-------------
    private string getCels() {
        newTemp= 5*(temp-32)/9;
        return newTemp.ToString() ;
    }
    //-------------
    private string getFahr() {
        newTemp = 9*temp/5 + 32;
        return Convert.ToString(newTemp) ;
    }
}
```

Note that the temperature variable *temp* is declared as *private* so it cannot be "seen" or accessed from outside the class. You can only put data into the class and get it back out using the constructor and the getConvTemp method. The main point to this code rearrangement is that the outer calling program does not have to know how the data are stored and how they are retrieved; that is only known inside the class.

The other important feature of the class is that it actually *holds data*. You can put data into it and it will return it at any later time. This class only holds the one temperature value, but classes can contain quite complex sets of data values. This is known as *encapsulation*.

We could easily modify this class to get temperature values out in other scales, still without requiring that the user of the class know anything about how the data are stored or how the conversions are performed.

Converting to Kelvin

Absolute zero on the Celsius scale is defined as −273.16°. This is the coldest possible temperature, since it is the point at which all molecular motion stops. The Kelvin scale is based on absolute zero, but the degrees are the same size as Celsius degrees. We can add the following function.

```
public string getKelvin() {
      newTemp = Convert.ToString (getCels() + 273.16)
}
```

What would the setKelvin method look like?

Putting the Decisions into the Temperature Class

At this point, we are still making decisions within the user interface about which methods of the Temperature class to use. It would be even better if all that complexity could disappear into the Temperature class. It would be nice if we just could write our Conversion button click method as follows.

```
private void btCompute_Click(object sender, System.EventArgs e) {
      Temperature temper =
            new Temperature(txEntry.Text , opCels.Checked);
      //put result in label text
      lbResult.Text = temper.getConvTemp();
      txEntry.Text ="";   //clear entry field
}
```

This removes the decision-making process to the Temperature class and reduces the calling interface program to just two lines of code.

The class that handles all this becomes somewhat more complex, however, but it then keeps track of what data have been passed in and what conversion must be done. We pass in the data and the state of the radio button in the constructor.

```
public Temperature(string sTemp, bool toCels)        {
       temp = Convert.ToSingle (sTemp);
       celsius =  toCels;
}
```

Now, the Celsius Boolean tells the class whether to convert and whether conversion is required on fetching the temperature value. The output routine is simply this.

```
public string getConvTemp(){
       if (celsius)
               return getCels();
       else
               return getFahr();
}
//-------------
private string getCels() {
       newTemp= 5*(temp-32)/9;
       return newTemp.ToString() ;
}
//-------------
private string getFahr() {
       newTemp = 9*temp/5 + 32;
       return Convert.ToString(newTemp) ;
}
```

In this class we have both public and private methods. The public ones are callable from other modules, such as the user interface form module. The private ones, getCels and getFahr, are used internally and operate on the temperature variable.

Note that we now also have the opportunity to return the output temperature as either a string or a single floating point value, and we could thus vary the output format as needed.

Using Classes for Format and Value Conversion

It is convenient in many cases to have a method for converting between formats and representations of data. You can use a class to handle and hide the details of such conversions. For example, you might design a program where you can enter an elapsed time in minutes and seconds with or without the colon.

```
315.20
3:15.20
315.2
```

Since all styles are likely, you'd like a class to parse the legal possibilities and keep the data in a standard format within. Figure 4-2 shows how the entries "112" and "102.3" are parsed.

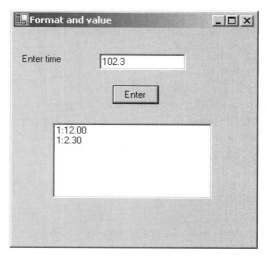

Figure 4-2 A simple parsing program that uses the Times class

Much of the parsing work takes place in the constructor for the class. Parsing depends primarily on looking for a colon. If there is no colon, then values greater than 99 are treated as minutes.

```
public FormatTime(string entry)                {
errflag = false;
if (! testCharVals(entry)) {
        int i = entry.IndexOf (":");
        if (i >= 0 ) {
                mins = Convert.ToInt32 (entry.Substring (0, i));
                secs = Convert.ToSingle (entry.Substring (i+1));
                if(secs >= 60.0F ) {
                        errflag = true;
                        t = NT;
                }
                t = mins *100 + secs;
        }
        else {
                float fmins = Convert.ToSingle (entry) / 100;
                mins = (int)fmins;
```

```
secs = Convert.ToSingle (entry) - 100 * mins;
if (secs >= 60) {
        errflag = true;
        t = NT;
}
else
        t = Convert.ToSingle(entry);
    }
    }
}
```

Since illegal time values might also be entered, we test for cases like 89.22 and set an error flag. (Remember that there are only 60 seconds in a minute.)

Depending on the kind of time measurements these represent, you might also have some non-numeric entries such as NT for no time, or in the case of athletic times, SC for scratch or DQ for disqualified. All of these are best managed inside the class. Thus, you never need to know what numeric representations of these values are used internally.

```
static public int NT = 10000;
static public int DQ = 20000;
```

Some of these are processed in the code represented by Figure 4-3.

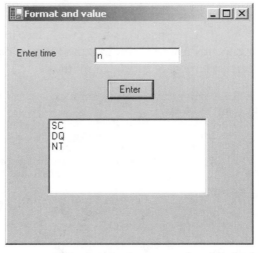

Figure 4-3   The time entry interface, showing the parsing of symbols for Scratch, Disqualification, and No Time

Handling Unreasonable Values

A class is also a good place to encapsulate error handling. For example, it might be that times greater than some threshold value are unlikely, and they could be times that were entered without a decimal point. If large times are unlikely, then a number such as 123473 could be assumed to be 12:34.73.

```
public void setSingle(float tm) {
      t = tm;
      if((tm > minVal) && (tm < NT)) {
            t = tm / 100.0f;
      }
}
```

The cutoff value minVal may vary with the domain of times being considered and thus should be a variable. You can also use the class constructor to set up default values for variables.

```
public class FormatTime {
  public FormatTime(string entry)          {
      errflag = false;
      minVal = 1000;
      t = 0;
```

A String Tokenizer Class

A number of languages provide a simple method for separating strings into tokens, where each token is separated by a specified character. While C# does not exactly provide a class for this feature, we can write one quite easily using the Split method of the String class. The goal of the Tokenizer class will be to pass in a string and obtain the successive string tokens back one at a time. For example, if we had the simple string

```
Now is the time
```

our tokenizer should return the following four tokens.

```
Now
is
the
time
```

The critical part of this class is that it holds the initial string and remembers which token is to be returned next.

We use the Split function, which approximates the Tokenizer but returns an array of substrings instead of having an object interface. The class we want to write will have a nextToken method that returns string tokens or a zero length string when we reach the end of the series of tokens. This is the entire class.

```
//String Tokenizer class
public class StringTokenizer       {
  private string data, delimiter;
  private string[] tokens; //token array
  private int index;              //index to next token
//----------
public StringTokenizer(string dataLine)                    {
     init(dataLine, " ");
}
//----------
//sets up initial values and splits string
private void init(String dataLine, string delim) {
     delimiter = delim;
     data = dataLine;
     tokens = data.Split (delimiter.ToCharArray() );
     index = 0;
}
//----------
public StringTokenizer(string dataLine, string delim) {
     init(dataLine, delim);
}
//----------
public bool hasMoreElements() {
     return (index < (tokens.Length));
}
//----------
public string nextElement() {
     //get the next token
     if( index > tokens.Length )
          return tokens[index++];
     else
          return "";      //or none
     }
}
```

The class is illustrated in use in Figure 4-4.
The code that uses the Tokenizer class is just this.

```
//call tokenizer when button is clicked
private void btToken_Click(object sender,
          System.EventArgs e) {
     StringTokenizer tok =
          new StringTokenizer (txEntry.Text );
     while(tok.hasMoreElements () ) {
          lsTokens.Items.Add (tok.nextElement());
     }
  }
```

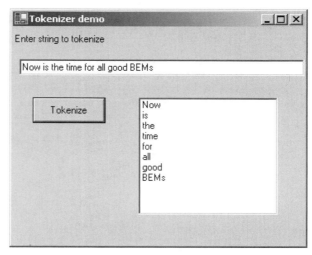

Figure 4-4 The Tokenizer in use

Classes as Objects

The primary difference between ordinary procedural programming and object-oriented (OO) programming is the presence of classes. A class is just a module, as we have previously shown, which has both public and private methods and that can contain data. However, classes are also unique in that there can be any number of *instances* of a class, each containing different data. We frequently refer to these instances as objects. We'll see some examples of single and multiple instances later.

Suppose we have a file of results from a swimming event stored in a text data file. Such a file might look, in part, like this, where the columns represent place, names, age, club, and time.

```
1 Emily Fenn              17    WRAT        4:59.54
2 Kathryn Miller          16    WYW         5:01.35
3 Melissa Sckolnik        17    WYW         5:01.58
4 Sarah Bowman            16    CDEV        5:02.44
5 Caitlin Klick           17    MBM         5:02.59
6 Caitlin Healey          16    MBM         5:03.62
```

If we wrote a program to display these swimmers and their times, we'd need to read in and parse this file. For each swimmer, we'd have a first and last name, an age, a club, and a time. An efficient way to group together the data for each swimmer is to design a Swimmer class and create an instance for each swimmer.

Here is how we read the file and create these instances. As each instance is created, we add it into an ArrayList object.

```
private void init() {
        ar = new ArrayList ();        //create array list
        csFile fl = new csFile ("500free.txt");
        //read in liens
        string s =  fl.readLine ();
        while (s != null) {
                //convert to tokens in swimmer object
                Swimmer swm = new Swimmer(s);
                ar.Add (swm);
                s= fl.readLine ();
        }
        fl.close();
        //add names to list box
        for(int i=0; i < ar.Count ; i++) {
                Swimmer swm = (Swimmer)ar[i];
                lsSwimmers.Items.Add (swm.getName ());
        }
}
```

The Swimmer class itself parses each line of data from the file and stores it for retrieval using the getXxx accessor functions.

```
public class Swimmer {
        private string frName, lName;
        private string club;
        private int age;
        private int place;
        private FormatTime tms;
//-----------
  public Swimmer(String dataLine) {
        StringTokenizer tok = new StringTokenizer (dataLine);
        place =  Convert.ToInt32 (tok.nextElement());
        frName = tok.nextElement ();
        lName = tok.nextElement ();
        string s = tok.nextElement ();
        age = Convert.ToInt32 (s);
        club = tok.nextElement ();
        tms = new FormatTime (tok.nextElement ());

  }
//-----------
  public string getName() {
        return frName+" "+lName;
  }
//-----------
public string getTime() {
        return tms.getTime();
  }
}
```

Class Containment

Each instance of the Swimmer class contains an instance of the StringTokenizer class that it uses to parse the input string and an instance of the Times class we wrote above to parse the time and return it in formatted form to the calling program. Having a class contain other classes is a very common ploy in OO programming and is one of the main ways we can build up more complicated programs from rather simple components. The program that displays these swimmers is shown in Figure 4-5.

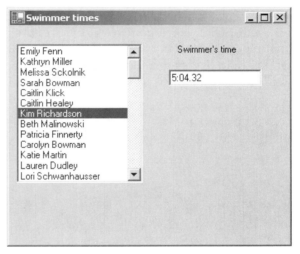

Figure 4-5   A list of swimmers and their times, using containment

When you click on any swimmer, her time is shown in the box on the right. The code for showing that time is extremely easy to write, since all the data are in the swimmer class.

```
private void lsSwimmers_SelectedIndexChanged(
          object sender, System.EventArgs e) {
  //get index of selected swimmer
      int i = lsSwimmers.SelectedIndex ;
      //get that swimmer
      Swimmer swm = (Swimmer)ar[i];
      //display her time
      txTime.Text =swm.getTime ();
}
```

Initialization

In our previous Swimmer class, note that the constructor in turn calls the constructor of the StringTokenizer class.

```
public Swimmer(String dataLine)              {

        StringTokenizer tok =
              new StringTokenizer (dataLine);
```

Classes and Properties

Classes in C# can have Property methods as well as public and private functions and subs. These correspond to the kinds of properties you associate with Forms, but they can store and fetch any kinds of values you care to use. For example, rather than having methods called getAge and setAge, you could have a single age property that then corresponds to a get and a set method.

```
private int Age;
//age property
public int age {
      get {
            return Age;
      }
      set {
            Age = value;
      }
}
```

Note that a property declaration does *not* contain parentheses after the property name and that the special keyword *value* is used to obtain the data to be stored.

To use these properties, you refer to the age property on the left side of an equal sign to set the value and refer to the age property on the right side to get the value back.

```
age = sw.Age;       //Get this swimmer's age
sw.Age = 12;        //Set a new age for this swimmer
```

Properties are somewhat vestigial, since they originally applied more to Forms in the VB language, but many programmers find them quite useful. They do not provide any features that are not already available using get and set methods, and both generate equally efficient code.

In the revised version of our SwimmerTimes display program, we convert all of the get and set methods to properties and then allow users to vary the times of each swimmer by typing in new ones. Here is the Swimmer class.

```
public class Swimmer
{
      private string frName, lName;
      private string club;
      private int Age;
      private int place;
      private FormatTime tms;
//-----------
public Swimmer(String dataLine)              {
      StringTokenizer tok = new StringTokenizer (dataLine);
      place =  Convert.ToInt32 (tok.nextElement());
      frName = tok.nextElement ();
      lName = tok.nextElement ();
      string s = tok.nextElement ();
      Age = Convert.ToInt32 (s);
      club = tok.nextElement ();
      tms = new FormatTime (tok.nextElement ());
}
//-----------
public string name {
      get{
      return frName+" "+lName;
      }
}
//-----------
public string time {
      get{
          return tms.getTime();
      }
      set  {
          tms = new FormatTime (value);
      }
}
//-------------------
//age property
public int age {
      get {
          return Age;

      set {
          Age = value;
      }
}
}
```

Then we can type in a new time for any swimmer, and when the txTime text entry field loses focus, we can store a new time as follows.

```
private void txTime_OnLostFocus(
      object sender, System.EventArgs e) {
      //get index of selected swimmer
      int i = lsSwimmers.SelectedIndex ;
```

```
        //get that swimmer
        Swimmer swm = (Swimmer)ar[i];
        swm.time =txTime.Text ;
}
```

One distinct advantage of properties is the ability to write statements like this.

```
sw.age += 10;
```

This is far more readable and friendly than this.

```
sw.setAge (sw.getAge() + 10);
```

Programming Style in C#

You can develop any of a number of readable programming styles for C#. The one we use here is partly influenced by Microsoft's Hungarian notation (named after its originator, Charles Simonyi) and partly on styles developed for Java.

We favor using names for C# controls such as buttons and ListBoxes that have prefixes that make their purpose clear, and we will use them whenever there is more than one of them on a single form.

We will not generally create new names for labels, frames, and forms if they are never referred to directly in the code. We will begin class names with capital letters and instances of classes with lowercase letters. We will also spell instances and classes with a mixture of lowercase and capital letters to make their purpose clearer:

```
swimmerTime
```

Control Name	Prefix	Example
Buttons	bt	btCompute
ListBoxes	ls	lsSwimmers
Radio (option buttons)	op	opFSex
ComboBoxes	cb	cbCountry
Menus	mnu	mnuFile
TextBoxes	tx	txTime

Delegates

C# introduces a unique feature among the C-like languages, called a delegate. Basically, a delegate is a reference to a function in another class that you can pass around and use without knowing what class it came from as long as it satisfies the same interface.

Consider the simple program in Figure 4-6. When you click on the Process button, the text in the entry field is copied into the ListBox as either all uppercase characters or all lowercase characters. While there are a number of simple ways to write this program, we will use it here to illustrate delegates.

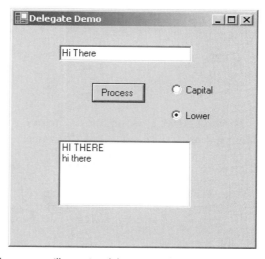

Figure 4-6   A simple program illustrating delegates

A delegate is a prototype of a class method to which you assign an actual identity later. The method can be either static or from some class instance. You declare the delegate as a sort of type declaration.

```
private delegate string fTxDelegate(string s);
```

Then you can declare one or more instances of that type and assign values to them. Here is a single delegate variable.

```
fTxDelegate ftx;    //instance of delegate
```

Note that the variable ftx represents the instance of a particular method in some class that takes a string for an input and returns a string for output.

Now we will choose the function to put in this delegate variable by determining which radio button was selected. We build a class called Capital that has a fixText method as follows.

```
public class Capital
{
      public string fixText(string s) {
            return s.ToUpper ();
      }
}
```

We also construct a Lower class that also has a fixText method, only in this case it is a static method.

```
public class Lower
{
      public static string fixText(string s) {
            return s.ToLower();
      }
}
```

Now when we click on one of the two radio buttons, we assign one of these fixText methods to this delegate reference.

```
private void opCap_CheckedChanged(object sender, EventArgs e) {
      btProcess.Enabled =true;
      //assign an instance method to the delegate
      //create an instance of the Capital class
      ftx = new fTxDelegate (new Capital().fixText);
}
//-----
private void opLower_CheckedChanged(object sender, EventArgs e) {
      btProcess.Enabled =true;
      //assign a static method to the delegate
      //the Lower class has a static method fixText
      ftx = new fTxDelegate (Lower.fixText);
}
```

Note that the syntax for creating a delegate from a class instance and from a static method varies slightly.

```
ftx = new fTxDelegate (new Capital().fixText); //instance
ftx = new fTxDelegate (Lower.fixText);         //static
```

Then when we click on the Process button, we simply execute that method using the ftx delegate.

```
private void btProcess_Click(object sender, EventArgs e) {
      string s  = ftx(txName.Text);
```

```
                lsBox.Items.Add ( s );
        }
```

The ftx method then resolves to call one fixText method or the other.

While the delegate approach can give you added flexibility in programming, it is really not an entirely new approach, since you could accomplish the same thing using interfaces and calling the fixText methods directly.

Indexers

C# introduces a special kind of class method called an indexer. This allows you to access elements of data inside a class using a method that makes the data look like array elements. In the BitList class that follows, the indexer returns the value of the *ith* bit of the number stored in the class.

```
public class BitList
{
        private int number;
        public BitList(string snum) {
                number = Convert.ToInt32 (snum);
        }
        //-----
        // here is an indexer that
        // returns the i-th bit of a value
        public int this[int index] {
                get{
                        int val = number >> index;
                        return val & 1;
                }
        }
}
```

In Figure 4-7, each time you click on the numerical up-down control, the value of that index is used to get the value of that bit from the number in the bit class, using this simple code.

```
private void numericUpDown1_ValueChanged(
                object sender, EventArgs e) {
        //get the index value from the updown control
        int index = Convert.ToInt32 (numericUpDown1.Value );
        //create an instance of the BitList class
        BitList bits = new BitList(txNum.Text );

        //get that bit value using the indexer
        int bit = bits[index];
        //add it to the list box
        lsBits.Items.Add (Convert.ToString (bit));
}
```

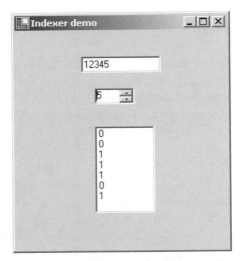

Figure 4-7   Demonstration of use of indexer to get bits from a number

As you can see, this is a convenient trick for making arraylike references, but it offers no function that could not be implemented just as easily with a class method.

Operator Overloading

Along with the ability to use pointers within *unsafe* sections of C# code, the C# language also lets you overload most of the common operators.

+ - * / % & | ^ << >> == != > < >=, and <=

For any given class, you can specify a new meaning for any of these operators. For a hypothetical Complex class, you could define the +-operator like this.

```
public static Complex operator +(Complex c1, Complex c2)
  {
    return new Complex(c1.real + c2.real,
              c1.imaginary + c2.imaginary);
  }
```

This tends to lead to highly unreadable code, and we will not use this feature in this book.

Summary

In this chapter, we've introduced C# classes and shown how they can contain public and private methods and can contain data. Each class can have many instances, and each could contain different data values. Classes can also have Property methods for setting and fetching data. These Property methods provide a simpler syntax over the usual getXxx and setXxx accessor methods but have no other substantial advantages.

Programs on the CD-ROM

Temperature Conversion	`\UsingClasses\CalcTemp`
Temperature Conversion Using Classes	`\UsingClasses\ClsCalcTemp`
Temperature Conversion Using Classes	`\UsingClasses\AllClsCalcTemp`
Time Conversion	`\UsingClasses\Formatvalue`
String Tokenizer	`\UsingClasses\TokenDemo`
Swimmer times	`\UsingClasses\SwimmerTokenizer`
Delegate	`\UsingClasses\Delegate`
Indexer	`\UsingClasses\Indexer`

CHAPTER 5

Inheritance

Now we will take up the most important feature of OO languages like C# (and VB.NET): inheritance. When we create a Windows form, such as our Hello form, the IDE (VS.NET Integrated Development Environment) creates a declaration of the following type.

```
public class  Form1 : System.Windows.Forms.Form
```

This says that the form we create is a child class of the Form class, rather than being an instance of it. This has some very powerful implications. You can create visual objects and override some of their properties so that each behaves a little differently. We'll see some examples of this in the following.

Constructors

All classes have specific *constructors* that are called when you create an instance of a class. These constructors always have the same name as the class. This applies to Form classes as well as nonvisual classes. Here is the constructor the system generates for our simple hello window in the class Form1.

```
public class Form1 {
    public Form1(){              //constructor
        InitializeComponent();
    }
```

When you create your own classes, you must create constructor methods to initialize them, and you can pass arguments into the class to initialize class parameters to specific values. If you do not specifically include a constructor in any class you write, a constructor having no arguments is generated for you under the covers.

The InitializeComponent method is generated by the IDE as well, and it contains code that creates and positions all the visual controls in that window. If we need to set up additional code as part of the initialization of a Form class, we will always write a private *init* method that we call *after* the Initialize-Component method call.

```
public Form1(){
      InitializeComponent();
      init();
}

private void init() {
      x = 12.5f;           //set initial value of x
}
```

Drawing and Graphics in C#

In our first example, we'll write a program to draw a rectangle in a PictureBox on a form. In C#, controls are repainted by the Windows system, and you can connect to the paint event to do your own drawing whenever a paint event occurs. Such a paint event occurs whenever the window is resized, uncovered, or refreshed. To illustrate this, we'll create a Form containing a PictureBox, as shown in Figure 5-1.

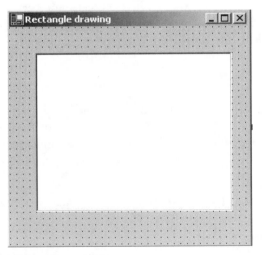

Figure 5-1   Inserting a PictureBox on a Form

Then we'll select the PictureBox in the designer and select the Events button (with the lightning icon) in the Properties window. This brings up a list of all the events that can occur on a PictureBox as shown in Figure 5-2.

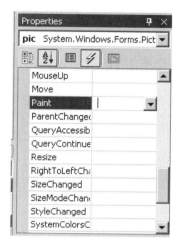

Figure 5-2   Selecting the Paint Event for the PictureBox window

Double-clicking on the Paint Event creates the following empty method in the Form's code.

```
private void pic_Paint(object sender, PaintEventArgs e) {
}
```

It also generates code that connects this method to the Paint Event for that picture box inside the *InitializeComponents* method.

```
this.pic.Paint += new PaintEventHandler(this.pic_Paint);
```

The PaintEventArgs object is passed into the subroutine by the underlying system, and you can obtain the graphics surface to draw on from that object. To do drawing, you must create an instance of a Pen object and define its color and, optionally, its width. This is illustrated here for a black pen with a default width of 1.

```
private void pic_Paint(object sender, PaintEventArgs e) {

  Graphics g = e.Graphics;                //get Graphics surface
  Pen rpen = new Pen(Color.Black);        //create a Pen
  g.drawLine(rpen, 10,20,70,80);          //draw the line
}
```

In this example, we show the Pen object being created each time a Paint Event occurs. We might also create the pen once in the window's constructor or in the init method we usually call from within it.

Using Inheritance

Inheritance in C# gives us the ability to create classes that are derived from existing classes. In new derived classes, we only have to specify the methods that are new or changed. All the others are provided automatically from the base class we inherit. To see how this works, let's consider writing a simple Rectangle class that draws itself on a form window. This class has only two methods: the constructor and the draw method.

```
namespace CsharpPats
{
public class Rectangle        {
       private int x, y, w, h;
       protected Pen rpen;
       public Rectangle(int x_, int y_, int w_, int h_)
       {
              x = x_;          //save coordinates
              y = y_;
              w = w_;
              h = h_;
              //create a pen
              rpen = new Pen(Color.Black);
       }
       //---------------
       public void draw(Graphics g) {
              //draw the rectangle
              g.DrawRectangle (rpen, x, y, w, h);
       }
   }
}
```

Namespaces

We already mentioned the System namespaces. Visual Studio.NET also creates a namespace for each project equal to the name of the project itself. You can change this namespace on the property page, or you can make it blank so that the project is not in a namespace. However, you can create namespaces of your own, and the Rectangle class shows a good reason for doing so. The System.Drawing namespace that this program requires to use the Graphics object also contains a Rectangle class. Rather than renaming our new Rectangle class to avoid this name overlap or "collision," we can just put the whole Rectangle class in its own namespace, as we saw previously.

Then when we declare the variable in the main Form window, we can declare it as a member of that namespace.

```
CsharpPats.Rectangle rec;
```

In this main Form window, we create an instance of our Rectangle class.

```
private void init() {
      rect = new CsharpPats.Rectangle (10, 20, 70, 100);
}
//---------------
public Form1() {
      InitializeComponent();
      init();
}
```

Then we add the drawing code to our Paint event handler to do the drawing and pass the graphics surface on to the Rectangle instance.

```
private void pic_Paint(object sender, PaintEventArgs e) {
      Graphics g =  e.Graphics;
      rect.draw (g);
}
```

This gives us the display we see in Figure 5-3.

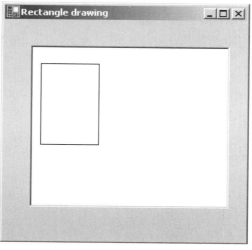

Figure 5-3   The Rectangle drawing program

Creating a Square from a Rectangle

A square is just a special case of a rectangle, and we can derive a Square class from the Rectangle class without writing much new code. Here is the entire class.

```
namespace CsharpPats {
    public class Square : Rectangle      {
    public Square(int x, int y, int w):base(x, y, w, w) {
        }
    }
}
```

This Square class contains only a constructor, which passes the square dimensions on to the underlying Rectangle class by calling the constructor of the parent Rectangle class as part of the Square constructor.

```
base(x, y, w, w)
```

Note the unusual syntax: The call to the parent class's constructor follows a colon and is *before* the opening brace of the constructor itself.

The Rectangle class creates the pen and does the actual drawing. Note that there is no draw method at all for the Square class. If you don't specify a new method, the parent class's method is used automatically, and this is what we want to have happen here.

The program that draws both a rectangle and a square has a simple constructor where instances of these objects are created.

```
private void init() {
    rect = new Rectangle (10, 20, 70, 100);
    sq = new Square (150,100,70);
}
```

The program also has a paint routine where instances of these objects are drawn.

```
private void pic_Paint(object sender, PaintEventArgs e) {
    Graphics g =  e.Graphics;
    rect.draw (g);
    sq.draw (g);
}
```

The display is shown in Figure 5-4 for the square and rectangle.

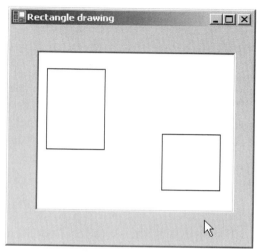

Figure 5-4   The Rectangle class and the Square class derived from it

Public, Private, and Protected

In C#, you can declare both variables and class methods as public, private, or protected. A public method is accessible from other classes, and a private method is accessible only inside that class. Usually, you make all class variables private and write getXxx and setXxx accessor functions to set or obtain their values. It is generally a bad idea to allow variables inside a class to be accessed directly from outside the class, since this violates the principle of *encapsulation*. In other words, the class is the only place where the actual data representation should be known, and you should be able to change the algorithms inside a class without anyone outside the class being any the wiser.

C# uses the *protected* keyword as well. Both variables and methods can be protected. Protected variables can be accessed within the class and from any subclasses you derive from it. Similarly, protected methods are only accessible from that class and its derived classes. They are not publicly accessible from outside the class. If you do not declare any level of accessibility, private accessibility is assumed.

Overloading

In C#, as well as in other object-oriented languages, you can have several class methods with the same name as long as they have different calling arguments or *signatures*. For example, we might want to create an instance of a StringTokenizer class where we define both the string and the separator.

```
tok = new StringTokenizer("apples, pears", ",");
```

By declaring constructors with different numbers of arguments, we say we are *overloading* the constructor. Here are the two constructors.

```
public StringTokenizer(string dataLine)              {
      init(dataLine, " ");
}
//----------
public StringTokenizer(string dataLine, string delim) {
      init(dataLine, delim);
}
private void init(string data, string delim) {
      //...
}
```

Of course, C# allows us to overload any method as long as we provide arguments that allow the compiler to distinguish between the various overloaded (or *polymorphic*) methods.

Virtual and Override Keywords

If you have a method in a base class that you want to allow derived classes to override, you must declare it as *virtual*. This means that a method of the same name and argument signature in a derived class will be called rather than the one in the base class. Then you must declare the method in the derived class, using the *override* keyword.

If you use the *override* keyword in a derived class without declaring the base class's method as *virtual*, the compiler will flag this as an error. If you create a method in a derived class that is identical in name and argument signature to one in the base class and do not declare it as *override*, this also is an error. If you create a method in the derived class and do *not* declare it as *override* and also do *not* declare the base class's method as *virtual*, the code will compile with a warning but will work correctly, with the derived class's method called as you intended.

Overriding Methods in Derived Classes

Suppose we want to derive a new class called DoubleRect from Rectangle, which draws a rectangle in two colors offset by a few pixels. We must declare the base class draw method as virtual.

```
public virtual void draw(Graphics g) {
  g.DrawRectangle (rpen, x, y, w, h);
}
```

In the derived DoubleRect constructor, we will create a red pen in the constructor for doing the additional drawing.

```
public class DoubleRect:Rectangle            {
private Pen rdPen;
public DoubleRect(int x, int y, int w, int h):
            base(x,y,w,h) {
      rdPen  = new Pen (Color.Red, 2);
}
```

This means that our new class DoubleRect will need its own draw method. However, this draw method will use the parent class's draw method but add more drawing of its own.

```
public override void draw(Graphics g) {
      base.draw (g);         //draw one rectangle using parent class
      g.DrawRectangle (rdPen, x +5, y+5, w, h);
}
```

Note that we want to use the coordinates and size of the rectangle that was specified in the constructor. We could keep our own copy of these parameters in the DoubleRect class, or we could change the protection mode of these variables in the base Rectangle class to protected from private.

```
protected int x, y, w, h;
```

The final rectangle drawing window is shown in Figure 5-5.

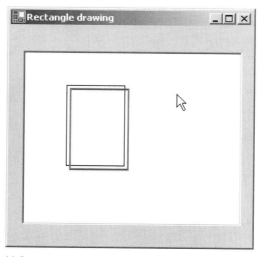

Figure 5-5   The DoubleRect classes

Replacing Methods Using New

Another way to replace a method in a base class when you cannot declare the base class method as *virtual* is to use the *new* keyword in declaring the method in the derived class. If you do this, it effectively hides any methods of that name (regardless of signature) in the base class. In that case, you cannot make calls to the base method of that name from the derived class and must put all the code in the replacement method.

```
public new void draw(Graphics g) {
        g.DrawRectangle (rpen, x, y, w, h);
        g.DrawRectangle (rdPen, x +5, y+5, w, h);
}
```

Overriding Windows Controls

In C# we can easily make new Windows controls based on existing ones, using inheritance. We'll create a TextBox control that highlights all the text when you tab into it. In C#, we can create that new control by just deriving a new class from the TextBox class.

We'll start by using the Windows Designer to create a window with two TextBoxes on it. Then we'll go to the Project | Add User Control menu and add an object called HiTextBox. We'll change this to inherit from TextBox instead of UserControl.

```
public class HiTextBox : Textbox {
```

Then before we make further changes, we compile the program. The new HiTextBox control will appear at the bottom of the Toolbox on the left of the development environment. You can create visual instances of the HiTextBox on any windows form you create. This is shown in Figure 5-6.

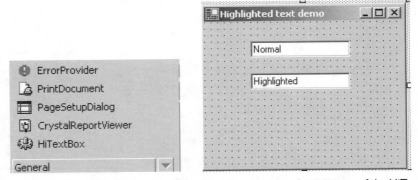

Figure 5-6   The Toolbox, showing the new control we created and an instance of the HiTextBox on the Windows Designer pane of a new form

Now we can modify this class and insert the code to do the highlighting.

```
public class HiTextBox : System.Windows.Forms.TextBox
{
       private Container components = null;
//-------------
private void init() {
       //add event handler to Enter event
       this.Enter += new System.EventHandler (highlight);
}
//-------------
//event handler for highlight event
private void highlight(object obj, System.EventArgs e) {
       this.SelectionStart =0;
       this.SelectionLength =this.Text.Length ;
}
//-------------
public HiTextBox()              {
       InitializeComponent();
       init();
}
```

And that's the whole process. We have derived a new Windows control in about ten lines of code. That's pretty powerful. You can see the resulting program in Figure 5-6. If you run this program, you might at first think that the ordinary TextBox and the HiTextBox behave the same because tabbing between them makes them both highlight. This is the "autohighlight" feature of the C# TextBox. However, if you *click* inside the TextBox and the HiTextBox and tab back and forth, you will see in Figure 5-7 that only our derived HiTextBox continues to highlight.

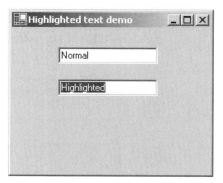

Figure 5-7 A new derived HiTextBox control and a regular TextBox control

Interfaces

An interface is a declaration that a class will contain a specific set of methods with specific arguments. If a class has those methods, it is said to *implement* that interface. It is essentially a contract or promise that a class will contain all the methods described by that interface. Interfaces declare the signatures of public methods but do not contain method bodies.

If a class implements an interface called Xyz, you can refer to that class as if it were of type Xyz as well as by its own type. Since C# only allows a single tree of inheritance, this is the only way for a class to be a member of two or more base classes.

Let's take the example of a class that provides an interface to a multiple select list like a ListBox or a series of check boxes.

```
//an interface to any group of components
//that can return zero or more selected items
//the names  are returned in an Arraylist
     public interface Multisel   {
            void clear();
            ArrayList getSelected();
            Panel getWindow();
     }
```

When you implement the methods of an interface in concrete classes, you must declare that the class uses that interface, and you must provide an implementation of each method in that interface as well, as we illustrate here.

```
/// ListSel  class implements MultiSel interface
     public class ListSel : Multisel {
            public ListSel() {
            }
            public void clear() {
            }
            public ArrayList getSelected() {
                 return new ArrayList ();
            }
            public Panel getWindow() {
                 return new Panel ();
            }
     }
```

We'll see how to use this interface when we discuss the Builder pattern.

Abstract Classes

An *abstract* class declares one or more methods but leaves them unimplemented. If you declare a method as abstract, you must also declare the class as abstract. Suppose, for example, that we define a base class called Shape. It will save some parameters and create a Pen object to draw with. However, we'll leave the actual *draw* method unimplemented, since every different kind of shape will need a different kind of drawing procedure.

```
public abstract class Shape        {
       protected int height, width;
       protected int xpos, ypos;
       protected Pen bPen;
       //-----
       public Shape(int x, int y, int h, int w)           {
              width = w;
              height = h;
              xpos = x;
              ypos = y;
              bPen = new Pen(Color.Black );
       }
       //-----
       public abstract void draw(Graphics g);
       //-----
       public virtual float getArea() {
              return height * width;
       }
   }
```

Note that we declare the *draw* method as *abstract* and end it with a semicolon rather than include any code between braces. We also must declare the overall class as abstract.

However, you can't create an instance of an abstract class like Shape. You can only create instances of derived classes in which the abstract methods are filled in. So, let's create a Rectangle class that does just that.

```
public class Rectangle:Shape          {
      public Rectangle(int x, int y,int h, int w):
                    base(x,y,h,w) {}
      //-----
      public override void draw(Graphics g) {
             g.DrawRectangle (bPen, xpos, ypos, width, height);
      }
}
```

This is a complete class that you can instantiate. It has a real draw method.

In the same way, we could create a Circle class that has its own draw method.

```
public class Circle :Shape         {
      public Circle(int x, int y, int r):
             base(x,y,r,r) {         }
```

```
        //-----
        public override void draw(Graphics g) {
                g.DrawEllipse (bPen, xpos, ypos, width, height);
        }
}
```

Now if we want to draw the circle and rectangle, we just create instances of them in the init method we call from our constructor. Note that since they are both of base type Shape, we can treat them as Shape objects.

```
public class Form1 : System.Windows.Forms.Form        {
        private PictureBox pictureBox1;
        private Container components = null;
        private Shape rect, circ;
        //-----
        public Form1()                {
                InitializeComponent();
                init();
        }
        //-----
        private void init() {
                rect = new CsharpPats.Rectangle (50, 60, 70, 100);
                circ = new Circle (100,60, 50);
        }
```

Finally, we draw the two objects by calling their draw methods from the Paint Event handler we created as we did previously.

```
private void pictureBox1_Paint(object sender, PaintEventArgs e) {
        Graphics g = e.Graphics ;
        rect.draw (g);
        circ.draw (g);
}
```

We see this program executing in Figure 5-8.

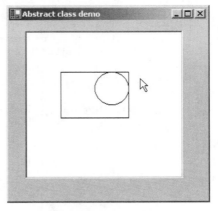

Figure 5-8   An abstract class system drawing a rectangle and circle

Comparing Interfaces and Abstract Classes

When you create an *interface,* you are creating a set of one or more method definitions that you must write in each class that implements that interface. There is no default method code generated; you must include that yourself. The advantage of interfaces is that they provide a way for a class to appear to be part of two classes: one inheritance hierarchy and one from the interface. If you leave an interface method out of a class that is supposed to implement that interface, the compiler will generate an error.

When you create an abstract class, you are creating a base class that might have one or more complete, working methods, but at least it is one that is left unimplemented and declared abstract. You can't instantiate an abstract class, but you must derive from it classes that contain implementations of the abstract methods. If all the methods of an abstract class are unimplemented in the base class, it is essentially the same as an interface but with the restriction that you can't make a class inherit from it as well as from another class hierarchy as you could with an interface. The purpose of abstract classes is to provide a base class definition for how a set of derived classes will work and then allow the programmer to fill in these implementations in the various derived classes.

Another related approach is to create base classes with empty methods. These guarantee that all the derived classes will compile but that the default action for each event is to do nothing at all. Here is a Shape class like that.

```
public class NullShape       {
        protected int height, width;
        protected int xpos, ypos;
        protected Pen bPen;
        //-----
        public Shape(int x, int y, int h, int w)   {
              width = w;
              height = h;
              xpos = x;
              ypos = y;
              bPen = new Pen(Color.Black );
        }
        //-----
        public virtual void draw(Graphics g){}
        //-----
        public virtual float getArea() {
              return height * width;
        }
   }
```

Note that the *draw* method is now an empty method. Derived classes will compile without error, but they won't do anything much. And there will be no hint of what method you are supposed to override, as you would get from using an abstract class.

Summary

We've seen the shape of most of the important features in C# in this chapter. C# provides inheritance, constructors, and the ability to overload methods to provide alternate versions. This leads to the ability to create new derived versions even of Windows controls. In the chapters that follow, we'll show you how you can write design patterns in C#.

Programs on the CD-ROM

Rectangle and Square	\Inheritance\RectDraw
DoubleRect	\Inheritance\DoubleRect
A Highlighted TextBox	\Inheritance\Hitext
Abstract Shape	\Inheritance\abstract

CHAPTER 6

UML Diagrams

The diagrams of the patterns in this book are drawn using the Unified Modeling Language (UML). This simple diagramming style was developed from work done by Grady Booch, James Rumbaugh, and Ivar Jacobson. This merging of ideas became a single specification and, eventually, a standard. You can read details of how to use UML in any number of books, such as those by Booch et al. (1999), Fowler and Scott (1997), and Grand (1998). We'll outline the basics you'll need in this introduction.

Basic UML diagrams consist of boxes representing classes. Let's consider the following class (which has very little actual function).

```
public class Person       {
      private string name;
      private int age;
      //-----
      public Person(string nm, int ag)       {
            name = nm;
            age = ag;
      }
      public string makeJob() {
            return "hired";
      }
      public int getAge() {
            return age;
      }
      public void splitNames() {
      }
}
```

We can represent this class in UML, as shown in Figure 6-1.

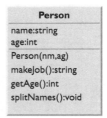

Figure 6-1   The Person class, showing private variables and public methods

The top part of the box contains the class name and package name (if any). The second compartment lists the class's variables, and the bottom compartment lists its methods. The symbols in front of the names indicate that member's visibility, where "+" means public, "–" means private, and "#" means protected. Static methods are underlined. Abstract methods may be in italics or have an "{abstract}" label.

You can also show all of the type information in a UML diagram where that is helpful, as illustrated in Figure 6-2a.

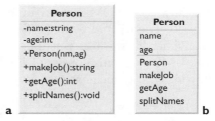

Figure 6-2   The Person class UML diagram, shown both with (a) and without (b) the
method types

UML does not require that you show all of the attributes of a class, and normally only those of interest to the discussion at hand are shown. For example, in Figure 6-2b, some of the method details have been omitted.

Inheritance

Let's consider a version of Person that has public, protected, and private variables and methods and an Employee class derived from it. We will also make the getJob method abstract in the base Person class, which means we indicate it with the *abstract* keyword.

```
public abstract class Person      {
            protected string name;
            private int age;
```

```
//-----
public Person(string nm, int ag)                    {
        name = nm;
        age = ag;
}
public string makeJob() {
        return "hired";
}
public int getAge() {
        return age;
}
public void splitNames() {
}
public abstract string getJob();   //must override
}
```

We now derive the Employee class from it and fill in some code for the getJob method.

```
public class Employee : Person     {
      public Employee(string nm, int ag):base(nm, ag){
      }
      public override string getJob() {
            return "Worker";
      }
}
```

You represent inheritance with a solid line and an open arrowhead. For the simple Employee class that is a subclass of Person, we represent this in UML, as shown in Figure 6-3.

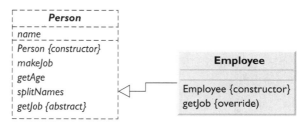

Figure 6-3   The UML diagram showing Employee derived from Person

Note that the name of the Employee class is not in italics because it is now a concrete class and because it includes a concrete method for the formerly abstract *getJob* method. While it has been conventional to show the inheritance with the arrow pointing *up* to the superclass, UML does not require this, and sometimes a different layout is clearer or uses space more efficiently.

Interfaces

An interface looks much like an inheritance, except that the arrow has a dotted line tail, as shown in Figure 6-4. The name *<<interface>>* may also be shown, enclosed in double angle brackets, or *guillamets*.

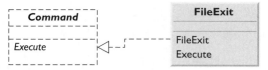

Figure 6-4   ExitCommand implements the Command interface.

Composition

Much of the time, a useful representation of a class hierarchy must include how objects are contained in other objects. For example, a small company might include one Employee and one Person (perhaps a contractor).

```
public class Company         {
        private Employee emp;
        private Person prs;
        public Company()             {

        }
}
```

We represent this in UML, as shown in Figure 6-5.

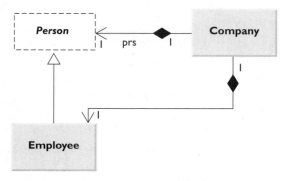

Figure 6-5   Company contains instances of Person and Employee.

The lines between classes show that there can be 0 to 1 instances of Person in Company and 0 to 1 instances of Employee in Company. The diamonds indicate the aggregation of classes within Company.

If there can be many instances of a class inside another, such as the array of Employees shown here

```
public class Company        {
    private Employee[] emps;
    private Employee emp;
    private Person prs;
    public Company()              {

    }
}
```

we represent that object composition as a single line with either an "*" or a "0, *" on it, as shown in Figure 6-6.

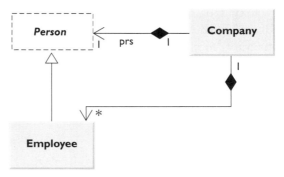

Figure 6-6   Company contains any number of instances of Employee.

Some writers use open and solid diamond arrowheads to indicate containment of aggregates and circle arrowheads for single object composition, but this is not required.

Annotation

You will also find it convenient to annotate your UML or insert comments to explain which class calls a method in which other class. You can place a comment anywhere you want in a UML diagram. Comments may be enclosed in a box with a turned corner or just entered as text. Text comments are usually shown along an arrow line, indicating the nature of the method that is called, as shown in Figure 6-7. You may also use a line to connect the comment to a particular element.

UML is a powerful way of representing object relationships in programs, and there are more diagram features in the full specification. However, the preceding brief discussion covers the markup methods we use in this text.

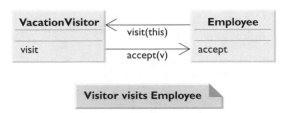

Figure 6-7   A comment is often shown in a box with a turned-down corner.

WithClass UML Diagrams

All of the UML programs in this book were drawn with the WithClass program from MicroGold. This program reads in the actual compiled classes and generates the UML class diagrams we show here. We have edited many of these class diagrams to show only the most important methods and relationships. However, the complete WithClass diagram files for each design pattern are stored in the diagram's directory. Thus, you can run your demo copy of WithClass on the enclosed CD and read in and investigate the detailed UML diagram starting with the same drawings you see here in the book.

C# Project Files

All of the programs in this book were written as projects using Visual Studio.NET. Each subdirectory of the CD-ROM contains the project file for that project so you can load the project and compile it as we did.

CHAPTER 7

Arrays, Files, and Exceptions in C#

C# makes handling arrays and files extremely easy and introduces exceptions to simplify error handling.

Arrays

In C#, all arrays are zero based. If you declare an array as

```
int[] x = new int[10];
```

such arrays have 10 elements, numbered from 0 to 9. Thus, arrays are in line with the style used in C, C++, and Java.

```
const int MAX = 10;
float[] xy = new float[MAX];
for (int i = 0; i < MAX; i++ ) {
      xy[i] = i;
}
```

You should get into the habit of looping through arrays from zero to the array bounds minus one, as we did in the preceding example.

All array variables have a length property so you can find out how large the array is.

```
float[] z = new float[20];
for (int j = 0; j< z.Length ; j++) {
      z[j] = j;
}
```

Arrays in C# are dynamic and space can be reallocated at any time. To create a reference to an array and allocate it later within the class, use this syntax.

```
float[] z;                    //declare here
z = new float[20];            //create later
```

Collection Objects

The System.Collections namespace contains a number of useful variable-length array objects you can use to add and obtain items in several ways.

ArrayLists

The ArrayList object is essentially a variable-length array that you can add items to as needed. The basic ArrayList methods allow you to add elements to the array and fetch and change individual elements.

```
float[] z = {1.0f, 2.9f, 5.6f} ;
ArrayList arl = new ArrayList ();
for (int j = 0; j< z.Length ; j++) {
        arl.Add (z[j]);
}
```

The ArrayList has a Count property you can use to find out how many elements it contains. You can then move from 0 to that count *minus one* to access these elements, treating the ArrayList just as if it were an array.

```
for (j = 0; j < arl.Count ; j++) {
        Console.WriteLine (arl[j]);
}
```

You can also access the members of ArrayList objects sequentially, using the *foreach* looping construct, without having to create an index variable or know the length of the ArrayList.

```
foreach (float a in arl) {
     Console.WriteLine (a);
}
```

You can also use the methods of the ArrayList shown in Table 7-1.

An object fetched from an ArrayList is always of type *object*. This means you usually need to cast the object to the correct type before using it.

```
float x = (float) arl[j];
```

Table 7-1 ArrayList Methods

`Clear`	Clears the contents of the ArrayList.
`Contains(object)`	Returns true if the ArrayList contains that value.
`CopyTo(array)`	Copies entire ArrayList into a one-dimensional array.
`IndexOf(object)`	Returns the first index of the value.
`Insert(index, object)`	Inserts the element at the specified index.
`Remove(object)`	Removes element from list.
`RemoveAt(index)`	Removes element from specified position.
`Sort`	Sorts ArrayList.

Hashtables

A Hashtable is a variable-length array where every entry can be referred to by a key value. Typically, keys are strings of some sort, but they can be any sort of object. Each element must have a unique key, although the elements themselves need not be unique. Hashtables are used to allow rapid access to one of a large and unsorted set of entries and can also be used by reversing the key and the entry values to create a list where each entry is guaranteed to be unique.

```
Hashtable hash = new Hashtable ();
float freddy = 12.3f;
hash.Add ("fred", freddy);  //add to table
//get this one back out
float temp = (float)hash["fred"];
```

Note that like the ArrayList, we must cast the values we obtain from a Hashtable to the correct type. Hashtables also have a count property, and you can obtain an enumeration of the keys or of the values.

SortedLists

The SortedList class maintains two internal arrays, so you can obtain the elements either by zero-based index or by alphabetic key.

```
float sammy = 44.55f;
SortedList slist = new SortedList ();
```

```
slist.Add ("fred", freddy);
slist.Add ("sam", sammy);
//get by index
float newFred = (float)slist.GetByIndex (0);
//get by key
float newSam = (float)slist["sam"];
```

You will also find the Stack and Queue objects in this namespace. They behave much as you'd expect, and you can find their methods in the system help documentation.

Exceptions

Error handling in C# is accomplished using *exceptions* instead of other, more awkward kinds of error checking. The thrust of exception handling is that you enclose the statements that could cause errors in a *try* block and then catch any errors using a *catch* statement.

```
try {
  //Statements
}
 catch (Exception e) {
  //do these if an error occurs
}
 finally {
   //do these anyway
}
```

Typically, you use this approach to test for errors around file handling statements, although you can also catch array index out-of-range statements and a large number of other error conditions. The way this works is that the statements in the try block are executed, and if there is no error, control passes to the finally statements if any and then out of the block. If errors occur, control passes to the catch statement, where you can handle the errors, and then control passes on to the finally statements and then out of the block.

The following example shows testing for any exception. Since we are moving one element beyond the end of the ArrayList, an error will occur.

```
try {
      //note- one too many
      for(int i = 0; i <= arl.Count ; i++)
            Console.WriteLine (arl[i]);
}
catch(Exception e) {
            Console.WriteLine (e.Message );
}
```

This code prints out the error message and the calling locations in the program and then goes on.

```
0123456789Index was out of range.
Must be non-negative and less than the size of the collection.
Parameter name: index
    at System.Collections.ArrayList.get_Item(Int32 index)
    at arr.Form1..ctor() in form1.cs:line 58
```

By contrast, if we do not catch the exception, we will get an error message from the runtime system, and the program will exit instead of going on.

Some of the more common exceptions are shown in Table 7-2.

Table 7-2   Common Exception classes in C#

`AccessException`	Error in accessing a method or field of a class.
`ArgumentException`	Argument to a method is not valid.
`ArgumentNullException`	Argument is null.
`ArithmeticException`	Overflow or underflow.
`DivideByZeroException`	Division by zero.
`IndexOutOfRangeException`	Array index out of range.
`FileNotFoundException`	File not found.
`EndOfStreamException`	Access beyond end of input stream (such as files).
`DirectoryNotFoundException`	Directory not found.
`NullReferenceException`	The object variable has not been initialized to a real value.

Multiple Exceptions

You can also catch a series of exceptions and handle them differently in a series of catch blocks.

```
try {
    for(int i =0; i<= arl.Count ; i++) {
        int k = (int)(float)arl[i];
        Console.Write(i + " "+ k / i);
```

```
        }
    }
    catch(DivideByZeroException e) {
          printZErr(e);
    }
    catch(IndexOutOfRangeException e) {
          printOErr(e);
    }
    catch(Exception e) {
          printErr(e);
    }
```

This gives you the opportunity to recover from various errors in different ways.

Throwing Exceptions

You don't have to deal with exceptions exactly where they occur. You can pass them back to the calling program using the throw statement. This causes the exception to be thrown in the calling program.

```
try {
//statements
}
catch(Exception e) {
          throw(e);      //pass on to calling program
}
```

Note that C# does not support the Java syntax *throws*, which allows you to declare that a method will throw an exception and that you therefore must provide an exception handler for it.

File Handling

The file handling objects in C# provide you with some fairly flexible methods of handling files.

The File Object

The File object represents a file and has useful methods for testing for a file's existence as well as renaming and deleting a file. All of its methods are *static*, which means that you do not (and cannot) create an instance of File using the new operator. Instead, you use its methods directly.

```
if (File.Exists ("Foo.txt"))
      File.Delete ("foo.txt");
```

You can also use the File object to obtain a FileStream for reading and writing file data.

```
//open text file for reading
    StreamReader ts = File.OpenText ("foo1.txt");

//open any type of file for reading
    FileStream fs = File.OpenRead ("foo2.any");
```

These are some of the more useful File methods.

Static Method	Meaning
File.FileExists(filename)	True if file exists
File.Delete(filename)	Delete the file
File.AppendText(String)	Append text
File.Copy(fromFile, toFile)	Copy a file
File.Move(fromFile, toFile)	Move a file, deleting old copy
File.GetExtension(filename)	Return file extension
File.HasExtension(filename)	True if file has an extension

Reading a Text File

To read a text file, use the File object to obtain a StreamReader object. Then use the text stream's read methods.

```
    StreamReader ts = File.OpenText ("foo1.txt");
    String s =ts.ReadLine ();
```

Writing a Text File

To create and write a text file, use the CreateText method to get a StreamWriter object.

```
//open for writing
    StreamWriter sw = File.CreateText ("foo3.txt");
    sw.WriteLine ("Hello file");
```

If you want to append to an existing file, you can create a StreamWriter object directly with the Boolean argument for append set to true.

```
//append to text file
StreamWriter asw = new StreamWriter ("foo1.txt", true);
```

Exceptions in File Handling

A large number of the most commonly occurring exceptions arise in handling file input and output. You can get exceptions for illegal filenames, files that do not exist, directories that do not exist, illegal filename arguments, and file protection errors. Thus, the best way to handle file input and output is to enclose file manipulation code in Try blocks to assure yourself that all possible error conditions are caught and thus prevent embarrassing fatal errors. All of the methods of the various file classes show in their documentation which methods they throw. You can be confident that you will catch all of them by just catching the general Exception object, but if you need to take different actions for different exceptions, you can test for them separately.

For example, you might open text files in the following manner.

```
try {
//open text file for reading
        StreamReader ts = File.OpenText ("foo1.txt");
        String s =ts.ReadLine ();
}
catch(Exception e ) {
        Console.WriteLine (e.Message );
}
```

Testing for End of File

There are two useful ways to make sure you do not pass the end of a text file: (1) look for a null exception and (2) look for the end of a data stream. When you read beyond the end of a text file, no error occurs and no end of file exception is thrown. However, if you read a string after the end of a file, it will return as a null value. You can use this to create an end-of-file function in a file reading class.

```
private StreamReader rf;
private bool eof;
//------------
public String readLine () {
        String s = rf.ReadLine ();
        if(s == null)
                eof = true;
        return s;
}
//------------
public bool fEof() {
        return eof;
}
```

The other way to ensure that you don't read past the end of a file is to peek ahead using the Stream's Peek method. This returns the ASCII code for the next character, or a −1 if no characters remain.

```
public String read_Line() {
        String s = ""
        if (rf.Peek() > 0) {
                s = rf.ReadLine ();
        }
        else {
                eof=true;
        }
        return s;
}
```

A csFile Class

It is sometimes convenient to wrap these file methods in a simpler class with easy-to-use methods. We have done that here in the csFile class. We'll be using this convenience class in some of the examples in later chapters.

We can include the filename and path in the constructor, or we can pass it in using the overloaded OpenForRead and OpenForWrite statements.

```
public class csFile
        {
                private string fileName;
                StreamReader ts;
                StreamWriter ws;
                private bool opened, writeOpened;
                //-----------
                public csFile() {
                        init();
                }
                //-----------
                private void init() {
                        opened = false;
                        writeOpened = false;
                }
                //-----------
                public csFile(string file_name)    {
                        fileName = file_name;
                        init();
                }
```

We can open a file for reading by either of two methods: one that includes the filename and one that uses a filename in the argument.

```
public bool OpenForRead(string file_name){
        fileName = file_name;
        try {
```

```
                ts = new StreamReader (fileName);
                opened=true;
        }
        catch(FileNotFoundException e) {
                return false;
        }
        return true;
}
//-----------
public bool OpenForRead() {
        return OpenForRead(fileName);
}
```

You can then read data from the text file using a readLine method.

```
public string readLine() {
        return ts.ReadLine ();
}
```

Likewise, the following methods allow you to open a file for writing and write lines of text to it.

```
public void writeLine(string s) {
        ws.WriteLine (s);
}
//-----------
public bool OpenForWrite() {
        return OpenForWrite(fileName);
}
//-----------
public bool OpenForWrite(string file_name) {
        try{
                ws = new StreamWriter (file_name);
                fileName = file_name;
                writeOpened = true;
                return true;
        }
        catch(FileNotFoundException e) {
                return false;
        }
}
```

We'll use this simplified file method wrapper class whenever we need to read in a file.

Program on the CD-ROM

Illustrates csFile class	\Files\FileReader

PART 2

Creational Patterns

With the foregoing description of objects, inheritance, and interfaces in hand, we are now ready to begin discussing design patterns in earnest. Recall that these are merely recipes for writing better object-oriented programs. We have divided them into the Gang of Four's three groups: creational, structural, and behavioral. We'll start out in this section with the creational patterns.

All of the creational patterns deal with ways to create instances of objects. This is important because your program should not depend on how objects are created and arranged. In C#, of course, the simplest way to create an instance of an object is by using the *new* operator.

```
Fred fred1 = new Fred();          //instance of Fred class
```

However, this really amounts to hard coding, depending on how you create the object within your program. In many cases, the exact nature of the object that is created could vary with the needs of the program, and abstracting the creation process into a special "creator" class can make your program more flexible and general.

The **Factory Method pattern** provides a simple decision-making class that returns one of several possible subclasses of an abstract base class, depending on the data that are provided. We'll start with the **Simple Factory pattern** as an introduction to factories and then introduce the **Factory Method pattern** as well.

The **Abstract Factory pattern** provides an interface to create and return one of several families of related objects.

The **Singleton pattern** is a class of which there can be no more than one instance. It provides a single global point of access to that instance.

The **Builder pattern** separates the construction of a complex object from its representation so that several different representations can be created, depending on the needs of the program.

The **Prototype pattern** starts with an instantiated class and copies or clones it to make new instances. These instances can then be further tailored using their public methods.

CHAPTER 8

The Simple Factory Pattern

One type of pattern that we see again and again in OO programs is the Simple Factory pattern. A Simple Factory pattern is one that returns an instance of one of several possible classes, depending on the data provided to it. Usually all of the classes it returns have a common parent class and common methods, but each of them performs a task differently and is optimized for different kinds of data. This Simple Factory is not, in fact, one of the 23 GoF patterns, but it serves here as an introduction to the somewhat more subtle Factory Method GoF pattern we'll discuss shortly.

How a Simple Factory Works

To understand the Simple Factory pattern, let's look at the diagram in Figure 8-1. In this figure, X is a base class, and classes XY and XZ are derived from it. The

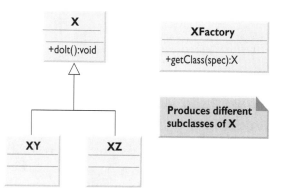

Figure 8-1 A Simple Factory pattern

XFactory class decides which of these subclasses to return, depending on the arguments you give it. On the right, we define a *getClass* method to be one that passes in some value *abc* and that returns some instance of the class x. Which one it returns doesn't matter to the programmer, since they all have the same methods but different implementations. How it decides which one to return is entirely up to the factory. It could be some very complex function, but it is often quite simple.

Sample Code

Let's consider a simple C# case where we could use a Factory class. Suppose we have an entry form and we want to allow the user to enter his name either as "firstname lastname" or as "lastname, firstname." We'll make the further simplifying assumption that we will always be able to decide the name order by whether there is a comma between the last and first names.

This is a pretty simple decision to make, and you could make it with a simple *if* statement in a single class, but let's use it here to illustrate how a factory works and what it can produce. We'll start by defining a simple class that takes the name string in using the constructor and allows you to fetch the names back.

```
//Base class for getting split names
    public class Namer   {
            //parts stored here
            protected string frName, lName;

            //return first name
            public string getFrname(){
                return frName;
            }
            //return last name
            public string getLname() {
                return lName;
            }
        }
```

Note that our base class has no constructor for setting the name.

The Two Derived Classes

Now we can write two very simple derived classes that implement that interface and split the name into two parts in the constructor. In the FirstFirst class, we make the simplifying assumption that everything before the last space is part of the first name.

```
public class FirstFirst : Namer {
    public FirstFirst(string name)    {
    int i = name.Trim().IndexOf (" ");
    if(i > 0) {
        frName = name.Substring (0, i).Trim ();
        lName = name.Substring (i + 1).Trim ();
    }
    else {
        lName = name;
        frName = "";
    }
  }
}
```

And in the LastFirst class, we assume that a comma delimits the last name. In both classes, we also provide error recovery in case the space or comma does not exist.

```
public class LastFirst : Namer {
    public LastFirst(string name)    {
        int i = name.IndexOf (",");
        if(i > 0) {
            lName = name.Substring (0, i);
            frName = name.Substring (i + 1).Trim ();
        }
        else {
            lName = name;
            frName = "";
        }
    }
}
```

In both cases, we store the split name in the protected lName and frName variables in the base Namer class. Note that we don't even need any getFrname or getLname methods, since we have already written them in the base class.

Building the Simple Factory

Now our Simple Factory class is easy to write. We just test for the existence of a comma and then return an instance of one class or the other.

```
public class NameFactory    {
    public NameFactory() {}

    public Namer getName(string name) {
        int i = name.IndexOf (",");
        if(i > 0)
            return new LastFirst (name);
        else
```

```
                    return new FirstFirst (name);
        }
}
```

Using the Factory

Let's see how we put this together. In response to the Compute button click, we use an instance of the NameFactory to return the correct derived class.

```
private void btCompute_Click(
          object sender, System.EventArgs e) {
     Namer nm = nameFact.getName (txName.Text );
     txFirst.Text = nm.getFrname ();
     txLast.Text = nm.getLname ();
}
```

Then we call the getFrname and getLname methods to get the correct splitting of the name. We don't need to know which derived class this is. The Factory has provided it for us, and all we need to know is that it has the two get methods. The complete class diagram is shown in Figure 8-2.

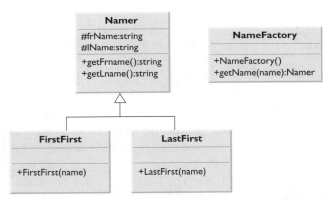

Figure 8-2   The Name Factory program

We have constructed a simple user interface that allows you to enter the names in either order and see the two names separately displayed. You can see this program in Figure 8-3.

You type in a name and then click on the "Get name" button, and the divided name appears in the text fields below. The crux of this program is the compute method that fetches the text, obtains an instance of a Namer class, and displays the results.

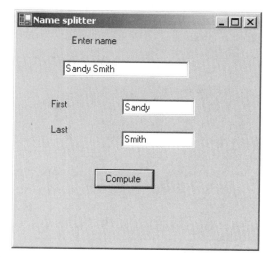

Figure 8-3   The Namer program executing

And that's the fundamental principle of the Simple Factory pattern. You create an abstraction that decides which of several possible classes to return, and it returns one. Then you call the methods of that class instance without ever knowing which subclass you are actually using. This approach keeps the issues of data dependence separated from the classes' useful methods.

Factory Patterns in Math Computation

Most people who use Factory patterns tend to think of them as tools for simplifying tangled programming classes. But it is perfectly possible to use them in programs that simply perform mathematical computations. For example, in the Fast Fourier Transform (FFT), you evaluate the following four equations repeatedly for a large number of point pairs over many passes through the array you are transforming. Because of the way the graphs of these computations are drawn, the following four equations constitute one instance of the FFT "butterfly." These are shown as Equations 1–4.

$$R_1' = R_1 + R_2 \cos(y) - I_2 \sin(y) \quad (1)$$
$$R_2' = R_1 - R_2 \cos(y) + I_2 \sin(y) \quad (2)$$
$$I_1' = I_1 + R_2 \sin(y) + I_2 \cos(y) \quad (3)$$
$$I_2' = I_1 - R_2 \sin(y) - I_2 \cos(y) \quad (4)$$

However, there are a number of times during each pass through the data where the angle y is zero. In this case, your complex math evaluation reduces to Equations 5–8.

$$R_1' = R_1 + R_2 \quad (5)$$
$$R_2' = R_1 - R_2 \quad (6)$$
$$I_1' = I_1 + I_2 \quad (7)$$
$$I_2' = I_1 - I_2 \quad (8)$$

We first define a class to hold complex numbers.

```
public class Complex          {
      float real;
      float imag;
//---------------------------------
public Complex(float r, float i) {
      real = r; imag = i;
}
//---------------------------------
public void setReal(float r) { real = r;}
//---------------------------------
public void setImag(float i) {imag= i;}
//---------------------------------
public float getReal() {return real;}
//---------------------------------
public float getImag() {return imag;}
}
```

Our basic Buttefly class is an abstract class that can be filled in by one of the implementations of the Execute command.

```
public abstract class Butterfly {
      float y;
      public Butterfly() {
      }
      public Butterfly(float angle) {
            y = angle;
      }
      abstract public void Execute(Complex x, Complex y);
}
```

We can then make a simple addition Butterfly class that implements the add and subtract methods of Equations 5–8.

```
class AddButterfly : Butterfly    {
   float oldr1, oldi1;
      public AddButterfly(float angle) {
            }
```

```
      public override void Execute(Complex xi, Complex xj) {
            oldr1 = xi.getReal();
            oldi1 = xi.getImag();
            xi.setReal(oldr1 + xj.getReal());
            xj.setReal(oldr1 - xj.getReal());
            xi.setImag(oldi1 + xj.getImag());
            xj.setImag(oldi1 - xj.getImag());
      }
}
```

The TrigButterfly class is analogous except that the Execute method contains the actual trig functions of Equations 1–4.

```
public class TrigButterfly:Butterfly    {
      float y, oldr1, oldi1;
      float cosy, siny;
      float r2cosy, r2siny, i2cosy, i2siny;

      public TrigButterfly(float angle) {
            y = angle;
            cosy = (float) Math.Cos(y);
            siny = (float)Math.Sin(y);
      }
      public override void Execute(Complex xi, Complex xj) {
            oldr1 = xi.getReal();
            oldi1 = xi.getImag();
            r2cosy = xj.getReal() * cosy;
            r2siny = xj.getReal() * siny;
            i2cosy = xj.getImag()*cosy;
            i2siny = xj.getImag()*siny;
            xi.setReal(oldr1 + r2cosy +i2siny);
            xi.setImag(oldi1 - r2siny +i2cosy);
            xj.setReal(oldr1 - r2cosy - i2siny);
            xj.setImag(oldi1 + r2siny - i2cosy);
      }
}
```

Then we can make a simple factory class that decides which class instance to return. Since we are making Butterflies, we'll call our Factory a Cocoon. We never really need to instantiate Cocoon, so we will make its one method static.

```
public class Cocoon          {
      static public Butterfly getButterfly(float y) {
            if (y != 0)
                  return new TrigButterfly(y);
            else
                  return new addButterfly(y);
      }
}
```

Summary

We have seen that the simple Factory returns instances of classes that have the same methods. They may be instances of different derived subclasses, or they may in fact be unrelated classes that just share the same *interface*. Either way, the methods in these class instances are the same and can be used interchangeably.

Thought Questions

1. Consider a personal checkbook management program like Quicken. It manages several bank accounts and investments and can handle your bill paying. Where could you use a Factory pattern in designing a program like that?

2. Suppose you are writing a program to assist homeowners in designing additions to their houses. What objects might a Factory be used to produce?

Programs on the CD-ROM

The Name Factory	\Factory\Namer
An FFT Example	\Factory\FFT

CHAPTER 9

The Factory Method

We've just seen a couple of examples of the simplest of factories. The factory concept recurs throughout object-oriented programming, and we find a few examples embedded in C# itself and in other design patterns (such as the Builder pattern). In these cases a single class acts as a traffic cop and decides which subclass of a single hierarchy will be instantiated.

The Factory Method pattern is a clever but subtle extension of this idea, where no single class makes the decision as to which subclass to instantiate. Instead, the superclass defers the decision to each subclass. This pattern does not actually have a decision point where one subclass is directly selected over another class. Instead, programs written to this pattern define an abstract class that creates objects but lets each subclass decide which object to create.

We can draw a pretty simple example from the way that swimmers are seeded into lanes in a swim meet. When swimmers compete in multiple heats in a given event, they are sorted to compete from slowest in the early heats to fastest in the last heat and arranged within a heat with the fastest swimmers in the center lanes. This is referred to as *straight seeding*.

Now, when swimmers swim in championships, they frequently swim the event twice. During preliminaries everyone competes, and the top 12 or 16 swimmers return to compete against one another at finals. In order to make the preliminaries more equitable, the top heats are *circle* seeded: The fastest three swimmers are in the center lane in the fastest three heats, the second fastest three swimmers are in the next to center lane in the top three heats, and so forth.

So how do we build some objects to implement this seeding scheme and illustrate the Factory Method? First, let's design an abstract Event class.

```
public abstract class Event     {
    protected int numLanes;
    protected ArrayList swimmers;
```

```
        public Event(string filename, int lanes) {
                numLanes = lanes;
                swimmers = new ArrayList();
                //read in swimmers from file
                 csFile f = new csFile(filename);
                f.OpenForRead ();
                string s = f.readLine();
                while (s != null) {
                        Swimmer sw = new Swimmer(s);
                        swimmers.Add (sw);
                        s = f.readLine();
                }
                f.close();
        }
        public abstract Seeding getSeeding();
        public abstract bool isPrelim();
        public abstract bool isFinal();
        public abstract bool isTimedFinal();
}
```

Note that this class is not entirely without content. Since all the derived classes will need to read data from a file, we put that code in the base class.

These abstract methods simply show the rest of a complete implementation of an Event class. Then we can implement concrete classes from the Event class, called PrelimEvent and TimedFinalEvent. The only difference between these classes is that one returns one kind of seeding and the other returns a different kind of seeding.

We also define an abstract Seeding class with the following methods.

```
public abstract class Seeding      {
                protected int        numLanes;
                protected int[]      lanes;
                public abstract IEnumerator getSwimmers();
                public abstract int getCount();
                public abstract int getHeats();
                protected abstract void seed();
                //-------------------------------
                protected void calcLaneOrder() {
                //complete code on CD
                }
        }
```

Note that we actually included code for the calcLaneOrder method but omit the code here for simplicity. The derived classes then each create an instance of the base Seeding class to call these functions.

We can then create two concrete seeding subclasses: StraightSeeding and CircleSeeding. The PrelimEvent class will return an instance of CircleSeeding, and the TimedFinalEvent class will return an instance of StraightSeeding. Thus, we see that we have two hierarchies: one of Events and one of Seedings.

In the Events hierarchy (Figure 9-1), you will see that both derived Events classes contain a *getSeeding* method. One of them returns an instance of StraightSeeding and the other an instance of CircleSeeding. So you can see that there is no real factory decision point as we had in our simple example. Instead, the decision as to which Event class to instantiate is the one that determines which Seeding class will be instantiated.

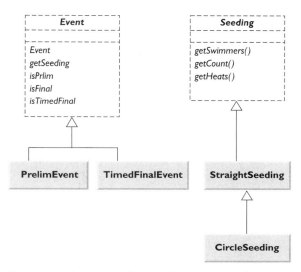

Figure 9-1   Seeding diagram showing Seeding interface and derived classes

While it looks like there is a one-to-one correspondence between the two class hierarchies, there needn't be. There could be many kinds of Events and only a few kinds of Seeding used.

The Swimmer Class

We haven't said much about the Swimmer class, except that it contains a name, club, age, seed, time, and place to put the heat and lane after seeding. The Event class reads in the Swimmers from some database (a file in our example) and then passes that collection to the Seeding class when you call the getSeeding method for that event.

The Events Classes

We have seen the previous abstract base Events class. In actual use, we use it to read in the swimmer data and pass it on to instances of the Swimmer class to parse.

The base Event class has empty methods for whether the event is a prelim, final, or timed final event. We fill in the event in the derived classes.

Our PrelimEvent class just returns an instance of CircleSeeding.

```
public class PrelimEvent:Event    {
    public PrelimEvent(string filename, int lanes):
            base(filename,lanes) {}
            //return circle seeding
    public override Seeding getSeeding() {
            return new CircleSeeding(swimmers, numLanes);
    }
    public override bool isPrelim() {
            return true;
    }
    public override bool isFinal() {
            return false;
    }
    public override bool isTimedFinal() {
            return false;
    }
}
```

Our TimedFinalEvent class returns an instance of StraightSeeding.

```
public class TimedFinalEvent:Event  {

    public TimedFinalEvent(string filename,
            int lanes):base(filename, lanes) {}
    //return StraightSeeding class
    public override Seeding getSeeding() {
            return new StraightSeeding(swimmers, numLanes);
    }
    public override bool isPrelim() {
            return false;
    }
    public override bool isFinal() {
            return false;
    }
    public override bool isTimedFinal() {
            return true;
    }
}
```

In both cases our events classes contain an instance of the base Events class, which we use to read in the data files.

StraightSeeding

In actually writing this program, we'll discover that most of the work is done in straight seeding. The changes for circle seeding are pretty minimal. So we instantiate our StraightSeeding class and copy in the Collection of swimmers and the number of lanes.

```
protected override void seed() {
        //loads the swmrs array and sorts it
        sortUpwards();

        int lastHeat = count % numLanes;
        if (lastHeat < 3)
                lastHeat = 3;    //last heat must have 3 or more
        int lastLanes = count - lastHeat;
        numHeats = count / numLanes;
        if (lastLanes > 0)
                numHeats++;
        int heats = numHeats;
        //place heat and lane in each swimmer's object
        //Add in last partial heat
        //copy from array back into ArrayList
        //details on CDROM
}
```

This makes the entire array of seeded Swimmers available when you call the getSwimmers method.

Circle Seeding

The CircleSeeding class is derived from StraightSeeding, so it starts by calling the parent class's seed method and then rearranges the top heats.

```
protected override void seed() {
        int circle;
        base.seed();         //do straight seed as default
        if (numHeats >= 2 ) {
                if (numHeats >= 3)
                        circle = 3;
                else
                        circle = 2;
                int i = 0;
        for (int j = 0; j < numLanes; j++) {
                for (int k = 0; k < circle; k++) {
                        swmrs[i].setLane(lanes[j]);
                        swmrs[i++].setHeat(numHeats - k);
                }
        }
    }
}
```

Our Seeding Program

In this example, we took a list of swimmers from the Web who competed in the 500-yard freestyle and the 100-yard freestyle and used them to build our

TimedFinalEvent and PrelimEvent classes. You can see the results of these two seedings in Figure 9-2. In the top box, the 500 Free event is selected, and you can see that the swimmers are seeded in straight seeding from slowest to fastest. In the bottom box, the 100 Free event is selected and is circle seeded, with the last 3 heats seeded in a rotating fashion.

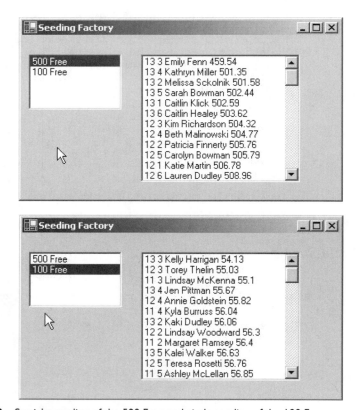

Figure 9-2   Straight seeding of the 500 Free and circle seeding of the 100 Free

Other Factories

One issue that we have skipped over is how the program that reads in the swimmer data decides which kind of event to generate. We finesse this here by simply creating the correct type of event when we read in the data. This code is in our init method of our form.

```
private void init() {
    //create array of events
    events = new ArrayList ();
```

```
            lsEvents.Items.Add ("500 Free");
            lsEvents.Items.Add ("100 Free");
            //and read in their data
            events.Add (new TimedFinalEvent ("500free.txt", 6));
            events.Add (new PrelimEvent ("100free.txt", 6));
        }
```

Clearly, this is an instance where an EventFactory may be needed to decide which kind of event to generate. This revisits the simple factory with which we began the discussion.

When to Use a Factory Method

You should consider using a Factory method in the following situations.

- A class can't anticipate which kind of class of objects it must create.
- A class uses its subclasses to specify which objects it creates.
- You want to localize the knowledge of which class gets created.

There are several variations on the factory pattern to recognize.

1. The base class is abstract, and the pattern must return a complete working class.

2. The base class contains default methods, and these methods are called unless the default methods are insufficient.

3. Parameters are passed to the factory telling it which of several class types to return. In this case the classes may share the same method names but may do something quite different.

Thought Question

Seeding in track is carried out from inside to outside lanes. What classes would you need to develop to carry out tracklike seeding as well?

Program on the CD-ROM

Seeding Program	\FactoryMethod\Seeder

CHAPTER 10

The Abstract Factory Pattern

The Abstract Factory pattern is one level of abstraction higher than the Factory pattern. You can use this pattern when you want to return one of several related classes of objects, each of which can return several different objects on request. In other words, the Abstract Factory is a factory object that returns one of several groups of classes. You might even decide which class to return from that group using a Simple Factory.

Common thought experiment–style examples might include automobile factories. You would expect a Toyota factory to work exclusively with Toyota parts and a Ford factory to use Ford parts. You can consider each auto factory as an Abstract Factory and the parts the groups of related classes.

A GardenMaker Factory

Let's consider a practical example where you might want to use the abstract factory in your application. Suppose you are writing a program to plan a garden design. This could include annual, vegetable, or perennial gardens. However, no matter which kind of garden you are planning, you will have the same questions.

1. What are good border plants?

2. What are good center plants?

3. What plants do well in partial shade?

(You would probably have a lot more plant questions, but we won't get into them here.)

We want a base C# Garden class that can answer these questions as class methods.

```
public class Garden {
     protected Plant center, shade, border;
     protected bool showCenter, showShade, showBorder;
     //select which ones to display
     public void setCenter() {showCenter = true;}
     public void setBorder() {showBorder =true;}
     public void setShade() {showShade =true;}
     //draw each plant
     public void draw(Graphics g) {
          if (showCenter) center.draw (g, 100, 100);
          if (showShade) shade.draw (g, 10, 50);
          if (showBorder) border.draw (g, 50, 150);
     }
}
```

Our Plant object sets the name and draws itself when its draw method is called.

```
public class Plant   {
     private string name;
     private Brush br;
     private Font font;

     public Plant(string pname) {
          name = pname;      //save name
          font = new Font ("Arial", 12);
          br = new SolidBrush (Color.Black );
     }
     //-------------
     public void draw(Graphics g, int x, int y) {
          g.DrawString (name, font, br, x, y);
     }
}
```

In *Design Patterns* terms, the Garden interface is the Abstract Factory. It defines the methods of concrete class that can return one of several classes. Here, we return central, border, and shade-loving plants as those three classes. The abstract factory could also return more specific garden information, such as soil pH or watering requirements.

In a real system, each type of garden would probably consult an elaborate database of plant information. In our simple example we'll return one kind of each plant. So, for example, for the vegetable garden we simply write the following.

```
public class VeggieGarden : Garden          {
     public VeggieGarden() {
          shade = new Plant("Broccoli");
          border = new Plant ("Peas");
          center = new Plant ("Corn");
     }
}
```

In a similar way, we can create Garden classes for PerennialGarden and AnnualGarden. Each of these concrete classes is known as a Concrete Factory, since it implements the methods in the parent class. Now we have a series of Garden objects, each of which creates one of several Plant objects. This is illustrated in the class diagram in Figure 10-1.

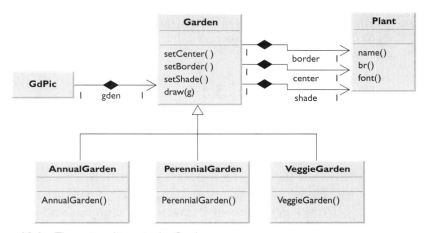

Figure 10-1   The major objects in the Gardener program

We can easily construct our Abstract Factory driver program to return one of these Garden objects based on the radio button that a user selects, as shown in the user interface in Figure 10-2.

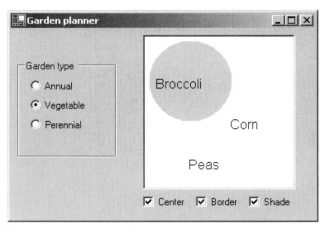

Figure 10-2   The user interface of the Gardener program

Each time you select a new garden type, the screen is cleared and the check boxes unchecked. Then, as you select each checkbox, that plant type is drawn in.

Remember that in C# you do not draw on the screen directly from your code. Instead, the screen is updated when the next paint event occurs, and you must tell the paint routine what objects to paint.

Since each garden (and Plant) knows how to draw itself, it should have a draw method that draws the appropriate plant names on the garden screen. And since we provided check boxes to draw each of the types of plants, we set a Boolean that indicates that you can now draw each of these plant types.

Our Garden object contains three set methods to indicate that you can draw each plant.

```
public void setCenter() {showCenter = true;}
public void setBorder() {showBorder =true;}
public void setShade() {showShade =true;}
```

The PictureBox

We draw the circle representing the shady area inside the PictureBox and draw the names of the plants inside this box as well. This is best accomplished by deriving a new GardenPic class from PictureBox and giving it the knowledge to draw the circle and the garden plant names. Thus, we need to add a paint method not to the main GardenMaker window class but to the PictureBox it contains. This overrides the base OnPaint event of the underlying Control class.

```
public class GdPic : System.Windows.Forms.PictureBox  {
      private Container components = null;
      private Brush br;
      private Garden gden;
      //-----------
      private void init () {
            br = new SolidBrush (Color.LightGray );
      }
      //-----------
      public GdPic()        {
            InitializeComponent();
            init();
      }
      //-----------
      public void setGarden(Garden garden) {
            gden = garden;
      }
      //-----------
      protected override void OnPaint ( PaintEventArgs pe ){
            Graphics g = pe.Graphics;
            g.FillEllipse (br, 5, 5, 100, 100);
            if(gden != null)
                  gden.draw (g);
      }
```

Note that we do not have to erase the plant name text each time because OnPaint is only called when the whole picture needs to be repainted.

Handling the RadioButton and Button Events

When one of the three radio buttons is clicked, you create a new garden of the correct type and pass it into the picture box class. You also clear all the check boxes.

```
private void opAnnual_CheckedChanged(
          object sender, EventArgs e) {
    setGarden( new AnnualGarden ());
}
//-----
private void opVegetable_CheckedChanged(
          object sender, EventArgs e) {
    setGarden( new VeggieGarden ());
}
//-----
private void opPerennial_CheckedChanged(
          object sender, EventArgs e) {
    setGarden( new PerennialGarden ());
}
//-----
private void setGarden(Garden gd) {
    garden = gd;                    //save current garden
    gdPic1.setGarden ( gd);         //tell picture bos
    gdPic1.Refresh ();              //repaint it
    ckCenter.Checked =false;        //clear all
    ckBorder.Checked = false;       //check
    ckShade.Checked = false;        //boxes
}
```

When you click on one of the check boxes to show the plant names, you simply call that garden's method to set that plant name to be displayed and then call the picture box's Refresh method to cause it to repaint.

```
private void ckCenter_CheckedChanged(
          object sender, System.EventArgs e) {
    garden.setCenter ();
    gdPic1.Refresh ();
}
//-----
private void ckBorder_CheckedChanged(
          object sender, System.EventArgs e) {
    garden.setBorder();
    gdPic1.Refresh ();
}
//-----
```

```
private void ckShade_CheckedChanged(
          object sender, System.EventArgs e) {
    garden.setShade ();
    gdPic1.Refresh ();
}
```

Adding More Classes

One of the great strengths of the Abstract Factory is that you can add new subclasses very easily. For example, if you needed a GrassGarden or a Wild-FlowerGarden, you can subclass Garden and produce these classes. The only real change you'd need to make in any existing code is to add some way to choose these new kinds of gardens.

Consequences of Abstract Factory

One of the main purposes of the Abstract Factory is that it isolates the concrete classes that are generated. The actual class names of these classes are hidden in the factory and need not be known at the client level at all.

Because of the isolation of classes, you can change or interchange these product class families freely. Further, since you generate only one kind of concrete class, this system keeps you from inadvertently using classes from different families of products. However, it is some effort to add new class families, since you need to define new, unambiguous conditions that cause such a new family of classes to be returned.

While all of the classes that the Abstract Factory generates have the same base class, there is nothing to prevent some subclasses from having additional methods that differ from the methods of other classes. For example, a BonsaiGarden class might have a Height or WateringFrequency method that is not in other classes. This presents the same problem that occurs in any subclass: You don't know whether you can call a class method unless you know whether the subclass is one that allows those methods. This problem has the same two solutions as in any similar case: You can either define all of the methods in the base class, even if they don't always have an actual function, or you can derive a new base interface that contains all the methods you need and subclass that for all of your garden types.

Thought Question

If you are writing a program to track investments, such as stocks, bonds, metal futures, derivatives, and the like, how might you use an Abstract Factory?

Program on the CD-ROM

The Gardener Program	\AbstractFactory\GardenPlanner

CHAPTER 11

The Singleton Pattern

The Singleton pattern is grouped with the other Creational patterns, although to some extent it is a pattern that limits, rather than promotes, the creation of classes. Specifically, the Singleton assures that there is one and only one instance of a class and provides a global point of access to it. There are any number of cases in programming where you need to make sure that there can be only one instance of a class. For example, your system can have only one window manager or print spooler, or a single point of access to a database engine. Your PC might have several serial ports but there can only be one instance of "COM1."

Creating Singleton Using a Static Method

The easiest way to make a class that can have only one instance is to embed a static variable inside the class, which we set on the first instance and check for each time we enter the constructor. A static variable is one for which there is only one instance, no matter how many instances there are of the class. To prevent instantiating the class more than once, we make the constructor private so an instance can only be created from within the static method of the class. Then we create a method called getSpooler that will return an instance of Spooler, or null if the class has already been instantiated.

```
public class Spooler        {
    private static bool instance_flag= false;
    private Spooler()  {
    }
    public static Spooler getSpooler() {
            if (! instance_flag)
                    return new Spooler ();
            else
```

```
                           return null;
              }
}
```

One major advantage to this approach is that you don't have to worry about exception handling if the Singleton already exists—you simply get a null return from the getSpooler method.

```
Spooler sp = Spooler.getSpooler();
if (sp != null)
      Console.WriteLine ("Got 1 spooler");
Spooler sp2 = Spooler.getSpooler ();
if (sp2 == null)
      Console.WriteLine ("Can\'t get spooler");
}
```

Also, should you try to create instances of the Spooler class directly, this will fail at compile time because the constructor has been declared as private.

```
//fails at compiler time
Spooler sp3 = new Spooler ();
```

Finally, if you need to change the program to allow two or three instances, this class can be modified easily to allow this.

Exceptions and Instances

The preceding approach has the disadvantage that it requires the programmer to check the getSpooler method return to make sure it is not null. Assuming that programmers will always remember to check errors is the beginning of a slippery slope that many prefer to avoid.

Instead, we can create a class that throws an Exception if you attempt to instantiate it more than once. This requires the programmer to take action and is thus a safer approach. Let's create our own exception class for this case.

```
public class SingletonException:Exception      {
      //new exception type for singleton classes
      public SingletonException(string s):base(s) {
      }
}
```

Note that other than calling its parent classes through the base constructor, this new exception type doesn't do anything in particular. However, it is convenient to have our own named exception type so that the runtime system will warn us if this type of exception is thrown when we attempt to create an instance of Spooler.

Throwing the Exception

Let's write the skeleton of our PrintSpooler class. We'll omit all of the printing methods and just concentrate on correctly implementing the Singleton pattern.

```
public class Spooler      {
     static bool instance_flag = false; //true if one instance
     public Spooler()   {
     if (instance_flag)
           throw new SingletonException(
                 "Only one printer allowed");
           else {
                 instance_flag = true;      //set flag
                 Console.WriteLine ("printer opened");
           }
      }
}
```

Creating an Instance of the Class

Now that we've created our simple Singleton pattern in the PrintSpooler class, let's see how we use it. Remember that we should enclose every method that may throw an exception in a try-catch block.

```
public class singleSpooler         {
     static void Main(string[] args) {
            Spooler pr1, pr2;
 //open one printer--this should always work
   Console.WriteLine ("Opening one spooler");
     try {
       pr1 = new Spooler();
       }
       catch (SingletonException e)        {
          Console.WriteLine (e.Message);
   }
       //try to open another printer --should fail
     Console.WriteLine ("Opening two spoolers");
      try {
        pr2 = new Spooler();
        }
        catch (SingletonException e) {
                Console.WriteLine (e.Message);
      }
}
```

Then if we execute this program, we get the following results.

```
Opening one spooler
printer opened
```

```
Opening two spoolers
Only one spooler allowed
```

The last line indicates than an exception was thrown, as expected.

Providing a Global Point of Access to a Singleton

Since a Singleton is used to provide a single point of global access to a class, your program design must provide a way to reference the Singleton throughout the program, even though there are no global variables in C#.

One solution is to create such Singletons at the beginning of the program and pass them as arguments to the major classes that might need to use them.

```
pr1 = iSpooler.Instance();
Customers cust = new Customers(pr1);
```

The disadvantage is that you might not need all the Singletons that you create for a given program execution, and this could have performance implications.

A more elaborate solution could be to create a registry of all the Singleton classes in the program and make the registry generally available. Each time a Singleton is instantiated, it notes that in the Registry. Then any part of the program can ask for the instance of any Singleton, using an identifying string, and get back that instance variable.

The disadvantage of the registry approach is that type checking may be reduced, since the table of Singletons in the registry probably keeps all of the Singletons as objects—for example, in a Hashtable object. And, of course, the registry itself is probably a Singleton and must be passed to all parts of the program using the constructor or various set functions.

Perhaps the most common way to provide a global point of access is by using static methods of a class. The class name is always available, and the static methods can only be called from the class and not from its instances. This approach is illustrated in the following example.

Returning the Same Instance

Another common approach for Singletons, is to create one and only one instance and always return that same instance. In this revised Singleton class, you see that the constructor is again private and that there is a static getInstance method. However, the class creates one instance and always returns that instance.

```
public class Singleton   {
   private static Singleton single;
   static private bool created = false;
   //creates an instance privately
   private Singleton()  {
         single = this;
         created = true;
   }
   //always returns the same instance
   public static Singleton getInstance() {
         if (! created) {
                single = new Singleton ();
         }
         return single;
   }
   //carries out some operation
   public void doSomething() {
   }
}
```

Other Consequences of the Singleton Pattern

1. It can be difficult to subclass a Singleton, since this can only work if the base Singleton class has not yet been instantiated.

2. You can easily change a Singleton to allow a small number of instances where this is allowable and meaningful.

Programs on the CD-ROM

Shows how print spooler could be written thowing exception	\Singleton\SinglePrinter
Creates one instance or returns null	\Singleton\InstancePrinter

CHAPTER 12

The Builder Pattern

In this chapter we'll examine how to use the Builder pattern to construct objects from components. We have already seen that the Factory pattern returns one of several different subclasses, depending on the data passed in arguments to the creation methods. But suppose we don't want just a computing algorithm but a completely different user interface because of the data we need to display. A typical example might be your e-mail address book. You probably have both individual people and groups of people in your address book, and you would expect the display for the address book to change so that the People screen has places for first and last name, company, e-mail address, and phone number.

On the other hand, if you were displaying a group address page, you'd like to see the name of the group, its purpose, and a list of members and their e-mail addresses. You click on a person and get one display and on a group and get the other display. Let's assume that all e-mail addresses are kept in an object called an Address and that people and groups are derived from this base class, as shown in Figure 12-1.

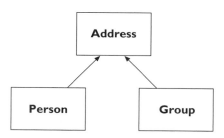

Figure 12-1   Both Person and Group are derived from Address.

Depending on which type of Address object we click on, we'd like to see a somewhat different display of that object's properties. This is a little more than just a Factory pattern because we aren't returning objects that are simple descendants of a base display object but totally different user interfaces made up of different combinations of display objects. The *Builder pattern* assembles a number of objects, such as display controls, in various ways, depending on the data. Furthermore, by using classes to represent the data and forms to represent the display, you can cleanly separate the data from the display methods into simple objects.

An Investment Tracker

Let's consider a somewhat simpler case where it would be useful to have a class build our UI for us. Suppose we are going to write a program to keep track of the performance of our investments. We might have stocks, bonds, and mutual funds, and we'd like to display a list of our holdings in each category so we can select one or more of the investments and plot their comparative performance.

Even though we can't predict in advance how many of each kind of investment we might own at any given time, we'd like to have a display that is easy to use for either a large number of funds (such as stocks) or a small number of funds (such as mutual funds). In each case, we want some sort of a multiple-choice display so that we can select one or more funds to plot. If there are a large number of funds, we'll use a multichoice list box, and if there are three or fewer funds, we'll use a set of check boxes. We want our Builder class to generate an interface that depends on the number of items to be displayed and yet have the same methods for returning the results.

Our displays are shown in Figure 12-2. The top display contains a large number of stocks, and the bottom contains a small number of bonds. Now let's consider how we can build the interface to carry out this variable display. We'll start with a *multiChoice* interface that defines the methods we need to implement.

```
public interface MultiChoice
{
     ArrayList getSelected();
     void clear();
     Panel getWindow();
}
```

The *getWindow* method returns a Panel containing a multiple-choice display. The two display panels we're using here—a check box panel or a list box panel—implement this interface.

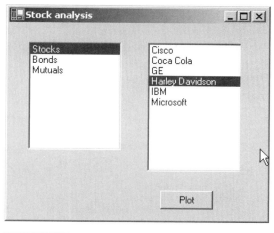

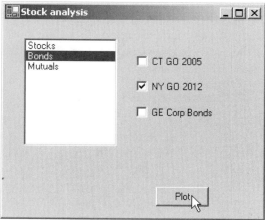

Figure 12-2   Stocks with the list interface and bonds with the check box interface

```
public class CheckChoice:MultiChoice {
```

or

```
public class ListChoice:MultiChoice {
```

C# gives us considerable flexibility in designing Builder classes, since we have direct access to the methods that allow us to construct a window from basic components. For this example, we'll let each builder construct a Panel containing whatever components it needs. We can then add that Panel to the form and position it. When the display changes, you remove the old Panel and add a new one. In C#, a Panel is just a unbordered container that can hold any number of Windows components. The two implementations of the Panel must satisfy the *multiChoice* interface.

We will create a base abstract class called Equities and derive the stocks, bonds, and mutual funds from it.

```
public abstract class Equities   {
     protected ArrayList array;
     public abstract string ToString();
     //----------
     public ArrayList getNames() {
          return array;
     }
     //----------
     public int count() {
          return array.Count ;
     }
}
```

Note the abstract ToString method. We'll use this to display each kind of equity in the list box. Now our Stocks class will just contain the code to load the ArrayList with the stock names.

```
public class Stocks:Equities      {
     public Stocks() {
          array = new ArrayList();
          array.Add ("Cisco");
          array.Add ("Coca Cola");
          array.Add ("GE");
          array.Add ("Harley Davidson");
          array.Add ("IBM");
          array.Add ("Microsoft");
     }
     public override string ToString() {
          return "Stocks";
     }
}
```

All the remaining code (getNames and count) is implemented in the base Equities class. The Bonds and Mutuals classes are entirely analogous.

The Stock Factory

We need a little class to decide whether we want to return a check box panel or a list box panel. We'll call this class the StockFactory class. However, we will never need more than one instance of this class, so we'll create the class so its one method is static.

```
public class StockFactory {
     public static MultiChoice getBuilder(Equities stocks) {
      if (stocks.count ()<=3) {
            return new CheckChoice (stocks);
      }
      else {
            return new ListChoice(stocks);
      }
     }
}
```

We never need more than one instance of this class, so we make the getBuilder method *static*. Then we can call it directly without creating a class instance. In the language of *Design Patterns*, this simple factory class is called the Director, and the actual classes derived from *multiChoice* are each Builders.

The CheckChoice Class

Our Check Box Builder constructs a panel containing 0 to 3 check boxes and returns that panel to the calling program.

```
//returns a panel of 0 to 3 check boxes
public class CheckChoice:MultiChoice      {
     private ArrayList stocks;
     private Panel panel;
     private ArrayList boxes;
//------
     public CheckChoice(Equities stks)                        {
     stocks = stks.getNames ();
     panel = new Panel ();
     boxes = new ArrayList ();
     //add the check boxes to the panel
     for (int i=0; i< stocks.Count; i++) {
            CheckBox ck = new CheckBox ();
            //position them
            ck.Location = new Point (8, 16 + i * 32);
            string stk = (string)stocks[i];
            ck.Text =stk;
            ck.Size = new Size (112, 24);
            ck.TabIndex =0;
            ck.TextAlign = ContentAlignment.MiddleLeft ;
            boxes.Add (ck);
            panel.Controls.Add (ck);
     }
}
}
```

The methods for returning the window and the list of selected names are shown here. Note that we cast the object type returned by an ArrayList to the CheckBox type the method actually requires.

```
//------
//uncheck all check boxes
public  void clear() {
        for(int i=0; i< boxes.Count; i++) {
          CheckBox ck = (CheckBox)boxes[i];
              ck.Checked =false;
        }
}
//------
//return list of checked items
public ArrayList getSelected() {
        ArrayList sels = new ArrayList ();
        for(int i=0; i< boxes.Count ; i++) {
                CheckBox ck = (CheckBox)boxes[i];
                if (ck.Checked ) {
                        sels.Add (ck.Text );
                }
        }
        return sels;
}
//------
//return panel of check boxes
public Panel getWindow() {
        return panel;
}
```

The ListboxChoice Class

This class creates a multiselect list box, inserts it into a Panel, and loads the names into the list.

```
public class ListChoice:MultiChoice {
        private ArrayList stocks;
        private Panel panel;
        private ListBox list;
//------
//constructor creates and loads the list box
        public ListChoice(Equities stks) {
                stocks = stks.getNames ();
                panel = new Panel ();
                list = new ListBox ();
                list.Location = new Point (16, 0);
                list.Size = new Size (120, 160);
                list.SelectionMode =SelectionMode.MultiExtended ;
                list.TabIndex =0;
                panel.Controls.Add (list);
                for(int i=0; i< stocks.Count ; i++) {
```

```
                        list.Items.Add (stocks[i]);
            }
      }
```

Since this is a multiselect list box, we can get all the selected items in a single SelectedIndices collection. This method, however, only works for a multiselect list box. It returns a 1 for a single-select list box. We use it to load the array list of selected names as follows.

```
//returns the Panel
//------
public  Panel getWindow() {
        return panel;
}
//returns an array of selected elements
//------
public ArrayList getSelected() {
        ArrayList sels = new ArrayList ();
        ListBox.SelectedObjectCollection
              coll = list.SelectedItems  ;
        for(int i=0; i< coll.Count; i++) {
                string item = (string)coll[i];
                      sels.Add (item );
        }
        return sels;
}
//------
//clear selected elements
public void clear() {
        list.Items.Clear();
}
```

Using the Items Collection in the ListBox Control

You are not limited to populating a list box with strings in C#. When you add data to the Items collection, it can be any kind of object that has a ToString method.

Since we created our three Equities classes to have a ToString method, we can add these classes directly to the list box in our main program's constructor.

```
public class WealthBuilder : Form        {
    private ListBox lsEquities;
    private Container components = null;
    private Button btPlot;
    private Panel pnl;
    private MultiChoice mchoice;
    private void init() {
            lsEquities.Items.Add (new Stocks());
            lsEquities.Items.Add (new Bonds());
            lsEquities.Items.Add (new Mutuals());
```

```
        }
    public WealthBuilder()      {
            InitializeComponent();
            init();
    }
```

Whenever we click on a line of the list box, the click method obtains that instance of an Equities class and passes it to the MultiChoice factory, which in turn produces a Panel containing the items in that class. It then removes the old panel and adds the new one.

```
private void lsEquities_SelectedIndexChanged(object sender,
            EventArgs e) {
    int i = lsEquities.SelectedIndex ;
    Equities eq = (Equities)lsEquities.Items[i];
    mchoice= StockFactory.getBuilder (eq);
    this.Controls.Remove (pnl);
    pnl = mchoice.getWindow ();
    setPanel();

}
//------
private void setPanel() {
    pnl.Location = new Point(152, 24);
    pnl.Size = new Size(128, 168);
    pnl.TabIndex = 1;
    Controls.Add(pnl);
}
```

Plotting the Data

We don't really implement an actual plot in this example. However, we did provide a getSelected method to return the names of stocks from either MultiSelect implementation. The method returns an ArrayList of selected items. In the Plot click method, we load these names into a message box and display it.

```
private void btPlot_Click(object sender, EventArgs e) {
//display the selected items in a message box
    if(mchoice != null) {
            ArrayList ar  = mchoice.getSelected ();
            string ans = "";
            for(int i=0; i< ar.Count ; i++) {
                    ans += (string)ar[i] +" ";
            }
            MessageBox.Show (null, ans,
            "Selected equities", MessageBoxButtons.OK  );

    }
}
```

The Final Choice

Now that we have created all the needed classes, we can run the program. It starts with a blank panel on the right side, so there will always be some panel there to remove. Then each time we click on one of the names of the Equities, that panel is removed and a new one is added in its place. We see the three cases in Figure 12-3.

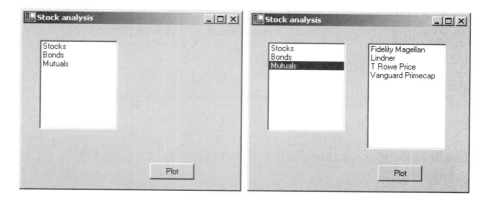

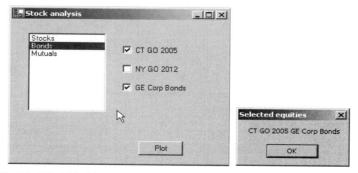

Figure 12-3 The WealthBuilder program, showing the list of equities, the list box, the check boxes, and the plot panel

You can see the relationships between the classes in the UML diagram in Figure 12-4.

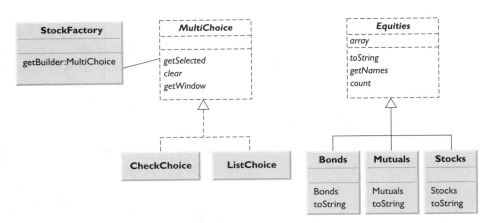

Figure 12-4   The inheritance relationships in the Builder pattern

Consequences of the Builder Pattern

1. A Builder lets you vary the internal representation of the product it builds. It also hides the details of how the product is assembled.

2. Each specific Builder is independent of the others and of the rest of the program. This improves modularity and makes the addition of other Builders relatively simple.

3. Because each Builder constructs the final product step by step, depending on the data, you have more control over each final product that a Builder constructs.

A Builder pattern is somewhat like an Abstract Factory pattern in that both return classes made up of a number of methods and objects. The main difference is that while the Abstract Factory returns a family of related classes, the Builder constructs a complex object step by step, depending on the data presented to it.

Thought Questions

1. Some word-processing and graphics programs construct menus dynamically based on the context of the data being displayed. How could you use a Builder effectively here?

2. Not all Builders must construct visual objects. What might you construct with a Builder in the personal finance industry? Suppose you were scoring a

track meet, made up of five or six different events. How can you use a Builder there?

Program on the CD-ROM

Basic Equities Builder	\Builders\Stocks

CHAPTER 13

The Prototype Pattern

The Prototype pattern is another tool you can use when you can specify the general class needed in a program but need to defer the exact class until execution time. It is similar to the Builder in that some class decides what components or details make up the final class. However, it differs in that the target classes are constructed by cloning one or more prototype classes and then changing or filling in the details of the cloned class to behave as desired.

Prototypes can be used whenever you need classes that differ only in the type of processing they offer—for example, in parsing of strings representing numbers in different radixes. In this sense, the prototype is nearly the same as the Examplar pattern described by Coplien (1992).

Let's consider the case of an extensive database where you need to make a number of queries to construct an answer. Once you have this answer as a result set, you might like to manipulate it to produce other answers without issuing additional queries.

In a case like the one we have been working on, we'll consider a database of a large number of swimmers in a league or statewide organization. Each swimmer swims several strokes and distances throughout a season. The "best times" for swimmers are tabulated by age group, and even within a single four-month season many swimmers will pass their birthdays and fall into new age groups. Thus, the query to determine which swimmers did the best in their age group that season is dependent on the date of each meet and on each swimmer's birthday. The computational cost of assembling this table of times is therefore fairly high.

Once we have an instance of a class containing this table sorted by sex, we could imagine wanting to examine this information sorted just by time or by actual age rather than by age group. It would not be sensible to recompute these data, and we don't want to destroy the original data order, so some sort of copy of the data object is desirable.

Cloning in C#

The idea of cloning a class instance (making an exact copy) is not a designed-in feature of C#, but nothing actually stops you from carrying out such a copy yourself. The only place the Clone method appears in C# is in ADO DataSet manipulation. You can create a DataSet as a result of a database query and move through it a row at a time. If for some reason you need to keep references to two places in this DataSet, you would need two "current rows." The simplest way to handle this in C# is to clone the DataSet.

```
DataSet cloneSet;
cloneSet = myDataSet.Clone();
```

Now this approach does not generate two *copies* of the data. It just generates two sets of row pointers to use to move through the records independently of each other. Any change you make in one clone of the DataSet is immediately reflected in the other because there is in fact only one data table. We discuss a similar problem in the following example.

Using the Prototype

Now let's write a simple program that reads data from a database and then clones the resulting object. In our example program, we just read these data from a file, but the original data were derived from a large database, as we discussed previously. That file has the following form.

```
Kristen Frost, 9, CAT, 26.31, F
Kimberly Watcke, 10, CDEV,27.37, F
Jaclyn Carey, 10, ARAC, 27.53, F
Megan Crapster, 10, LEHY, 27.68, F
```

We'll use the csFile class we developed earlier. First, we create a class called Swimmer that holds one name, club name, sex, and time, and read them in using the csFile class and the StringTokenizer class we developed in Chapter 4.

```
public class Swimmer      {
        private string name;                  //name
        private string lname, frname;         //split names
        private int age;                      //age
        private string club;                  //club initials
        private float time;                   //time achieved
        private bool female;                  //sex
```

```
//---------
public Swimmer(string line) {
     StringTokenizer tok = new StringTokenizer(line,",");
     splitName(tok);
     age = Convert.ToInt32 (tok.nextToken());
     club = tok.nextToken();
     time = Convert.ToSingle (tok.nextToken());
     string sx = tok.nextToken().ToUpper ();
     female = sx.Equals ("F");
}
//---------
private void splitName(StringTokenizer tok) {
     name = tok.nextToken();
     int i = name.IndexOf (" ");
     if(i >0 ) {
             frname = name.Substring (0, i);
             lname = name.Substring (i+1).Trim ();
     }
}
//---------
public bool isFemale() {
     return female;
}
//---------
public int getAge() {
     return age;
}
//---------
public float getTime() {
     return time;
}
//---------
public string getName() {
     return name;
}
//---------
public string getClub() {
     return club;
}
```

Then we create a class called SwimData that maintains an ArrayList of the Swimmers we read in from the database.

```
public class SwimData        {
     protected ArrayList swdata;
     private int index;
 //-----
 public SwimData() {
     swdata = new ArrayList ();
 }
 //-----
 public SwimData(ArrayList swd) {
```

```
            swdata = swd;
            index=0;
    }
    //-----
    public SwimData(string filename)                    {
            swdata = new ArrayList ();
            csFile fl = new csFile(filename);
            fl.OpenForRead ();
            string s = fl.readLine ();
            while(s != null) {
                    Swimmer sw = new Swimmer(s);
                    swdata.Add (sw);
                    s = fl.readLine ();
            }
            fl.close ();
    }
    //-----
    public void moveFirst() {
            index = 0;
    }
    //-----
    public bool hasMoreElements() {
            return (index < swdata.Count-1 );
    }
    //-----
    public void sort() {
    }
    //-----
    public Swimmer getSwimmer() {
            if(index < swdata.Count )
                    return (Swimmer)swdata[index++];
            else
                    return null;
    }
}
```

We can then use this class to read in the swimmer data and display it in a list box.

```
private void init() {
        swdata = new SwimData ("swimmers.txt");
        reload();
}
//-----
private void reload() {
        lsKids.Items.Clear ();
        swdata.moveFirst ();
        while (swdata.hasMoreElements() ) {
                Swimmer sw = swdata.getSwimmer ();
                lsKids.Items.Add (sw.getName() );
        }
}
```

This is illustrated in Figure 13-1.

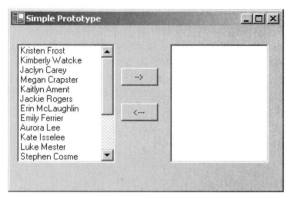

Figure 13-1   A simple prototype program

When we click on the → button, we are cloning this class and sorting the data differently in the new class. Again, we clone the data because creating a new class instance would be much slower, and we want to keep the data in both forms.

```
private void btClone_Click(object sender, EventArgs e) {
    SwimData newSd = (SwimData)swdata.Clone ();
    newSd.sort ();
    while(newSd.hasMoreElements() ) {
        Swimmer sw = (Swimmer)newSd.getSwimmer ();
        lsNewKids.Items.Add (sw.getName() );
    }
}
```

We show the sorted results in Figure 13-2.

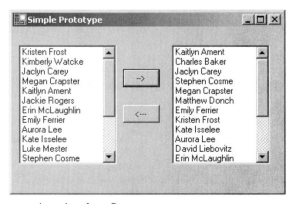

Figure 13-2   The sorted results of our Prototype program

Cloning the Class

While it may not be strictly required, we can make the SwimData class implement the ICloneable interface.

```
public class SwimData:ICloneable    {
```

All this means is that the class must have a Clone method that returns an object.

```
public object Clone() {
     SwimData newsd = new SwimData(swdata);
     return newsd;
}
```

Of course, using this interface implies that we must cast the object type back to the SwimData type when we receive the clone as we did previously.

```
SwimData newSd = (SwimData)swdata.Clone ();
```

Now, let's click on the ← button to reload the left-hand list box from the original data. The somewhat disconcerting result is shown in Figure 13-3.

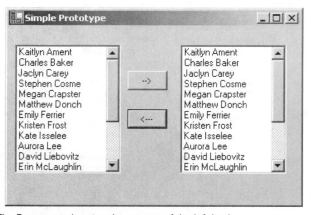

Figure 13-3   The Prototype showing the re-sort of the left list box

Why have the names in the left-hand list box also been re-sorted? Our sort routine looks like this.

```
public void sort() {
     //sort using IComparable interface of Swimmer
     swdata.Sort (0,swdata.Count ,null);
}
```

Note that we are sorting the actual ArrayList in place. This sort method assumes that each element of the ArrayList implements the IComparable interface.

```
public class Swimmer:IComparable      {
```

All this means is that it must have an integer CompareTo method that returns −1, 0, or 1, depending on whether the comparison between the two objects returns less than, equal or greater than. In this case, we compare the two last names using the string class's CompareTo method and return that.

```
public int CompareTo(object swo) {
      Swimmer sw = (Swimmer)swo;
      return lname.CompareTo (sw.getLName() );
}
```

Now we can understand the unfortunate result in Figure 13-3. The original array is re-sorted in the new class, and there is really only one copy of this array. This occurs because the clone method is a *shallow copy* of the original class. In other words, the references to the data objects are copies, but they refer to the same underlying data. Thus, any operation we perform on the copied data will also occur on the original data in the Prototype class.

In some cases, this shallow copy may be acceptable, but if you want to make a deep copy of the data, you must write a deep cloning routine of your own as part of the class you want to clone. In this simple class, you just create a new ArrayList and copy the elements of the old class's ArrayList into the new one.

```
public object Clone() {
      //create a new ArrayList
      ArrayList swd = new ArrayList ();
      //copy in swimmer objects
      for(int i = 0; i < swdata.Count ; i++)
            swd.Add (swdata[i]);
      //create new SwimData object with this array
      SwimData newsd = new SwimData (swd);
      return newsd;
}
```

Using the Prototype Pattern

You can use the Prototype pattern whenever any of a number of classes might be created or when the classes are modified after being created. As long as all the classes have the same interface, they can actually carry out rather different operations.

Let's consider a more elaborate example of the listing of swimmers we just discussed. Instead of just sorting the swimmers, let's create subclasses that operate on that data, modifying it and presenting the result for display in a list box. We start with the same basic class, SwimData.

Then it becomes possible to write different derived SwimData classes, depending on the application's requirements. We always start with the SwimData class and then clone it for various other displays. For example, the SexSwimData class re-sorts the data by sex and displays only one sex. This is shown in Figure 13-4.

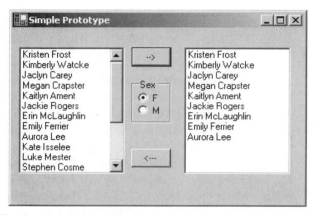

Figure 13-4   The OneSexSwimData class displays only one sex on the right.

In the SexSwimData class, we sort the data by name but return them for display based on whether girls or boys are supposed to be displayed. This class has this polymorphic sort method.

```
public void sort(bool isFemale) {
     ArrayList swd = new ArrayList();
     for (int i = 0; i < swdata.Count ; i++) {
          Swimmer sw =(Swimmer)swdata[i];
          if (isFemale == sw.isFemale() ) {
               swd.Add (sw);
          }
     }
     swdata = swd;
}
```

Each time you click on the one of the sex option buttons, the class is given the current state of these buttons.

```
private void btClone_Click(object sender, System.EventArgs e) {
     SexSwimData newSd = (SexSwimData)swdata.Clone ();
```

```
newSd.sort (opFemale.Checked );
lsNewKids.Items.Clear() ;
while(newSd.hasMoreElements() ) {
        Swimmer sw = (Swimmer)newSd.getSwimmer ();
        lsNewKids.Items.Add (sw.getName() );
    }
}
```

Note that the btClone_Click event clones the general SexSwimdata class instance swdata and casts the result to the type SexSwimData. This means that the Clone method of SexSwimData must override the general SwimData Clone method because it returns a different data type.

```
public object Clone() {
    //create a new ArrayList
    ArrayList swd = new ArrayList ();
    //copy in swimmer objects
    for(int i=0; i< swdata.Count ; i++)
        swd.Add (swdata[i]);
    //create new SwimData object with this array
    SexSwimData newsd = new SexSwimData (swd);
    return newsd;
}
```

Having to rewrite the Clone method each time we derive a new highly similar class is not a satisfactory approach. A better solution is to do away with implementing the ICloneable interface where each class has a Clone method and reverse the process where each receiving class clones the data inside the sending class. Here we show a revised portion of the SwimData class that contains the *cloneMe* method. It takes the data from another instance of SwimData and copies it into the ArrayList inside this instance of the class.

```
public class SwimData       {
        protected ArrayList swdata;
        private int index;
        //-----
        public void cloneMe(SwimData swdat) {
                swdata = new ArrayList ();
                ArrayList swd=swdat.getData ();
                //copy in swimmer objects
                for(int i=0; i < swd.Count ; i++)
                        swdata.Add (swd[i]);

        }
```

This approach will then work for all child classes of SwimData without having to cast the data between subclass types.

Dissimilar Classes with the Same Interface

Classes, however, do not have to be even that similar. The AgeSwimData class takes the cloned input data array and creates a simple histogram by age. If you click on "F," you see the girls' age distribution, and if you click on "M," you see the boys' age distribution, as shown in Figure 13-5.

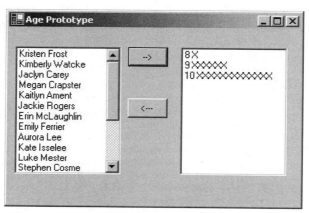

Figure 13-5   The AgeSwimData class displays an age distribution.

This is an interesting case: The AgeSwimData class inherits the cloneMe method from the base SwimData class but overrides the sort method with one that creates a proto-swimmer with a name made up of the number of kids in that age group.

```
public class AgeSwimData:SwimData  {
     ArrayList swd;
     public AgeSwimData() {
          swdata = new ArrayList ();
     }
     //------
     public AgeSwimData(string filename):base(filename){}
     public AgeSwimData(ArrayList ssd):base(ssd){}
     //------
     public override void cloneMe(SwimData swdat) {
          swd = swdat.getData ();
     }
     //------
     public override void sort() {
          Swimmer[] sws = new Swimmer[swd.Count ];
          //copy in swimmer objects
          for(int i=0; i < swd.Count ; i++) {
               sws[i] = (Swimmer)swd[i];
          }
```

```
//sort into increasing order
for( int i=0; i< sws.Length ; i++) {
        for (int j = i; j< sws.Length ; j++) {
                if (sws[i].getAge ()>sws[j].getAge ())
                        Swimmer sw = sws[i];
                        sws[i]=sws[j];
                        sws[j]=sw;
                }
        }
}
int age = sws[0].getAge ();
int agecount = 0;
int k = 0;
swdata = new ArrayList ();
bool quit = false;


while( k < sws.Length && ! quit ) {
        while(sws[k].getAge() ==age && ! quit) {
                agecount++;
                if(k < sws.Length -1)
                        k++;
                else
                        quit= true;
        }
//create a new Swimmer with a series of X's for a name
//for each new age
        string name = "";
        for(int j = 0; j < agecount; j++)
                name +="X";
        Swimmer sw = new Swimmer(age.ToString() + " " +
                name + "," + age.ToString() +
                ",club,0,F");
                swdata.Add (sw);
                agecount = 0;
                if(quit)
                        age = 0;
                else
                        age = sws[k].getAge ();
        }
    }
}
```

Now, since our original classes display first and last names of selected swimmers, note that we achieve this same display, returning Swimmer objects with the first name set to the age string and the last name set to the histogram.

The UML diagram in Figure 13-6 illustrates this system fairly clearly. The main GUI class keeps two instances of SwimData but does not specify which ones. AgeSwimData is derived from SwimData, and both contain instances of the Swimmer class.

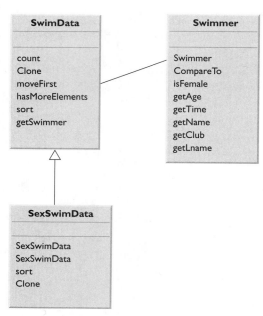

Figure 13-6   The UML diagram for the various SwimData classes

You should also note that you are not limited to the few subclasses we demonstrated here. It would be quite simple to create additional concrete classes and register them with whatever code selects the appropriate concrete class. In our example program, the user is the deciding point or Factory because he or she simply clicks on one of several buttons. In a more elaborate case, each concrete class could have an array of characteristics, and the decision point could be a class registry or *prototype manager* that examines these characteristics and selects the most suitable class. You could also combine the Factory Method pattern with the Prototype, where each of several concrete classes uses a different concrete class from those available.

Prototype Managers

A prototype manager class can be used to decide which of several concrete classes to return to the client. It can also manage several sets of prototypes at once. For example, in addition to returning one of several classes of swimmers, it could return different groups of swimmers who swam certain strokes and distances. It could also manage which of several types of list boxes are returned in which to display them, including tables, multicolumn lists, and graphical displays. It is best that whichever subclass is returned, it not require conversion to a new class type to be used in the program. In other words, the methods of the parent abstract or base class should be sufficient, and the client should never need to know which actual subclass it is dealing with.

Consequences of the Prototype Pattern

Using the Prototype pattern, you can add and remove classes at runtime by cloning them as needed. You can revise the internal data representation of a class at runtime, based on program conditions. You can also specify new objects at runtime without creating a proliferation of classes.

One difficulty in implementing the Prototype pattern in C# is that if the classes already exist, you may not be able to change them to add the required clone methods. In addition, classes that have circular references to other classes cannot really be cloned.

Like the registry of Singletons discussed before, you can also create a registry of Prototype classes that can be cloned and ask the registry object for a list of possible prototypes. You may be able to clone an existing class rather than writing one from scratch.

Note that every class that you might use as a prototype must itself be instantiated (perhaps at some expense) in order for you to use a Prototype Registry. This can be a performance drawback.

Finally, the idea of having prototype classes to copy implies that you have sufficient access to the data or methods in these classes to change them after cloning. This may require adding data access methods to these prototype classes so that you can modify the data once you have cloned the class.

Thought Question

An entertaining banner program shows a slogan starting at different places on the screen at different times and in different fonts and sizes. Design the program using a Prototype pattern.

Programs on the CD-ROM

Age Plot	\Prototype\Ageplot
Deep Prototype	\Prototype\DeepProto
Display by Sex	\Prototype\OneSex
Shallow Copy	\Prototype\SimpleProto
Age and Sex Display	\Prototype\TwoclassAgePlot

Summary of Creational Patterns

The **Factory pattern** is used to choose and return an instance of a class from a number of similar classes, based on data you provide to the factory.

The **Abstract Factory pattern** is used to return one of several groups of classes. In some cases, it actually returns a Factory for that group of classes.

The **Builder pattern** assembles a number of objects to make a new object, based on the data with which it is presented. Frequently, the choice of which way the objects are assembled is achieved using a Factory.

The **Prototype pattern** copies or clones an existing class, rather than creating a new instance, when creating new instances is more expensive.

The **Singleton pattern** is a pattern that ensures there is one and only one instance of an object and that it is possible to obtain global access to that one instance.

PART 3

Structural Patterns

Structural patterns describe how classes and objects can be combined to form larger structures. The difference between *class* patterns and *object* patterns is that class patterns describe how inheritance can be used to provide more useful program interfaces. Object patterns, on the other hand, describe how objects can be composed into larger structures using object composition or the inclusion of objects within other objects.

For example, we'll see that the **Adapter pattern** can be used to make one class interface match another to make programming easier. We'll also look at a number of other structural patterns where we combine objects to provide new functionality. The **Composite,** for instance, is exactly that—a composition of objects, each of which may be either simple or itself a composite object. The **Proxy pattern** is frequently a simple object that takes the place of a more complex object that may be invoked later—for example, when the program runs in a network environment.

The **Flyweight pattern** is used for sharing objects, where each instance does not contain its own state but stores it externally. This allows efficient sharing of objects to save space when there are many instances but only a few different types.

The **Façade pattern** is used to make a single class represent an entire subsystem, and the **Bridge pattern** separates an object's interface from its implementation so you can vary them separately. Finally, we'll look at the **Decorator pattern,** which can be used to add responsibilities to objects dynamically.

You'll see that there is some overlap among these patterns and even some overlap with the behavioral patterns in the next chapter. We'll summarize these similarities after we describe the patterns.

CHAPTER 14

The Adapter Pattern

The Adapter pattern is used to convert the programming interface of one class into that of another. We use adapters whenever we want unrelated classes to work together in a single program. The concept of an adapter is thus pretty simple: We write a class that has the desired interface and then make it communicate with the class that has a different interface.

There are two ways to do this: by inheritance and by object composition. In the first case, we derive a new class from the nonconforming one and add the methods we need to make the new derived class match the desired interface. The other way is to include the original class inside the new one and create the methods to translate calls within the new class. These two approaches, called class adapters and object adapters, are both fairly easy to implement.

Moving Data between Lists

Let's consider a simple program that allows you to select some names from a list to be transferred to another list for a more detailed display of the data associated with them. Our initial list consists of a team roster, and the second list has names with times or scores.

In this simple program, shown in Figure 14-1, the program reads in the names from a roster file during initialization. To move a name to the right-hand list box, you click on the name and then click on the arrow button. To move a name from the right-hand list box to the left-hand list, click on the name and then click on the back-arrow button.

This is a very simple program to write in C#. It consists of the visual layout and action routines for each of the button clicks. When we read in the file of team roster data, we store each child's name and score in a Swimmer object and

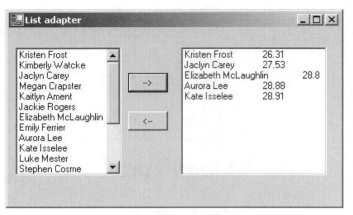

Figure 14-1   A simple program to choose names for display

then store all of these objects in an ArrayList collection called *swdata*. When you select one of the names to display in expanded form, you simply obtain the list index of the selected child from the left-hand list and get that child's data to display in the right-hand list.

```
private void btClone_Click(object sender, EventArgs e) {
int i = lskids.SelectedIndex ();
  if( i >= 0) {
      Swimmer sw = swdata.getSwimmer (i);
      lsnewKids.Item.Add (sw.getName() +"\t"+sw.getTime ());
      lskids.SelectedIndex = -1;

  }
}
```

In a similar fashion, if we want to remove a name from the right-hand list, we just obtain the selected index and remove the name.

```
private void putBack_Click(object sender, EventArgs e) {
      int i = lsnewKids.SelectedIndex ();
      if(i >= 0)
            lsNewKids.Items.RemoveAt (i);
}
```

Note that we obtain the column spacing between the two rows using the tab character. This works fine as long as the names are more or less the same length. However, if one name is much longer or shorter than the others, the list may end up using a different tab column, which is what happened here for the third name in the list.

Making an Adapter

It may be a little difficult to remember to use the Items collection of the list box for some operations but not for others. For this reason, we might prefer to have a class that hides some of these complexities and *adapts* the interface to the simpler one we wish we had, rather like the ListBox interface in VB6. We'll create a simpler interface in a ListAdapter class that then operates on an instance of the ListBox class.

```
public class ListAdapter     {
      private ListBox listbox;    //operates on this one
      public ListAdapter(ListBox lb)            {
            listbox = lb;
      }
      //-----
      public void Add(string s) {
            listbox.Items.Add (s);
      }
      //-----
      public int SelectedIndex() {
            return listbox.SelectedIndex;
      }
      //-----
      public void Clear() {
            listbox.Items.Clear ();
      }
      //-----
      public void clearSelection() {
            int i = SelectedIndex();
            if(i >= 0) {
                  listbox.SelectedIndex =-1;
            }
      }
}
```

Then we can make our program a little simpler.

```
private void btClone_Click(object sender, EventArgs e) {
      int i = lskids.SelectedIndex ();
      if( i >= 0) {
            Swimmer sw = swdata.getSwimmer (i);
            lsnewKids.Add (sw.getName() + "\t" + sw.getTime ());
            lskids.clearSelection ();
      }
}
```

Now let's recognize that if we are always adding swimmers and times spaced apart like this, maybe there should be a method in our ListAdapter that handles the Swimmer object directly.

```
public void Add(Swimmer sw) {
    listbox.Items.Add (sw.getName() + "" + sw.getTime());
}
```

This simplifies the Click Event handler even more.

```
private void btClone_Click(object sender, EventArgs e) {
    int i = lskids.SelectedIndex ();
    if( i >= 0) {
            Swimmer sw = swdata.getSwimmer (i);
            lsnewKids.Add (sw);
            lskids.clearSelection ();
    }
}
```

What we have done is create an Adapter class that contains a ListBox class and simplifies how you use the ListBox. Next, we'll see how we can use the same approach to create adapters for two of the more complex visual controls.

Using the DataGrid

To circumvent the problem with the tab columns in the simple list box, we can turn to a grid display. The grid table that comes with Visual Studio.NET is called the DataGrid. It can be bound to a database or to an in-memory data array. To use the DataGrid without a database, you create an instance of the DataTable class and add DataColumns to it. DataColumns are by default of string type, but you can define them to be of any type when you create them. Here is the general outline of how you create a DataGrid using a DataTable.

```
DataTable dTable = new DataTable("Kids");
dTable.MinimumCapacity = 100;
dTable.CaseSensitive = false;

DataColumn column =
new DataColumn("Frname",System.Type.GetType("System.String"));
dTable.Columns.Add(column);
column = new DataColumn("Lname",
      System.Type.GetType("System.String"));
dTable.Columns.Add(column);
column = new DataColumn("Age",
        System.Type.GetType("System.Int16"));

dTable.Columns.Add(column);

dGrid.DataSource = dTable;
dGrid.CaptionVisible = false;     //no caption
dGrid.RowHeadersVisible = false; //no row headers
dGrid.EndInit();
```

To add text to the DataTable, you ask the table for a row object and then set
the elements of the row object to the data for that row. If the types are all String,
then you copy the strings, but if one of the columns is of a different type, such as
the integer age column here, you must be sure to use that type in setting that column's data. Note that you can refer to the columns by name or by index number.

```
DataRow row = dTable.NewRow();
row["Frname"] = sw.getFrname();
row[1] = sw.getLName();
row[2] = sw.getAge();   //This one is an integer
dTable.Rows.Add(row);
dTable.AcceptChanges();
```

However, we would like to be able to use the grid without changing any of the
code we used for the simple list box. We do this by creating a GridAdapter that
follows that same interface.

```
public interface LstAdapter      {
       void Add(Swimmer sw) ;
       int SelectedIndex() ;
       void Clear() ;
       void clearSelection() ;
}
```

The GridAdapter class implements this interface and is instantiated with an
instance of the grid.

```
public class GridAdapter:LstAdapter      {
     private DataGrid grid;
     private DataTable dTable;
     private int row;
     //-----
     public GridAdapter(DataGrid grd)            {
            grid = grd;
            dTable = (DataTable)grid.DataSource;
            grid.MouseDown +=
                  new System.Windows.Forms.MouseEventHandler
                  (Grid_Click);
            row = -1;
     }
     //-----
     public void Add(Swimmer sw) {
            DataRow row = dTable.NewRow();
            row["Frname"] = sw.getFrname();
            row[1] = sw.getLName();
            row[2] = sw.getAge();   //This one is an integer
            dTable.Rows.Add(row);
            dTable.AcceptChanges();
     }
     //-----
```

```
       public int SelectedIndex() {
               return row;
       }
       //-----
       public void Clear() {
               int  count = dTable.Rows.Count ;
               for(int i=0; i< count; i++) {
                       dTable.Rows[i].Delete ();
               }
       }
       //-----
       public void clearSelection() {}
}
```

Detecting Row Selection

The DataGrid does not have a SelectedIndex property, and the rows do not
have Selected properties. Instead, you must detect a MouseDown event with
a MouseEvent handler and then get the HitTest object and see if the user has
clicked on a cell.

```
public void Grid_Click(object sender, MouseEventArgs  e) {
     DataGrid.HitTestInfo hti = grid.HitTest (e.X, e.Y);
     if(hti.Type   == DataGrid.HitTestType.Cell ){
             row = hti.Row ;
     }
}
```

Note that we can now simply call the GridAdapter class's Add method
when we click on the → button, regardless of which display control we are
using.

```
private void btClone_Click(object sender, System.EventArgs e) {
     int i = lskids.SelectedIndex ();
     if( i >= 0) {
             Swimmer sw = swdata.getSwimmer (i);
             lsNewKids.Add (sw);
             lskids.clearSelection ();
     }
}
```

We see the final grid display in Figure 14-2.

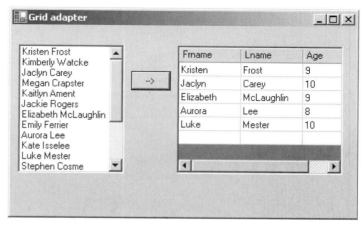

Figure 14-2 A grid adapter

Using a TreeView

If, however, you choose to use a TreeView control to display the data you select, you will find that there is no convenient interface that you can use to keep your code from changing.

For each node you want to create, you create an instance of the TreeNode class and add the root TreeNode collection to another node. In our example version using the TreeView, we'll add the swimmer's name to the root node collection and the swimmer's time as a subsidiary node. Here is the entire TreeAdapter class.

```
public class TreeAdapter:LstAdapter       {
    private TreeView tree;
    //------
    public TreeAdapter(TreeView tr)             {
        tree=tr;
    }
    //------
    public void Add(Swimmer sw) {
        TreeNode nod;
     //add a root node
        nod = tree.Nodes.Add(sw.getName());
     //add a child node to it
     nod.Nodes.Add(sw.getTime().ToString ());
     tree.ExpandAll ();
    }
    //------
    public int SelectedIndex() {
```

```
            return tree.SelectedNode.Index ;
     }
     //------
     public void Clear() {
            TreeNode nod;
            for (int i=0; i< tree.Nodes.Count ; i++) {
                    nod = tree.Nodes [i];
                    nod.Remove ();
            }
     }
     //------
     public void clearSelection() {}
     }
```

The TreeDemo program is shown in Figure 14-3.

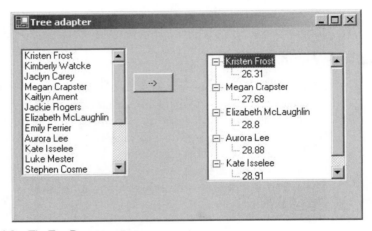

Figure 14-3   The TreeDemo program

The Class Adapter

In the class adapter approach, we derive a new class from ListBox (or the grid or tree control) and add the desired methods to it. In this class adapter example, we create a new class called MyList, which is derived from the ListBox class and that implements the following interface.

```
public interface ListAdapter {
     void Add(Swimmer sw) ;
     void Clear() ;
     void clearSelection() ;
}
```

The derived MyList class is as follows.

```
public class MyList : System.Windows.Forms.ListBox, ListAdapter {
    private System.ComponentModel.Container components = null;
//-----
    public MyList()              {
            InitializeComponent();
    }
    //-----
    public void Add(string s) {
            this.Items.Add (s);
    }
    //-----
    public void Add(Swimmer sw) {
            this.Items.Add (sw.getName() +
                    "\t" + sw.getAge ().ToString () );
    }
    //-----
    public void Clear() {
            this.Items.Clear ();
    }
    //-----
    public void clearSelection() {
            this.SelectedIndex = -1;
    }
```

The class diagram is shown in Figure 14-4. The remaining code is much the same as in the object adapter version.

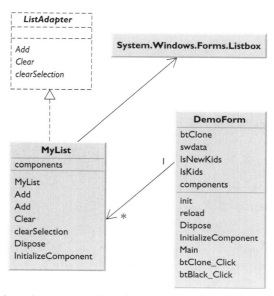

Figure 14-4 The class adapter approach to the list adapter

There are also some differences between the class and the object adapter approaches, although they are less significant than in C++.

- *The class adapter* won't work when we want to adapt a class and all of its subclasses, since you define the class it derives from when you create it.
- *The class adapter* lets the adapter change some of the adapted class's methods but still allows the others to be used unchanged.
- *The object adapter* could allow subclasses to be adapted by simply passing them in as part of a constructor.
- *The object adapter* requires that you specifically bring any of the adapted object's methods to the surface that you wish to make available.

Two-Way Adapters

The two-way adapter is a clever concept that allows an object to be viewed by different classes as being either of type ListBox or type DataGrid. This is most easily done with a class adapter, since all of the methods of the base class are automatically available to the derived class. However, this can only work if you do not override any of the base class's methods with any that behave differently.

Object versus Class Adapters in C#

The C# List, Tree, and Grid adapters illustrated previously are all object adapters. That is, they are all classes that *contain* the visual component we are adapting. However, it is equally easy to write a List or Tree Class adapter that is derived from the base class and contains the new add method.

In the case of the DataGrid, this is probably not a good idea because we would have to create instances of DataTables and Columns inside the DataGrid class, which makes one large complex class with too much knowledge of how other classes work.

Pluggable Adapters

A pluggable adapter is one that adapts dynamically to one of several classes. Of course, the adapter can only adapt to classes it can recognize, and usually the adapter decides which class it is adapting based on differing constructors or set-Parameter methods.

Thought Question

How would you go about writing a class adapter to make the DataGrid look like a two-column list box?

Programs on the CD-ROM

Tree Adapter	\Adapter\TreeAdapter
List Adapter	\Adapter\ListAdapter
Grid Adapter	\Adapter\GridAdapter
Class-Based List Adapter	\Adapter\ClassAdapter

CHAPTER 15

The Bridge Pattern

At first sight, the Bridge pattern looks a lot like the Adapter pattern in that a class is used to convert one kind of interface to another. However, the intent of the Adapter pattern is to make one or more classes' interfaces look the same as that of a particular class. The Bridge pattern is designed to separate a class's interface from its implementation so you can vary or replace the implementation without changing the client code.

The participants in the Bridge pattern are the Abstraction, which defines the class's interface; the Refined Abstraction, which extends and implements that interface; the Implementor, which defines the interface for the implementation classes; and the ConcreteImplementors, which are the implementation classes.

Suppose we have a program that displays a list of products in a window. The simplest interface for that display is a simple ListBox. But once a significant number of products have been sold, we may want to display the products in a table along with their sales figures.

Since we have just discussed the Adapter pattern, you might think immediately of the class-based Adapter, where we adapt the interface of the ListBox to our simpler needs in this display. In simple programs, this will work fine, but as we'll see, there are limits to that approach.

Let's further suppose that we need to produce two kinds of displays from our product data: a customer view that is just the list of products we've mentioned and an executive view that also shows the number of units shipped. We'll display the product list in an ordinary ListBox and the executive view in a Data-Grid table display. These two displays are the implementations of the display classes, as shown in Figure 15-1.

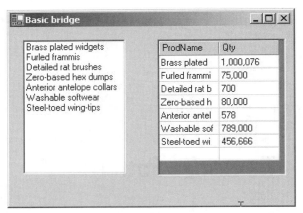

Figure 15-1   Two displays of the same information using a Bridge pattern

The Bridger Interface

Now we want to define a single interface that remains the same regardless of the type and complexity of the actual implementation classes. We'll start by defining a Bridger interface.

```
//Bridge interface to display list classes
    public interface Bridger   {
          void addData(ArrayList col);
    }
```

This class just receives an ArrayList of data and passes it on to the display classes.

We also define a Product class that holds the names and quantities and parses the input string from the data file.

```
public class Product : IComparable      {
    private string quantity;
    private string name;
    //-----
    public Product(string line)              {
          int i = line.IndexOf ("--");
          name =line.Substring (0, i).Trim ();
          quantity = line.Substring (i+2).Trim ();
    }
    //-----
    public string getQuantity() {
          return quantity;
    }
    //-----
    public string getName() {
          return name;
    }
}
```

On the other side of the bridge are the implementation classes, which usually have a more elaborate and somewhat lower-level interface. Here we'll have them add the data lines to the display one at a time.

```
public interface VisList   {
        //add a line to the display
        void addLine(Product p);
        //remove a line from the display
        void removeLine(int num);
}
```

The bridge between the interface on the left and the implementation on the right is the ListBridge class, which instantiates one or the other of the list display classes. Note that it implements the Bridger interface for use of the application program.

```
public class ListBridge : Bridger         {
        protected VisList vis;
        //------
        public ListBridge(VisList v)               {
                vis = v;
        }
        //-----
        public virtual void addData(ArrayList ar) {
                for(int i=0; i< ar.Count ; i++) {
                        Product p = (Product)ar[i];
                        vis.addLine (p);
                }
        }
}
```

Note that we make the VisList variable protected and the addData method virtual so we can extend the class later. At the top programming level, we just create instances of a table and a list using the ListBridge class.

```
private void init() {
        products = new ArrayList ();
        readFile(products);  //read in the data file
        //create the product list
        prodList = new ProductList(lsProd);
        //Bridge to product VisList
        Bridger lbr = new ListBridge (prodList);
        //put the data into the product list
        lbr.addData (products);
        //create the grid VisList
        gridList = new GridList(grdProd);
        //Bridge to the grid list
        Bridger gbr = new ListBridge (gridList);
        //put the data into the grid display
        gbr.addData (products);
}
```

The VisList Classes

The two VisList classes are really quite similar. The customer version operates on a ListBox and adds the names to it.

```
//A VisList class for the ListBox
public class ProductList : VisList     {
     private ListBox list;
     //-----
     public ProductList(ListBox lst)            {
          list = lst;
     }
     //-----
     public void addLine(Product p) {
          list.Items.Add (p.getName() );
     }
     //-----
     public void removeLine(int num) {
          if(num >=0 && num < list.Items.Count ){
               list.Items.Remove (num);
          }
     }
}
```

The ProductTable version of the VisList is quite similar except that it adds both the product name and quantity to the two columns of the grid.

```
public class GridList:VisList     {
     private DataGrid grid;
     private DataTable dtable;
     private GridAdapter gAdapter;
     //-----
     public GridList(DataGrid grd) {
          grid = grd;
          dtable = new DataTable("Products");
          DataColumn column = new DataColumn("ProdName");
          dtable.Columns.Add(column);
          column = new DataColumn("Qty");
          dtable.Columns.Add(column);
          grid.DataSource = dtable;
          gAdapter = new GridAdapter (grid);
     }
     //-----
     public void addLine(Product p) {
          gAdapter.Add (p);
     }
```

The Class Diagram

The UML diagram in Figure 15-2 for the Bridge class shows the separation of the interface and the implementation quite clearly. The *Bridger* class on the left is the Abstraction, and the *ListBridge* class is the implementation of that abstraction. The *VisList* interface describes the public interface to the list classes *ProductList* and *GridList*. The *VisList* interface defines the interface of the Implementor, and the Concrete Implementors are the *ProductList* and *GridList* classes.

Note that these two Concrete Implementors are quite different in their specifics even though they both support the *VisList* interface.

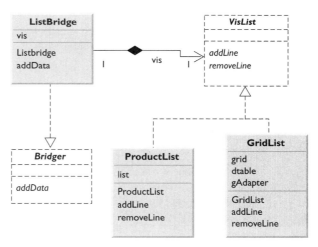

Figure 15-2   The UML diagram for the Bridge pattern used in the two displays of product information

Extending the Bridge

Now suppose we need to make some changes in the way these lists display the data. For example, maybe you want to have the products displayed in alphabetical order. You might think you'd need to either modify or subclass *both* the list and table classes. This can quickly get to be a maintenance nightmare, especially if more than two such displays are needed at some point. Instead, we simply derive a new *SortBridge* class similar to the *ListBridge* class.

In order to sort Product objects, we have the Product class implement the IComparable interface, which means it has a CompareTo method.

```
public class Product : IComparable     {
        private string quantity;
```

```
      private string name;
      //-----
      public Product(string line)             {
            int i = line.IndexOf ("--");
            name =line.Substring (0, i).Trim ();
            quantity = line.Substring (i+2).Trim ();
      }
      //-----
      public string getQuantity() {
            return quantity;
      }
      //-----
      public string getName() {
            return name;
      }
      //-----
      public int CompareTo(object p) {
            Product prod =(Product) p;
            return name.CompareTo (prod.getName ());
      }
```

With that change, sorting of the Product objects is much easier.

```
public class SortBridge:ListBridge        {
      //-----
      public SortBridge(VisList v):base(v){
      }
      //-----
      public override void addData(ArrayList ar) {
            int max = ar.Count ;
            Product[] prod = new Product[max];
            for(int i=0; i< max ; i++) {
                  prod[i] = (Product)ar[i];
            }
            for(int i=0; i < max ; i++) {
                  for (int j=i; j < max; j++) {
                        if(prod[i].CompareTo (prod[j])>0)   {
                              Product pt = prod[i];
                              prod[i]= prod[j];
                              prod[j] = pt;
                        }
                  }
            }
            for(int i = 0; i< max; i++) {
                  vis.addLine (prod[i]);
            }
      }
}
```

You can see the sorted result in Figure 15-3.

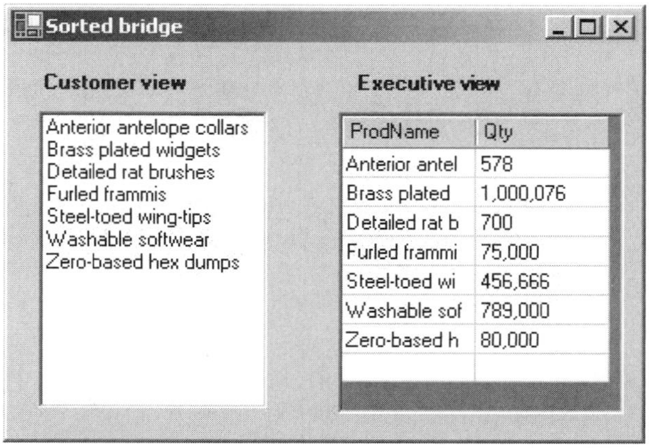

Figure 15-3 The sorted list generated using the SortBridge class

This clearly shows that you can vary the interface without changing the implementation. The converse is also true. For example, you could create another type of list display and replace one of the current list displays without any other program changes as long as the new list also implements the *VisList* interface. Here is the TreeList class.

```
public class TreeList:VisList    {
     private TreeView tree;
     private TreeAdapter gAdapter;
     //-----
     public TreeList(TreeView tre) {
          tree = tre;
          gAdapter = new TreeAdapter (tree);
     }
     //-----
     public void addLine(Product p) {
          gAdapter.Add (p);
     }
}
```

Note that we take advantage of the TreeAdapter we wrote in the previous chapter and modify it to work on Product objects.

```
public class TreeAdapter  {
     private TreeView tree;
     //------
     public TreeAdapter(TreeView tr)          {
          tree=tr;
     }
     //------
```

```
public void Add(Product p) {
      TreeNode nod;
 //add a root node
nod = tree.Nodes.Add(p.getName());
 //add a child node to it
 nod.Nodes.Add(p.getQuantity ());
 tree.ExpandAll ();
}
```

In Figure 15-4, we have created a tree list component that implements the *VisList* interface and replaced the ordinary list without any change in the public interface to the classes.

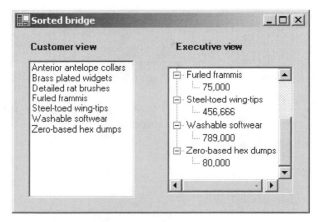

Figure 15-4   Another display using a Bridge to a tree list

Windows Forms as Bridges

The .NET visual control is itself an ideal example of a Bridge pattern implementation. A Control is a reusable software component that can be manipulated visually in a builder tool. All of the C# Controls support a query interface that enables builder programs to enumerate their properties and display them for easy modification. Figure 15-5 is a screen from Visual Studio.NET displaying a panel with a text field and a check box. The builder panel to the right shows how you can modify the properties of either of those components using a simple visual interface.

In other words, all ActiveX controls have the same interface used by the Builder program, and you can substitute any control for any other and still manipulate its properties using the same convenient interface. The actual program you construct uses these classes in a conventional way, each having its own rather different methods, but from the builder's point of view, they all appear to be the same.

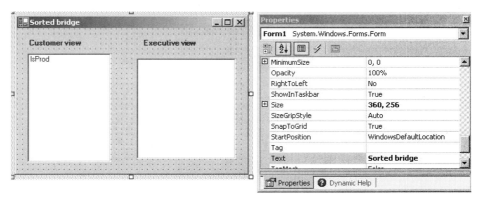

Figure 15-5   A screen from Visual Studio.NET showing a properties interface

Consequences of the Bridge Pattern

1. The Bridge pattern is intended to keep the interface to your client program constant while allowing you to change the actual kind of class you display or use. This can prevent you from recompiling a complicated set of user interface modules and only require that you recompile the bridge itself and the actual end display class.

2. You can extend the implementation class and the Bridge class separately, and usually without much interaction with each other.

3. You can hide implementation details from the client program much more easily.

Thought Question

In plotting a stock's performance, you usually display the price and price-earnings ratio over time, whereas in plotting a mutual fund, you usually show the price and the earnings per quarter. Suggest how you can use a Bridge to do both.

Programs on the CD-ROM

Bridge from List to Grid	\Bridge\BasicBridge
Sorted Bridge	\Bridge\SortBridge

CHAPTER 16

The Composite Pattern

Frequently, programmers develop systems in which a component may be either an individual object or a collection of objects. The Composite pattern is designed to accommodate both cases. You can use the Composite to build part-whole hierarchies or to construct data representations of trees. In summary, a composite is a collection of objects, any one of which may be either a composite or just a primitive object. In tree nomenclature, some objects may be nodes with additional branches and some may be leaves.

The problem that develops is the dichotomy between having a single, simple interface to access all the objects in a composite and the ability to distinguish between nodes and leaves. Nodes have children and can have children added to them, whereas leaves do not at the moment have children, and in some implementations they may be prevented from having children added to them.

Some authors have suggested creating a separate interface for nodes and leaves where a leaf could have the methods, such as the following.

```
public string getName();
public float getValue();
```

And a node could have these additional methods.

```
public ArrayList elements();
public Node getChild(string nodeName);
public void add(Object obj);
public void remove(Object obj);
```

This then leaves us with the programming problem of deciding which elements will be which when we construct the composite. However, *Design Patterns* suggests that each element should have the *same* interface whether it is a composite or a primitive element. This is easier to accomplish, but we are left with the question of what the *getChild* operation should accomplish when the object is actually a leaf.

C# can make this quite easy for us, since every node or leaf can return an ArrayList of the child nodes. If there are no children, the count property returns zero. Thus, if we simply obtain the ArrayList of child nodes from each element, we can quickly determine whether it has any children by checking the *count* property.

Just as difficult is the issue of adding or removing leaves from elements of the composite. A nonleaf node can have child-leaves added to it, but a leaf node cannot. However, we would like all of the components in the composite to have the same interface. We must prevent attempts to add children to a leaf node, and we can design the leaf node class to raise an error if the program attempts to add to such a node.

An Implementation of a Composite

Let's consider a small company that began with a single person. He was, of course, the CEO, although he may have been too busy to think about it at first. Then he hired a couple of people to handle the marketing and manufacturing. Soon each of them hired some additional assistants to help with advertising, shipping, and so forth, and they became the company's first two vice-presidents. As the company's success increased, the firm continued to grow until it had the organizational chart in Figure 16-1.

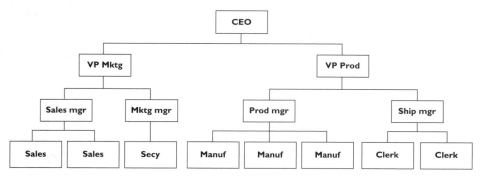

Figure 16-1   A typical organizational chart

Computing Salaries

If the company is successful, each of these company members receives a salary, and we could at any time ask for the cost of the control span of any employee to the company. We define this control cost as the salary of that person and those of all subordinates. Here is an ideal example for a composite.

- The cost of an individual employee is simply his or her salary (and benefits).
- The cost of an employee who heads a department is his or her salary plus those of subordinates.

We would like a single interface that will produce the salary totals correctly whether the employee has subordinates or not.

```
float getSalaries();    //get salaries of all
```

At this point, we realize that the idea of all Composites having the same standard method names in their interface is probably unrealistic. We'd prefer that the public methods be related to the kind of class we are actually developing. So rather than have generic methods like *getValue*, we'll use *getSalaries*.

The Employee Classes

We could now imagine representing the company as a Composite made up of nodes: managers and employees. It would be possible to use a single class to represent all employees, but since each level may have different properties, it might be more useful to define at least two classes: Employees and Bosses. Employees are leaf nodes and cannot have employees under them. Bosses are nodes that may have employee nodes under them.

We'll start with the AbstractEmployee class and derive our concrete Employee classes from it.

```
public interface AbstractEmployee     {
    float getSalary();                    //get current salary
    string getName();                     //get name
    bool isLeaf();                        //true if leaf
    void add(string nm, float salary);     //add subordinate
    void add(AbstractEmployee emp);        //add subordinate
    IEnumerator getSubordinates();         //get subordinates
    AbstractEmployee getChild();           //get child
    float getSalaries();                  //get sum of salaries
}
```

In C# we have a built-in enumeration interface called IEnumerator. This interface consists of these methods.

```
bool MoveNext();        //False if no more left
object Current()        //get current object
void Reset();           //move to first
```

So we can create an AbstractEmployee interface that returns an Enumerator. You move through an enumeration, allowing for the fact that it might be empty, using the following approach.

```
e.Reset();
while (e.MoveNext()) {
  Emp = (Employee)e.Current();
  //..do computation..
}
```

This Enumerator may, of course, be empty and can thus be used for both nodes and leaves of the composite.

Our concrete Employee class will store the name and salary of each employee and allow us to fetch them as needed.

```
public class Employee :AbstractEmployee        {
      protected float salary;
      protected string name;
      protected ArrayList subordinates;
      //------
      public Employee(string nm, float salary)              {
            subordinates = new ArrayList();
            name = nm;
            salary = salry;
      }
      //------
      public float getSalary() {
            return salary;
      }
      //------
      public string getName() {
            return name;
      }
      //------
      public bool isLeaf() {
            return subordinates.Count == 0;
      }
      //------
      public virtual AbstractEmployee getChild() {
            return null;
      }
```

The Employee class must have concrete implementations of the *add, remove, getChild,* and *subordinates* classes. Since an Employee is a leaf, all of these will return some sort of error indication. The subordinates method could return a null, but programming will be more consistent if *subordinates* returns an empty enumeration.

```
      public IEnumerator getSubordinates() {
            return subordinates.GetEnumerator ();
      }
```

The *add* and *remove* methods must generate errors, since members of the basic Employee class cannot have subordinates. We throw an Exception if you call these methods in the basic Employee class.

```
public virtual void add(string nm, float salary) {
   throw new Exception(
       "No subordinates in base employee class");
}
//------
public virtual void add(AbstractEmployee emp) {
       throw new Exception(
       "No subordinates in base employee class");
}
```

The Boss Class

Our Boss class is a subclass of Employee and allows us to store subordinate employees as well. We'll store them in an ArrayList called *subordinates* and return them through an enumeration. Thus, if a particular Boss has temporarily run out of Employees, the enumeration will just be empty.

```
public class Boss:Employee {
       public Boss(string name, float salary):base(name,salary) {}
       //------
       public override void add(string nm, float salary) {
               AbstractEmployee emp = new Employee(nm,salary);
               subordinates.Add (emp);
       }
       //------
       public override void add(AbstractEmployee emp){
               subordinates.Add(emp);
       }
       //------
```

If you want to get a list of employees of a given supervisor, you can obtain an Enumeration of them directly from the ArrayList. Similarly, you can use this same ArrayList to return a sum of salaries for any employee and his or her subordinates.

```
public float getSalaries() {
     float sum;
     AbstractEmployee esub;
     //get the salaries of the boss and subordinates
     sum = getSalary();
     IEnumerator enumSub = subordinates.GetEnumerator() ;
     while (enumSub.MoveNext())  {
             esub = (AbstractEmployee)enumSub.Current;
             sum += esub.getSalaries();
     }
  return sum;
}
```

Note that this method starts with the salary of the current Employee and then calls the *getSalaries()* method on each subordinate. This is, of course, recursive, and any employees who have subordinates will be included. A diagram of these classes is shown in Figure 16-2.

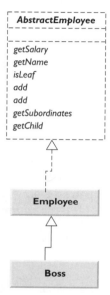

Figure 16-2   The AbstractEmployee class and how Employee and Boss are derived from it

Building the Employee Tree

We start by creating a CEO Employee and then add his or her subordinates and their subordinates, as follows.

```
private void buildEmployeeList() {
     prez = new Boss("CEO", 200000);
     marketVP = new Boss("Marketing VP", 100000);
     prez.add(marketVP);
     salesMgr = new Boss("Sales Mgr", 50000);
     advMgr = new Boss("Advt Mgr", 50000);
     marketVP.add(salesMgr);
     marketVP.add(advMgr);
     prodVP = new Boss("Production VP", 100000);
     prez.add(prodVP);
     advMgr.add("Secy", 20000);
     //add salesmen reporting to sales manager
     for (int i = 1; i<=5; i++){
          salesMgr.add("Sales" + i.ToString(),
```

```
                        rand_sal(30000));
    }

    prodMgr = new Boss("Prod Mgr", 40000);
    shipMgr = new Boss("Ship Mgr", 35000);
    prodVP.add(prodMgr);
    prodVP.add(shipMgr);

    for (int i = 1; i<=3; i++){
        shipMgr.add("Ship" + i.ToString(), rand_sal(25000));
    }
    for (int i = 1; i<=4; i++){
        prodMgr.add("Manuf" + i.ToString(), rand_sal(20000));
    }
}
```

Once we have constructed this Composite structure, we can load a visual TreeView list by starting at the top node and calling the *addNode()* method recursively until all the leaves in each node are accessed.

```
private void buildTree() {
    EmpNode nod;
    nod = new EmpNode(prez);
    rootNode = nod;
    EmpTree.Nodes.Add(nod);
    addNodes(nod, prez);
}
```

To simplify the manipulation of the TreeNode objects, we derive an EmpNode class that takes an instance of Employee as an argument.

```
public class EmpNode:TreeNode    {
    private AbstractEmployee emp;
    public EmpNode(AbstractEmployee aemp ):
                base(aemp.getName ()) {
        emp = aemp;
    }
    //-----
    public AbstractEmployee getEmployee() {
        return emp;
    }
}
```

The final program display is shown in Figure 16-3.

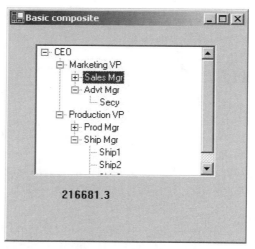

Figure 16-3   The corporate organization shown in a TreeView control

In this implementation, the cost (sum of salaries) is shown in the bottom bar for any employee you click on. This simple computation calls the *getChild()* method recursively to obtain all the subordinates of that employee.

```
private void EmpTree_AfterSelect(object sender,
             TreeViewEventArgs e) {
    EmpNode node;
    node = (EmpNode)EmpTree.SelectedNode;
    getNodeSum(node);
}
//------
private void getNodeSum(EmpNode node) {
    AbstractEmployee emp;
    float sum;

    emp = node.getEmployee();
    sum = emp.getSalaries();
    lbSalary.Text = sum.ToString ();
}
```

Self-Promotion

We can imagine cases where a simple Employee would stay in his current job but have new subordinates. For example, a Salesman might be asked to supervise sales trainees. For such a case, it is convenient to provide a method in the Boss class that creates a Boss from an Employee. We just provide an additional constructor that converts an employee into a boss.

```
public Boss(AbstractEmployee emp):
            base(emp.getName() , emp.getSalary())        {
```

Doubly Linked Lists

In the preceding implementation, we keep a reference to each subordinate in the Collection in each Boss class. This means that you can move down the chain from the president to any employee, but there is no way to move back up to find out who an employee's supervisor is. This is easily remedied by providing a constructor for each AbstractEmployee subclass that includes a reference to the parent node.

```
public class Employee :AbstractEmployee        {
      protected float salary;
      protected string name;
      protected AbstractEmployee parent;
      protected ArrayList subordinates;
      //------
      public Employee(AbstractEmployee parnt,
                  string nm, float salry)              {
            subordinates = new ArrayList();
            name = nm;
            salary = salry;
            parent = parnt;
}
```

Then you can quickly walk up the tree to produce a reporting chain.

```
private void btShowBoss_Click(object sender, System.EventArgs e) {
      EmpNode node;
      node = (EmpNode)EmpTree.SelectedNode;
      AbstractEmployee emp = node.getEmployee ();
      string bosses = "";
      while(emp != null) {
            bosses += emp.getName () +"\n";
            emp = emp.getBoss();
      }
      MessageBox.Show (null, bosses,"Reporting chain");
}
```

See Figure 16-4.

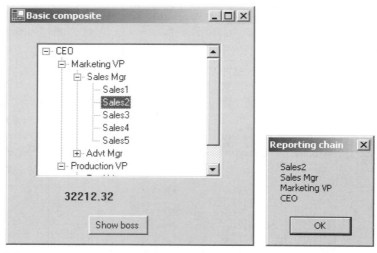

Figure 16-4   The tree list display of the composite with a display of the parent nodes
on the right

Consequences of the Composite Pattern

The Composite pattern allows you to define a class hierarchy of simple objects and more complex composite objects so they appear to be the same to the client program. Because of this simplicity, the client can be that much simpler, since nodes and leaves are handled in the same way.

The Composite pattern also makes it easy for you to add new kinds of components to your collection as long as they support a similar programming interface. On the other hand, this has the disadvantage of making your system overly general. You might find it harder to restrict certain classes where this would normally be desirable.

A Simple Composite

The intent of the Composite pattern is to allow you to construct a tree of various related classes, even though some have different properties than others and some are leaves that do not have children. However, for very simple cases, you can sometimes use just a single class that exhibits both parent and leaf behavior. In the SimpleComposite example, we create an Employee class that always contains the ArrayList *subordinates*. This collection of employees will either be empty or populated, and this determines the nature of the values that you return from the *getChild* and *remove* methods. In this simple case, we do not raise errors and always allow leaf nodes to be promoted to have child nodes. In other words, we always allow execution of the *add* method.

While you may not regard this automatic promotion as a disadvantage, in systems where there are a very large number of leaves, it is wasteful to keep a Collection initialized and unused in each leaf node. In cases where there are relatively few leaf nodes, this is not a serious problem.

Composites in .NET

In .NET, you will note that the *Node* object class we use to populate the Tree-View is in fact just such a simple Composite pattern. You will also find that the Composite describes the hierarchy of Form, Frame, and Controls in any user interface program. Similarly, toolbars are containers, and each may contain any number of other containers.

Any container may then contain components such as buttons, check boxes, and TextBoxes, each of which is a leaf node that cannot have further children. They may also contain ListBoxes and grids that may be treated as leaf nodes or that may contain further graphical components. You can walk down the Composite tree using the *Controls* collection.

Other Implementation Issues

Ordering components.   In some programs, the order of the components may be important. If that order is somehow different from the order in which they were added to the parent, then the parent must do additional work to return them in the correct order. For example, you might sort the original collection alphabetically and return a new sorted collection.

Caching results.   If you frequently ask for data that must be computed from a series of child components, as we did here with salaries, it may be advantageous to cache these computed results in the parent. However, unless the computation is relatively intensive and you are quite certain that the underlying data have not changed, this may not be worth the effort.

Thought Questions

1. A baseball team can be considered an aggregate of its individual players. How could you use a Composite to represent individual and team performance?

2. The produce department of a supermarket needs to track its sales performance by food item. Suggest how a Composite might be helpful.

Programs on the CD-ROM

Composite shows tree	\Composite\Composite
Composite that uses both child links and parent links	\Composite\DlinkComposite
Simple Composite of same employee tree that allows any employee to move from leaf to node	\Composite\SimpleComposite

CHAPTER 17

The Decorator Pattern

The Decorator pattern provides us with a way to modify the behavior of individual objects without having to create a new derived class. Suppose we have a program that uses eight objects, but three of them need an additional feature. You could create a derived class for each of these objects, and in many cases this would be a perfectly acceptable solution. However, if each of these three objects requires *different* features, this would mean creating three derived classes. Further, if one of the classes has features of *both* of the other classes, you begin to create complexity that is both confusing and unnecessary.

For example, suppose we wanted to draw a special border around some of the buttons in a toolbar. If we created a new derived Button class, this means that all of the buttons in this new class would always have the same border, even if that isn't what we want.

Instead, we create a Decorator class that *decorates* the buttons. Then we derive any number of specific Decorators from the main Decorator class, each of which performs a specific kind of decoration. In order to decorate a button, the Decorator has to be an object derived from the visual environment so it can receive paint method calls and forward calls to other useful graphic methods to the object it is decorating. This is another case where object containment is favored over object inheritance. The Decorator is a graphical object, but it contains the object it is decorating. It may intercept some graphical method calls, perform some additional computation, and pass them on to the underlying object it is decorating.

Decorating a CoolButton

Recent Windows applications such as Internet Explorer and Netscape Navigator have a row of flat, unbordered buttons that highlight themselves with outline borders when you move your mouse over them. Some Windows programmers call this toolbar a CoolBar and the buttons CoolButtons. There is no comparable button behavior in C# controls, but we can obtain that behavior by *decorating* a Panel and using it to contain a button. In this case, we decorate it by drawing black and white border lines to highlight the button or gray lines to remove the button borders.

Let's consider how to create this Decorator. *Design Patterns* suggests that Decorators should be derived from some general visual component class, and then every message for the actual button should be forwarded from the Decorator. This is not all that practical in C#, but if we use containers as Decorators, all of the events are forwarded to the control being contained.

Design Patterns further suggests that classes such as Decorator should be abstract classes and that you should derive all of your actual working (or concrete) Decorators from the Abstract class. In our implementation, we define a Decorator interface that receives the mouse and paint events we need to intercept.

```
public interface Decorator      {
        void mouseMove(object sender, MouseEventArgs e);
        void mouseEnter(object sender, EventArgs e);
        void mouseLeave(object sender, EventArgs e);
        void paint(object sender, PaintEventArgs e);
}
```

For our actual implementation, we can derive a CoolDecorator from a Panel class and have it become the container that holds the button we are going to decorate.

Now, let's look at how we could implement a CoolButton. All we really need to do is to draw the white and black lines around the button area when it is highlighted and draw gray lines when it is not. When a MouseMove is detected over the button, the next paint event should draw the highlighted lines, and when the mouse leaves the button area, the next paint event should draw outlines in gray. We do this by setting a mouse_over flag and then forcing a repaint by calling the Refresh method.

```
public void mouseMove(object sender, MouseEventArgs e){
            mouse_over = true;
}
public void mouseEnter(object sender, EventArgs e){
        mouse_over = true;
        this.Refresh ();
}
public void mouseLeave(object sender, EventArgs e){
        mouse_over = false;
        this.Refresh ();
}
```

This is the actual paint event.

```
public virtual void paint(object sender, PaintEventArgs e){
      //draw over button to change its outline
      Graphics g = e.Graphics;
      const int  d = 1;
      //draw over everything in gray first
      g.DrawRectangle(gPen, 0, 0, x2 - 1, y2 - 1);
      //draw black and white boundaries
      //if the mouse is over
      if( mouse_over) {
            g.DrawLine(bPen, 0, 0, x2 - d, 0);
            g.DrawLine(bPen, 0, 0, 0, y2 - 1);
            g.DrawLine(wPen, 0, y2 - d, x2 - d, y2 - d);
            g.DrawLine(wPen, x2 - d, 0, x2 - d, y2 - d);
      }
}
```

Handling Events in a Decorator

When we construct an actual Decorator containing the mouse and paint methods we just showed, we have to connect the event handling system to these methods. We do this in the constructor for the Decorator by creating an Event-Handler class for the mouse enter and hover events and a MouseEventHandler for the move and leave events. It is important to note that the events we are catching are events on the contained button, rather than on the surrounding Panel. So the control to which we add the handlers is the button itself.

```
public CoolDecorator(Control c) {
contl = c;              //copy in control
//mouse over, enter handler

EventHandler evh = new EventHandler(mouseEnter);
      c.MouseHover += evh;
      c.MouseEnter+= evh;
//mouse move handler
c.MouseMove += new MouseEventHandler(mouseMove);
c.MouseLeave += new EventHandler(mouseLeave);
```

Similarly, we create a PaintEventHandler for the paint event.

```
//paint handler catches button's paint
c.Paint += new PaintEventHandler( paint);
```

Layout Considerations

If you create a Windows form containing buttons, the GUI designer automatically generates code to add that Control to the Controls array for that Window. We want to change this by adding the button to the Controls array for the new panel, adding the panel to the Controls array for the Window, and removing the button from that array. Here is the code to add the panel and remove the button in the Form initialization method.

```
//add outside decorator to the layout
//and remove the button from the layout
this.Controls.AddRange(new System.Windows.Forms.Control[] {cdec} );
this.Controls.Remove (btButtonA);
```

This is the code to add the button to the Decorator panel.

```
public CoolDecorator(Control c) {
     contl = c;               //copy in control
     //add button to controls contained in panel
     this.Controls.AddRange(new Control[] {contl} );
```

Control Size and Position

When we decorate the button by putting it in a Panel, we need to change the coordinates and sizes so that the Panel has the size and coordinates of the button and the button has a location of (0, 0) within the panel. This also happens in the CoolDecorator constructor.

```
this.Location = p;
contl.Location =new Point(0,0);

this.Name = "deco"+contl.Name ;
this.Size = contl.Size;
x1 = c.Location.X - 1;
y1 = c.Location.Y - 1;
x2 = c.Size.Width;
y2 = c.Size.Height;
```

We also create instances of the Pens we will use in the Paint method in this constructor.

```
//create the overwrite pens
gPen = new Pen(c.BackColor, 2);     //gray pen overwrites borders
bPen = new Pen(Color.Black , 1);
wPen = new Pen(Color.White, 1);
```

This program is shown in Figure 17-1, with the mouse hovering over one of the buttons.

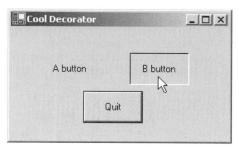

Figure 17-1 The A button and B button are CoolButtons, which are outlined when a mouse hovers over them. Here the B button is outlined.

Multiple Decorators

Now that we see how a single decorator works, what about multiple decorators? It could be that we'd like to decorate our CoolButtons with another decoration—say, a diagonal red line.

This is only slightly more complicated because we just need to enclose the CoolDecorator inside yet another Decorator panel for more decoration to occur. The only real change is that we not only need the instance of the panel we are wrapping in another but also the central object (here a button) being decorated, since we have to attach our paint routines to that central object's paint method.

So we need to create a constructor for our Decorator that has both the enclosing panel and the button as controls.

```
public class CoolDecorator :Panel, Decorator      {
    protected Control contl;
    protected Pen bPen, wPen, gPen;
    private bool mouse_over;
    protected float x1, y1, x2, y2;
//-------------------------------
    public CoolDecorator(Control c, Control baseC) {
    //the first control is the one laid out
    //the base control is the one whose paint method we extend
    //this allows for nesting of decorators
            contl = c;
            this.Controls.AddRange(new Control[] {contl} );
```

Then when we add the event handlers, the paint event handler must be attached to the base control.

```
//paint handler catches button's paint
    baseC.Paint += new PaintEventHandler( paint);
```

We make the paint method virtual so we can override it as we see here.

```
public virtual void paint(object sender, PaintEventArgs e){
    //draw over button to change its outline
    Graphics g = e.Graphics;
```

It turns out that the easiest way to write our SlashDecorator, which draws that diagonal red line, is to derive it from CoolDecorator directly. We can reuse all the base methods and extend only the paint method from the CoolDecorator and save a lot of effort.

```
public class SlashDeco:CoolDecorator      {
    private Pen rPen;
    //----------------
    public SlashDeco(Control c, Control bc):base(c, bc) {
      rPen = new Pen(Color.Red , 2);
    }
    //----------------
    public override void paint(object sender,
                PaintEventArgs e){

            Graphics g = e.Graphics ;
            x1=0; y1=0;
            x2=this.Size.Width ;
            y2=this.Size.Height ;
            g.DrawLine (rPen, x1, y1, x2, y2);
      }
    }
```

This gives us a final program that displays the two buttons, as shown in Figure 17-2. The class diagram is shown in Figure 17-3.

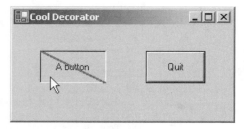

Figure 17-2   The A CoolButton is also decorated with a SlashDecorator.

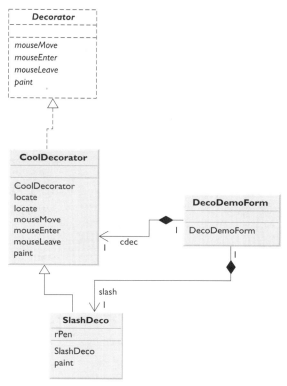

Figure 17-3   The UML class diagram for Decorators and two specific Decorator implementations

Nonvisual Decorators

Decorators, of course, are not limited to objects that enhance visual classes. You can add or modify the methods of any object in a similar fashion. In fact, nonvisual objects can be easier to decorate because there may be fewer methods to intercept and forward. Whenever you put an instance of a class inside another class and have the outer class operate on it, you are essentially "decorating" that inner class. This is one of the most common tools for programming available in Visual Studio.NET.

Decorators, Adapters, and Composites

As noted in *Design Patterns*, there is an essential similarity among these classes that you may have recognized. Adapters also seem to "decorate" an existing class. However, their function is to change the interface of one or more classes to one that is more convenient for a particular program. Decorators add methods to particular instances of classes rather than to all of them. You could also imagine that a composite consisting of a single item is essentially a Decorator. Once again, however, the intent is different.

Consequences of the Decorator Pattern

The Decorator pattern provides a more flexible way to add responsibilities to a class than by using inheritance, since it can add these responsibilities to selected instances of the class. It also allows you to customize a class without creating subclasses high in the inheritance hierarchy. *Design Patterns* points out two disadvantages of the Decorator pattern. One is that a Decorator and its enclosed component are not identical. Thus, tests for object types will fail. The second is that Decorators can lead to a system with "lots of little objects" that all look alike to the programmer trying to maintain the code. This can be a maintenance headache.

Decorator and Façade evoke similar images in building architecture, but in design pattern terminology, the Façade is a way of hiding a complex system inside a simpler interface, whereas Decorator adds function by wrapping a class. We'll take up the Façade next.

Thought Questions

1. When someone enters an incorrect value in a cell of a grid, you might want to change the color of the row to indicate the problem. Suggest how you could use a Decorator.

2. A mutual fund is a collection of stocks. Each one consists of an array, or Collection, of prices over time. Can you see how a Decorator can be used to produce a report of stock performance for each stock and for the whole fund?

Programs on the CD-ROM

C# Cool Button Decorator	\Decorator\Cooldecorator
C# Cool Button and Slash Decorator	\Decorator\Redecorator

CHAPTER 18

The Façade Pattern

The Façade pattern is used to wrap a set of complex classes into a simpler enclosing interface. As your programs evolve and develop, they grow in complexity. In fact, for all the excitement about using design patterns, these patterns sometimes generate so many classes that it is difficult to understand the program's flow. Furthermore, there may be a number of complicated subsystems, each of which has its own complex interface.

The Façade pattern allows you to simplify this complexity by providing a simplified interface to these subsystems. This simplification may in some cases reduce the flexibility of the underlying classes, but it usually provides all the function needed for all but the most sophisticated users. These users can still, of course, access the underlying classes and methods.

Fortunately, we don't have to write a complex system to provide an example of where a Façade can be useful. C# provides a set of classes that connect to databases, using an interface called ADO.NET. You can connect to any database for which the manufacturer has provided a ODBC connection class—almost every database on the market. Let's take a minute and review how databases are used and a little about how they work.

What Is a Database?

A *database* is a series of tables of information in some sort of file structure that allows you to access these tables, select columns from them, sort them, and select rows based on various criteria. Databases usually have *indexes* associated with many of the columns in these tables, so we can access them as rapidly as possible.

Databases are used more than any other kind of structure in computing. You'll find databases as central elements of employee records and payroll systems, in travel scheduling systems, and all through product manufacturing and marketing.

In the case of employee records, you could imagine a table of employee names and addresses and of salaries, tax withholding, and benefits. Let's consider how these might be organized. You can imagine one table of employee names, addresses, and phone numbers. Other information that you might want to store would include salary, salary range, last raise, next raise, employee performance ranking, and so forth.

Should this all be in one table? Almost certainly not. Salary ranges for various employee types are probably invariant between employees, and thus you would store only the employee type in the employee table and the salary ranges in another table that is pointed to by the type number. Consider the data in Table 18–1.

Table 18-1   Employee Names and Salary Type Tables

Key	Lastname	Salary Type
1	Adams	2
2	Johnson	1
3	Smyth	3
4	Tully	1
5	Wolff	2

Salary Type	Min	Max
1	30000	45000
2	45000	60000
3	60000	75000

The data in the SalaryType column refers to the second table. We could imagine many such tables for things like state of residence and tax values for each state, health plan withholding, and so forth. Each table will have a primary key column like the ones at the left of each table and several more columns of data. Building tables in a database has evolved to both an art and a science. The structure of these tables is referred to by their *normal form*. Tables are said to be in first, second, or third normal form, abbreviated as 1NF, 2NF, or 3NF.

- *First.* Each cell in a table should have only one value (never an array of values). (1NF)
- *Second.* 1NF and every nonkey column is fully dependent on the key column. This means there is a one-to-one relationship between the primary key and the remaining cells in that row. (2NF)

- *Third.* 2NF and all nonkey columns are mutually independent. This means that there are no data columns containing values that can be calculated from other columns' data. (3NF)

Today, nearly all databases are constructed so that all tables are in third normal form (3NF). This means that there are usually a fairly large number of tables, each with relatively few columns of information.

Getting Data Out of Databases

Suppose we wanted to produce a table of employees and their salary ranges for some planning exercise. This table doesn't exist directly in the database, but it can be constructed by issuing a query to the database. We'd like to have a table that looked like the data in Table 18-2.

Table 18-2   Employee Salaries Sorted by Name

Name	Min	Max
Adams	$45,000.00	$60,000.00
Johnson	$30,000.00	$45,000.00
Smyth	$60,000.00	$75,000.00
Tully	$30,000.00	$45,000.00
Wolff	$45,000.00	$60,000.00

Maybe we want data sorted by increasing salary, as shown in Table 18-3. We find that the query we issue to obtain these tables has this form.

Table 18-3   Employee Salaries Sorted by Magnitude

Name	Min	Max
Tully	$30,000.00	$45,000.00
Johnson	$30,000.00	$45,000.00
Wolff	$45,000.00	$60,000.00
Adams	$45,000.00	$60,000.00
Smyth	$60,000.00	$75,000.00

```
SELECT DISTINCTROW Employees.Name, SalaryRanges.Min,
SalaryRanges.Max FROM Employees INNER JOIN SalaryRanges ON
Employees.SalaryKey = SalaryRanges.SalaryKey
ORDER BY SalaryRanges.Min;
```

This language is called Structured Query Language or SQL (often pronounced "sequel"), and it is the language of virtually all databases currently available. There have been several standards issued for SQL over the years, and most PC databases support much of these ANSI standards. The SQL-92 standard is considered the floor standard, and there have been several updates since. However, not all databases support the later SQL versions perfectly, and most offer various kinds of SQL extensions to exploit various features unique to their database.

Kinds of Databases

Since the PC became a major office tool, there have been a number of popular databases developed that are intended to run by themselves on PCs. These include elementary databases like Microsoft Works and more sophisticated ones like Approach, dBase, Borland Paradox, Microsoft Access, and FoxBase.

Another category of PC databases includes databases intended to be accessed from a server by a number of PC clients. These include IBM DB/2, Microsoft SQL Server, Oracle, and Sybase. All of these database products support various relatively similar dialects of SQL, and thus all of them would appear at first to be relatively interchangeable. The reason they are *not* interchangeable, of course, is that each was designed with different performance characteristics involved and each with a different user interface and programming interface. While you might think that because they all support SQL, they are programmed the same way, quite the opposite is true. Each database has its own way of receiving the SQL queries and its own way of returning the results. This is where the next proposed level of standardization came about: ODBC.

ODBC

It would be nice if we could somehow write code that was independent of the particular vendor's database that would allow us to get the same results from any of these databases without changing our calling program. If we could only write some wrappers for all of these databases so that they all appeared to have similar programming interfaces, this would be quite easy to accomplish.

Microsoft first attempted this feat in 1992 when it released a specification called Object Database Connectivity. It was supposed to be the answer for connection to all databases under Windows. Like all first software versions, it suffered some growing pains, and another version was released in 1994 that was somewhat faster as well as more stable. It also was the first 32-bit version. In addition, ODBC began to move to platforms other than Windows and has by now become quite pervasive in the PC and Workstation world. Nearly every major database vendor provides ODBC drivers.

Database Structure

At the lowest level, then, a database consists of a series of tables, each having several named columns and some relationships between these tables. This can get pretty complicated to keep track of, and we would like to see some simplification of this in the code we use to manipulate databases.

C# and all of Visual Studio.NET use a new database access model, called ADO.NET, for ActiveX Data Objects. The design philosophy of ADO.NET is one in which you define a connection between your program and a database and use that connection sporadically, with much of the computation actually taking place in disconnected objects on your local machine. Further, ADO.NET uses XML for definition of the objects that are transmitted between the database and the program, primarily under the covers, although it is possible to access this data description using some of the built-in ADO.NET classes.

Using ADO.NET

ADO.NET as implemented in C# consists of a fairly large variety of interrelated objects. Since the operations we want to perform are still the same relatively simple ones, the Façade pattern will be an ideal way to manage them.

- **OleDbConnection**   This object represents the actual connection to the database. You can keep an instance of this class available but open and close the connection as needed. You must specifically close it when you are done, before it is garbage collected.
- **OleDbCommand**   This class represents an SQL command you send to the database, which may or may not return results.
- **OleDbDataAdapter**   Provides a bridge for moving data between a database and a local DataSet. You can specify an OleDbCommand, a Dataset, and a connection.
- **DataSet**   A representation of one or more database tables or results from a query on your local machine.
- **DataTable**   A single data table from a database or query.
- **DataRow**   A single row in a DataTable.

Connecting to a Database

To connect to a database, you specify a connection string in the constructor for the database you want to use. For example, for an Access database, your connection string would be the following.

```
string connectionString =
     "Provider=Microsoft.Jet.OLEDB.4.0;" +
     "Data Source=" + dbName;
```

The following makes the actual connection.

```
OleDbConnection conn =
     new OleDbConnection(connectionString);
```

You actually open that connection by calling the open method. To make sure that you don't reopen an already open connection, you can check its state first.

```
private void openConnection() {
     if (conn.State == ConnectionState.Closed){
          conn.Open ();
     }
}
```

Reading Data from a Database Table

To read data in from a database table, you create an ADOCommand with the appropriate Select statement and connection.

```
public DataTable openTable (string tableName) {
     OleDbDataAdapter adapter = new OleDbDataAdapter ();
     DataTable dtable = null;
     string query = "Select * from " + tableName;
     adapter.SelectCommand = new OleDbCommand (query, conn);
```

Then you create a dataset object into which to put the results.

```
DataSet dset = new DataSet ("mydata");
```

Then you simply tell the command object to use the connection to fill the dataset. You must specify the name of the table to fill in the FillDataSet method, as is shown here.

```
try {
     openConnection();
     adapter.Fill (dset);
}
```

```
catch(Exception e) {
     Console.WriteLine (e.Message );
}
```

The dataset then contains at least one table, and you can obtain it by index or by name and examine its contents.

```
//get the table from the dataset
dtable = dset.Tables [0];
```

Executing a Query

Executing a Select query is exactly identical to the preceding code, except the query can be an SQL Select statement of any complexity. Here we show the steps wrapped in a try block in case there are SQL or other database errors.

```
public DataTable openQuery(string query) {
     OleDbDataAdapter dsCmd = new OleDbDataAdapter ();
     DataSet dset = new DataSet ();
//create a dataset
     DataTable dtable = null;       //declare a data table
     try {
          //create the command
          dsCmd.SelectCommand =
               new OleDbCommand(query, conn);
//open the connection
          openConnection();
          //fill the dataset
          dsCmd.Fill(dset, "mine");
          //get the table
          dtable = dset.Tables[0];
          //always close it
          closeConnection();
          //and return it
          return dtable;
          catch (Exception e) {
               Console.WriteLine (e.Message);
               return null;
          }
}
```

Deleting the Contents of a Table

You can delete the contents of a table using the Delete * from Table SQL statement. However, since this is not a Select command, and there is no local table to bridge to, you can simply use the ExecuteNonQuery method of the OleDb Command object.

```
public void delete() {
     //deletes entire table
     conn = db.getConnection();
     openConn();
     if (conn.State == ConnectionState.Open ) {
          OleDbCommand adcmd =
          new OleDbCommand("Delete * from " + tableName, conn);
          try{
               adcmd.ExecuteNonQuery();
               closeConn();
          }
          catch (Exception e) {
               Console.WriteLine (e.Message);
          }
     }
}
```

Adding Rows to Database Tables Using ADO.NET

The process of adding data to a table is closely related. You generally start by getting the current version of the table from the database. If it is very large, you can get only the empty table by getting just its schema. We follow these steps.

1. Create a DataTable with the name of the table in the database.

2. Add it to a dataset.

3. Fill the dataset from the database.

4. Get a new row object from the DataTable.

5. Fill in its columns.

6. Add the row to the table.

7. When you have added all the rows, update the database from the modified DataTable object.

The process looks like this.

```
DataSet dset = new DataSet(tableName);   //create the data set
dtable = new DataTable(tableName);       //and a datatable
dset.Tables.Add(dtable);                 //add to collection
conn = db.getConnection();
openConn();                              //open the connection
OleDbDataAdapter adcmd = new OleDbDataAdapter();
//open the table
adcmd.SelectCommand =
     new OleDbCommand("Select * from " + tableName, conn);
OleDbCommandBuilder olecb = new OleDbCommandBuilder(adcmd);
adcmd.TableMappings.Add("Table", tableName);
//load current data into the local table copy
```

```
adcmd.Fill(dset, tableName);
//get the Enumerator from the Hashtable
IEnumerator ienum = names.Keys.GetEnumerator();
//move through the table, adding the names to new rows
while (ienum.MoveNext()) {
      string name = (string)ienum.Current;
      row = dtable.NewRow();     //get new rows
      row[columnName] = name;
      dtable.Rows.Add(row);        //add into table
}
//Now update the database with this table
try {
      adcmd.Update(dset);
      closeConn();
      filled = true;
}
catch (Exception e) {
      Console.WriteLine (e.Message);
}
```

It is this table editing and update process that is central to the ADO style of programming. You get the table, modify the table, and update the changes back to the database. You use this same process to edit or delete rows, and updating the database makes these changes as well.

Building the Façade Classes

This description is the beginning of the new Façade we are developing to handle creating, connecting to, and using databases. In order to carry out the rest, let's consider Table 18-4, grocery prices at three local stores.

It would be nice if we had this information in a database so we could easily answer the question, "Which store has the lowest prices for oranges?" Such a database should contain three tables: the supermarkets, the foods, and the prices. We also need to keep the relations among the three tables. One simple way to handle this is to create a Stores table with StoreName and StoreKey, a Foods table with a FoodName and a FoodKey, and a Price table with a PriceKey, a Price, and references to the StoreKey and Foodkey.

In our Façade, we will make each of these three tables its own class and have it take care of creating the actual tables. Since these three tables are so similar, we'll derive them all from the basic DBTable class.

Building the Price Query

For every food name, we'd like to get a report of which stores have the cheapest prices. This means writing a simple SQL query against the database. We can do

Table 18-4 Grocery Pricing Data

Store	Product	Price
Stop and Shop	Apples	0.27
Stop and Shop	Oranges	0.36
Stop and Shop	Hamburger	1.98
Stop and Shop	Butter	2.39
Stop and Shop	Milk	1.98
Stop and Shop	Cola	2.65
Stop and Shop	Green beans	2.29
Village Market	Apples	0.29
Village Market	Oranges	0.29
Village Market	Hamburger	2.45
Village Market	Butter	2.99
Village Market	Milk	1.79
Village Market	Cola	3.79
Village Market	Green beans	2.19
Waldbaum's	Apples	0.33
Waldbaum's	Oranges	0.47
Waldbaum's	Hamburger	2.29
Waldbaum's	Butter	3.29
Waldbaum's	Milk	1.89
Waldbaum's	Cola	2.99
Waldbaum's	Green beans	1.99

this within the Price class and have it return a Dataset with the store names and prices.

The final application simply fills one list box with the food names and fills the other list box with prices when you click on a food name, as shown in Figure 18-1.

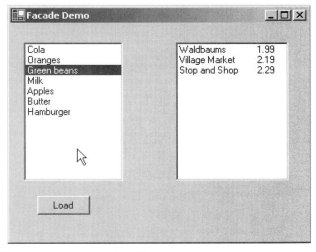

Figure 18-1   The grocery program using a Façade pattern

Making the ADO.NET Façade

In the Façade we will create for our grocery database, we start with an abstract DBase class that represents a connection to a database. This encapsulates making the connection and opening a table and an SQL query.

```
public abstract class DBase      {
      protected OleDbConnection conn;

private void openConnection() {
      if (conn.State == ConnectionState.Closed){
            conn.Open ();
      }
}
//------
private void closeConnection() {
      if (conn.State == ConnectionState.Open ){
            conn.Close ();
      }
}
//------
public DataTable openTable (string tableName) {
      OleDbDataAdapter adapter = new OleDbDataAdapter ();
      DataTable dtable = null;
      string query = "Select * from " + tableName;
      adapter.SelectCommand = new OleDbCommand (query, conn);
      DataSet dset = new DataSet ("mydata");
      try {
            openConnection();
```

```
                        adapter.Fill (dset);
                        dtable = dset.Tables [0];
                }
                catch(Exception e) {
                        Console.WriteLine (e.Message );
                }
                return dtable;
        }
        //------
        public DataTable openQuery(string query) {
                OleDbDataAdapter dsCmd = new OleDbDataAdapter ();
                DataSet dset = new DataSet ();      //create a dataset
                DataTable dtable = null;            //declare a data table
                try {
                        //create the command
                        dsCmd.SelectCommand = new OleDbCommand(query, conn);
                        openConnection();    //open the connection
                        //fill the dataset
                        dsCmd.Fill(dset, "mine");
                        //get the table
                        dtable = dset.Tables[0];
                        closeConnection();                  //always close it
                        return dtable;                      //and return it
                }
                catch (Exception e) {
                        Console.WriteLine (e.Message);
                        return null;
                }
        }
        //------
        public void openConnection(string connectionString) {
                conn = new OleDbConnection(connectionString);
        }
        //------
        public OleDbConnection getConnection() {
                return conn;
        }
}
```

Note that this class is complete except for constructors. We'll make derived classes that create the connection strings for various databases. Here we'll make a version for Access.

```
public class AxsDatabase :Dbase  {
        public AxsDatabase(string dbName)        {
                string connectionString =
                "Provider=Microsoft.Jet.OLEDB.4.0;Data Source=" +
                        dbName;
                openConnection(connectionString);
        }
}
```

Here is one for SQL Server.

```
public class SQLServerDatabase:DBase    {
     string connectionString;
     //-----
public SQLServerDatabase(String dbName)                    {
     connectionString = "Persist Security Info = False;" +
          "Initial Catalog =" + dbName + ";" +
          "Data Source = myDataServer;User ID = myName;" +
          "password=";
     openConnection(connectionString);
}
//-----
public SQLServerDatabase(string dbName, string serverName,
     string userid, string pwd) {
     connectionString = "Persist Security Info = False;" +
          "Initial Catalog =" + dbName + ";" +
          "Data Source =" + serverName + ";" +
          "User ID =" + userid + ";" +
          "password=" + pwd;
     openConnection(connectionString);
     }
}
```

The DBTable Class

The other major class we will need is the DBTable class. It encapsulates opening, loading, and updating a single database table. We will also use this class in this example to add the single values. Then we can derive food and store classes that do this addition for each class.

```
public class DBTable        {
     protected DBase db;
     protected string tableName;
     private bool filled, opened;
     private DataTable dtable;
     private int rowIndex;
     private Hashtable names;
     private string columnName;
     private DataRow row;
     private OleDbConnection conn;
     private int index;
//-----
public DBTable(DBase datab, string tb_Name)                {
     db = datab;
     tableName = tb_Name;
     filled =false;
     opened = false;
     names = new Hashtable();
}
//-----
```

```
public void createTable() {
    try {
            dtable = new DataTable(tableName);
            dtable.Clear();
    }
    catch (Exception e) {
            Console.WriteLine (e.Message );
    }
}
//-----
public bool hasMoreElements() {
    if(opened)
            return (rowIndex < dtable.Rows.Count) ;
    else
            return false;
}
//-----
public int getKey(string nm, string keyname){
    DataRow row;
    int key;
  if(! filled)
            return (int)names[ nm];
  else {
      string query = "select * from " + tableName + " where " +
            columnName + "=\'"+ nm + "\'";
      dtable = db.openQuery(query);
      row = dtable.Rows[0];
      key = Convert.ToInt32 (row[keyname].ToString());
      return key;
  }
}
//-----
public virtual void makeTable(string cName) {
    //shown below
//-----
private void closeConn() {
 if( conn.State == ConnectionState.Open) {
            conn.Close();
 }
}
//-----
private void openConn() {
    if(conn.State == ConnectionState.Closed ) {
            conn.Open();
    }
}
//-----
public void openTable() {
    dtable = db.openTable(tableName);
    rowIndex = 0;
    if(dtable != null)
            opened = true;
}
```

```
//-----
 public void delete() {
      //shown above
 }
}
```

Creating Classes for Each Table

We can derive the Store, Food, and Prices classes from DBTable and reuse much of the code. When we parse the input file, both the Store and Food classes will require that we create a table of unique names: store names in one class and food names in the other.

C# provides a very convenient way to create these classes using the Hashtable. A Hashtable is an unbounded array where each element is identified with a unique key. One way Hashtables are used is to add objects to the table with a short nickname as the key. Then you can fetch the object from the table by using its nickname. The objects need not be unique, but, of course, the keys must be.

The other place Hashtables are convenient is in making a list of unique names. If the names are the keys and some other numbers are the contents, we can add names to the Hashtable and assure ourselves that each will be unique. For them to be unique, the Hashtable must treat attempts to add a duplicate key in a predictable way. For example, the Java Hashtable simply replaces a previous entry having that key with the new one. The C# implementation of the Hashtable, on the other hand, throws an exception when we try to add a nonunique key value.

Now bearing in mind that we want to accumulate the entire list of names before adding them into the database, we can use the following method to add names to a Hashtable and make sure they are unique.

```
public void addTableValue(string nm) {
//accumulates names in hash table
     try {
            names.Add(nm, index++);
     }
     catch (ArgumentException) {}
     //do not allow duplicate names to be added
}
```

Then once we have added all the names, we can add each of them to the database table. Here we use the Enumerator property of the Hashtable to iterate though all the names we have entered in the list.

```
public virtual void makeTable(string cName) {
     columnName = cName;
     //stores current hash table values in data table
```

```
        DataSet dset = new DataSet(tableName);   //create dataset
        dtable = new DataTable(tableName);       //and a datatable
        dset.Tables.Add(dtable);                 //add to collection
        conn = db.getConnection();
        openConn();                                       //open the connection
        OleDbDataAdapter adcmd = new OleDbDataAdapter();
        //open the table
        adcmd.SelectCommand =
              new OleDbCommand("Select * from " + tableName, conn);
        OleDbCommandBuilder olecb = new OleDbCommandBuilder(adcmd);
        adcmd.TableMappings.Add("Table", tableName);
        //load current data into the local table copy
        adcmd.Fill(dset, tableName);
        //get the Enumerator from the Hashtable
        IEnumerator ienum = names.Keys.GetEnumerator();
        //move through the table, adding the names to new rows
        while (ienum.MoveNext()) {
              string name = (string)ienum.Current;
              row = dtable.NewRow();       //get new rows
              row[columnName] = name;
              dtable.Rows.Add(row);        //add into table
        }
         //Now update the database with this table
        try {
              adcmd.Update(dset);
              closeConn();
              filled = true;
        }
        catch (Exception e) {
              Console.WriteLine (e.Message);
        }
}
```

This simplifies our derived Stores table to just the following.

```
public class Stores :DBTable      {
     public Stores(DBase db):base(db, "Stores"){
     }
   //-----
   public void makeTable() {
              base.makeTable ("Storename");
              }
}
```

And it simplifies the Foods table to much the same thing.

```
public class Foods: DBTable       {
     public Foods(DBase db):base(db, "Foods"){
     }
     //-----
     public void makeTable() {
              base.makeTable ("Foodname");
```

```
        }
        //-----
        public string getValue() {
                return base.getValue ("FoodName");
        }
}
```

The getValue method allows us to enumerate the list of names of Stores or Foods, and we can put it in the base DBTable class.

```
public virtual string getValue(string cname) {
 //returns the next name in the table
 //assumes that openTable has already been called
        if (opened) {
                DataRow row = dtable.Rows[rowIndex++];
                return row[cname].ToString().Trim ();
        }
        else
                return "";
}
```

Note that we make this method *virtual* so we can override it where needed.

Building the Price Table

The Price table is a little more complicated because it contains keys from the other two tables. When it is completed, it will look like Table 18-5.

To create it, we have to reread the file, finding the store and food names, looking up their keys, and adding them to the Price table. The DBTable interface doesn't include this final method, but we can add additional specific methods to the Price class that are not part of that interface.

The Prices class stores a series of StoreFoodPrice objects in an ArrayList and then loads them all into the database at once. Note that we have overloaded the classes of DBTable to take arguments for the store and food key values as well as the price.

Each time we add a storekey, foodkey, and price to the internal ArrayList table, we create an instance of the StoreFoodPrice object and store it.

```
public class StoreFoodPrice {
        private int storeKey, foodKey;
        private float foodPrice;
        //-----
        public StoreFoodPrice(int sKey, int fKey, float fPrice) {
                storeKey = sKey;
                foodKey = fKey;
                foodPrice = fPrice;
        }
```

```
//-----
public int getStore() {
      return storeKey;
}
//-----
public int getFood() {
      return foodKey;
}
//-----
public float getPrice() {
      return foodPrice;
}
```
}

Table 18-5   The Price Table in the Grocery Database

Pricekey	Foodkey	StoreKey	Price
1	1	1	0.27
2	2	1	0.36
3	3	1	1.98
4	4	1	2.39
5	5	1	1.98
6	6	1	2.65
7	7	1	2.29
8	1	2	0.29
9	2	2	0.29
10	3	2	2.45
11	4	2	2.99
12	5	2	1.79
13	6	2	3.79
14	7	2	2.19
15	1	3	0.33
16	2	3	0.47
17	3	3	2.29
18	4	3	3.29
19	5	3	1.89
20	6	3	2.99
21	7	3	1.99

Then when we have them all, we create the actual database table.

```
public class Prices : DBTable    {
     private ArrayList priceList;
     public Prices(DBase db) : base(db, "Prices")    {
          priceList = new ArrayList ();
     }
     //-----
     public void makeTable() {
     //stores current array list values in data table
     OleDbConnection adc = new OleDbConnection();

     DataSet dset = new DataSet(tableName);
     DataTable dtable = new DataTable(tableName);

     dset.Tables.Add(dtable);
     adc = db.getConnection();
     if (adc.State == ConnectionState.Closed)
          adc.Open();
     OleDbDataAdapter adcmd = new OleDbDataAdapter();

      //fill in price table
      adcmd.SelectCommand =
          new OleDbCommand("Select * from " + tableName, adc);
      OleDbCommandBuilder custCB = new
          OleDbCommandBuilder(adcmd);
      adcmd.TableMappings.Add("Table", tableName);
      adcmd.Fill(dset, tableName);
      IEnumerator ienum = priceList.GetEnumerator();
      //add new price entries
     while (ienum.MoveNext() ) {
          StoreFoodPrice fprice =
               (StoreFoodPrice)ienum.Current;
          DataRow row = dtable.NewRow();
          row["foodkey"] = fprice.getFood();
          row["storekey"] = fprice.getStore();
          row["price"] = fprice.getPrice();
          dtable.Rows.Add(row);    //add to table
     }
      adcmd.Update(dset);      //send back to database
      adc.Close();
      }
     //-----
     public DataTable getPrices(string food) {
     string query=
          "SELECT Stores.StoreName, " +
          "Foods.Foodname, Prices.Price " +
          "FROM (Prices INNER JOIN Foods ON " +
          "Prices.Foodkey = Foods.Foodkey) " +
          "INNER JOIN Stores ON " +
          "Prices.StoreKey = Stores.StoreKey " +
          "WHERE(((Foods.Foodname) =\'" + food + "\'))" +
          "ORDER BY Prices.Price";
```

```
        return db.openQuery(query);
        }
        //-----
        public void addRow(int storeKey, int foodKey, float price)
                priceList.Add (
                        new StoreFoodPrice (storeKey,
                                foodKey, price));
        }
}
```

Loading the Database Tables

With all these classes derived, we can write a class to load the table from the
data file. It reads the file once and builds the Store and Food database tables.
Then it reads the file again and looks up the store and food keys and adds them
to the array list in the Price class. Finally, it creates the Price table.

```
public class DataLoader    {
        private csFile vfile;
        private Stores store;
        private Foods fods;
        private Prices price;
        private DBase db;
        //-----
        public DataLoader(DBase datab)    {
                db = datab;
                store = new Stores(db);
                fods = new Foods (db);
                price = new Prices(db);
        }
        //-----
        public void load(string dataFile) {
                string sline;
                int storekey, foodkey;
                StringTokenizer tok;
                //delete current table contents
                store.delete();
                fods.delete();
                price.delete();
                //now read in new ones
                vfile = new csFile(dataFile);
                vfile.OpenForRead();
                sline = vfile.readLine();
                while (sline != null){
                        tok = new StringTokenizer(sline, ",");
                        store.addTableValue(tok.nextToken()); //store
                        fods.addTableValue(tok.nextToken());  //food
                        sline = vfile.readLine();
                }
                vfile.close();
```

```
                        //construct store and food tables
                        store.makeTable();
                        fods.makeTable();
                        vfile.OpenForRead();
                        sline = vfile.readLine();
                while (sline != null) {
                        //get the gets and add to storefoodprice objects
                        tok = new StringTokenizer(sline, ",");
                        storekey = store.getKey(tok.nextToken(), "Storekey");
                        foodkey = fods.getKey(tok.nextToken(), "Foodkey");
                        price.addRow(storekey, foodkey,
                                Convert.ToSingle (tok.neXtToken()));
                                sline = vfile.readLine();
                }
                //add all to price table
                price.makeTable();
                vfile.close();
                }
        }
```

The Final Application

The program loads a list of food prices into a list box on startup.

```
private void loadFoodTable() {
        Foods fods =new Foods(db);
        fods.openTable();
        while (fods.hasMoreElements()){
            lsFoods.Items.Add(fods.getValue());
        }
}
```

And it displays the prices of the selected food when you click on it.

```
private void lsFoods_SelectedIndexChanged(object sender,
                System.EventArgs e) {
        string food  = lsFoods.Text;
        DataTable dtable = prc.getPrices(food);

        lsPrices.Items.Clear();
        foreach (DataRow rw in dtable.Rows) {
            lsPrices.Items.Add(rw["StoreName"].ToString().Trim() +
            "\t" + rw["Price"].ToString());
        }
}
```

The final program was shown in Figure 18-1.

What Constitutes the Façade?

The Façade in this case wraps the classes as follows.

- DBase
  Contains OleDbConnection, Database, DataTable, OleDbAdapter, DataSets
- DBTable
  Contains DataSet, DataRow, DataTable, OleDbConnection, OleDbCommandBuilder

You can quickly see the advantage of the Façade approach when dealing with such complicated data objects. This is illustrated in Figure 18-2.

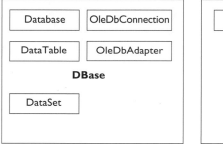 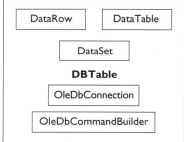

Figure 18-2   Façades wrapping classes make up the DBase and DBTable classes.

Consequences of the Façade

The Façade pattern shields clients from complex subsystem components and provides a simpler programming interface for the general user. However, it does not prevent the advanced user from going to the deeper, more complex classes when necessary.

In addition, the Façade allows you to make changes in the underlying subsystems without requiring changes in the client code and reduces compilation dependencies.

Thought Question

Suppose you had written a program with a File | Open menu, a text field, and some buttons controlling font (bold and italic). Now suppose that you need to have this program run from a line command with arguments. Suggest how to use a Façade pattern.

Program on the CD-ROM

C# Database Façade Classes	\Façade\

CHAPTER 19

The Flyweight Pattern

The Flyweight pattern is used to avoid the overhead of large numbers of very similar classes. There are cases in programming where it seems that you need to generate a very large number of small class instances to represent data. Sometimes you can greatly reduce the number of different classes that you need to instantiate if you can recognize that the instances are fundamentally the same except for a few parameters. If you can move those variables outside the class instance and pass them in as part of a method call, the number of separate instances can be greatly reduced by sharing them.

The Flyweight design pattern provides an approach for handling such classes. It refers to the instance's *intrinsic* data that makes the instance unique and the *extrinsic* data that is passed in as arguments. The Flyweight is appropriate for small, fine-grained classes like individual characters or icons on the screen. For example, you might be drawing a series of icons on the screen in a window, where each represents a person or data file as a folder, as shown in Figure 19-1.

In this case, it does not make sense to have an individual class instance for each folder that remembers the person's name and the icon's screen position. Typically, these icons are one of a few similar images, and the position where they are drawn is calculated dynamically based on the window's size in any case.

In another example in *Design Patterns*, each character in a document is represented as a single instance of a character class, but the positions where the characters are drawn on the screen are kept as external data. In this case there only has to be one instance of each character, rather than one for each appearance of that character.

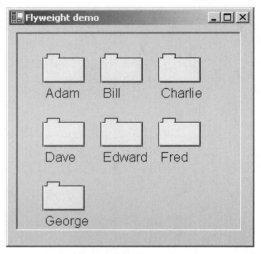

Figure 19-1   A set of folders representing information about various people. Since these are so
similar, they are candidates for the Flyweight pattern.

Discussion

Flyweights are sharable instances of a class. It might at first seem that each class
is a Singleton, but in fact there might be a small number of instances, such as
one for every character or one for every icon type. The number of instances that
are allocated must be decided as the class instances are needed, and this is usually accomplished with a FlyweightFactory class. This Factory class usually *is* a
Singleton, since it needs to keep track of whether a particular instance has been
generated yet. It then either returns a new instance or a reference to one it has
already generated.

To decide if some part of your program is a candidate for using Flyweights,
consider whether it is possible to remove some data from the class and make it
extrinsic. If this makes it possible to greatly reduce the number of different class
instances your program needs to maintain, this might be a case where Flyweights will help.

Example Code

Suppose we want to draw a small folder icon with a name under it for each person in an organization. If this is a large organization, there could be a large
number of such icons, but they are actually all the same graphical image. Even if
we have two icons—one for "is Selected" and one for "not Selected"—the number of different icons is small. In such a system, having an icon object for each

person, with its own coordinates, name, and selected state, is a waste of resources. We show two such icons in Figure 19-2.

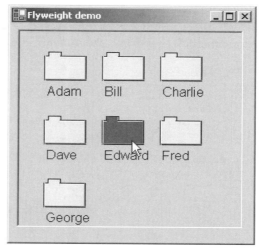

Figure 19-2 The Flyweight display with one folder selected

Instead, we'll create a FolderFactory that returns either the selected or the unselected folder drawing class but does not create additional instances once one of each has been created. Since this is such a simple case, we just create them both at the outset and then return one or the other.

```
public class FolderFactory {
     private Folder selFolder, unselFolder;
     //-----
     public FolderFactory()            {
          //create the two folders
          selFolder = new Folder(Color.Brown);
          unselFolder = new Folder(Color.Bisque);
     }
     //-----
     public Folder getFolder(bool selected) {
          if(selected)
               return selFolder;
          else
               return unselFolder;
     }
}
```

For cases where more instances could exist, the Factory could keep a table of those it had already created and only create new ones if they weren't already in the table.

The unique thing about using Flyweights, however, is that we pass the coordinates and the name to be drawn into the folder when we draw it. These coordinates are the extrinsic data that allow us to share the folder objects and, in this case, create only two instances. The complete folder class shown here simply creates a folder instance with one background color or the other and has a public draw method that draws the folder at the point you specify.

```
public class Folder {
        //Draws a folder at the specified coordinates
        private const int w  = 50;
        private const int h = 30;
        private Pen blackPen, whitePen;
        private Pen grayPen;

        private SolidBrush backBrush, blackBrush;
        private Font fnt;
        //------
        public Folder(Color col)              {
                backBrush = new SolidBrush(col);
                blackBrush = new SolidBrush(Color.Black);
                blackPen = new Pen(Color.Black);
                whitePen = new Pen(Color.White);
                grayPen = new Pen(Color.Gray);
                fnt = new Font("Arial", 12);
        }
        //-----
        public void draw(Graphics g, int x, int y, string title) {
                //color folder
                g.FillRectangle(backBrush, x, y, w, h);
                //outline in black
                g.DrawRectangle(blackPen, x, y, w, h);
                //left 2 sides have white line
                g.DrawLine(whitePen, x + 1, y + 1, x + w - 1, y + 1);
                g.DrawLine(whitePen, x + 1, y, x + 1, y + h);
                //draw tab
                g.DrawRectangle(blackPen, x + 5, y - 5, 15, 5);
                g.FillRectangle(backBrush, x + 6, y - 4, 13, 6);
                //gray line on right and bottom
                g.DrawLine(grayPen, x, y + h - 1, x + w, y + h - 1);
                g.DrawLine(grayPen, x + w - 1, y, x + w - 1,
                 y + h - 1);
                g.DrawString(title, fnt, blackBrush, x, y + h + 5);
        }
}
```

To use a Flyweight class like this, your main program must calculate the position of each folder as part of its paint routine and then pass the coordinates to the folder instance. This is actually rather common, since you need a different layout, depending on the window's dimensions, and you would not want to have to keep telling each instance where its new location is going to be. Instead, we compute it dynamically during the paint routine.

Here we note that we could have generated an ArrayList of folders at the outset and simply scanned through the array to draw each folder. Such an array is not as wasteful as a series of different instances because it is actually an array of references to one of only two folder instances. However, since we want to display one folder as "selected," and we would like to be able to change which folder is selected dynamically, we just use the FolderFactory itself to give us the correct instance each time.

There are two places in our display routine where we need to compute the positions of folders: when we draw them and when we check for a mouse hovering over them. Thus, it is convenient to abstract out the positioning code into a Positioner class.

```
public class Positioner    {
    private const int pLeft = 30;
    private const int pTop  = 30;
    private const int HSpace = 70;
    private const int VSpace = 80;
    private const int rowMax = 2;
    private int x, y, cnt;
    //-----
    public Positioner() {
        reset();
    }
    //-----
    public void reset() {
        x = pLeft;
        y = pTop;
        cnt = 0;
    }
    //-----
    public int nextX() {
        return x;
    }
    //-----
    public void incr() {
        cnt++;
        if (cnt > rowMax) { //reset to start new row
            cnt = 0;
            x = pLeft;
            y += VSpace;
        }
        else {
            x += HSpace;
        }
    }
    //-----
```

```
public int nextY() {
        return y;
}
}
```

Then we can write a much simpler paint routine.

```
private void picPaint(object sender,  PaintEventArgs e ) {
    Graphics g = e.Graphics;
    posn.reset ();
    for(int i = 0; i < names.Count; i++) {
            fol = folFact.getFolder(selectedName.Equals(
                    (string)names[i]));
            fol.draw(g, posn.nextX() , posn.nextY (),
                    (string)names[i]);
            posn.incr();
    }
}
```

The Class Diagram

The diagram in Figure 19-3 shows how these classes interact.

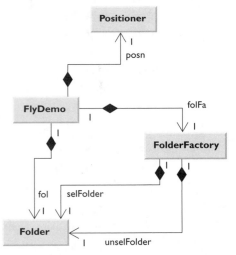

Figure 19-3   How Flyweights are generated

The FlyCanvas class is the main UI class, where the folders are arranged and drawn. It contains one instance of the FolderFactory and one instance of the Folder class. The FolderFactory class contains two instances of Folder: *selected* and *unselected*. One or the other of these is returned to the FlyCanvas by the FolderFactory.

Selecting a Folder

Since we have two folder instances, selected and unselected, we'd like to be able to select folders by moving the mouse over them. In the previous paint routine, we simply remember the name of the folder that was selected and ask the factory to return a "selected" folder for it. Since the folders are not individual instances, we can't listen for mouse motion within each folder instance. In fact, even if we did listen within a folder, we'd need a way to tell the other instances to deselect themselves.

Instead, we check for mouse motion at the Picturebox level, and if the mouse is found to be within a Rectangle, we make that corresponding name the selected name. We create a single instance of a Rectangle class where the testing can be done as to whether a folder contains the mouse at that instant. Note that we make this class part of the csPatterns namespace to make sure it does not collide with the Rectangle class in the System.Drawing namespace.

```
namespace csPatterns {
    public class Rectangle     {
    private int x1, x2, y1, y2;
    private int w, h;
    public Rectangle()           {                     }
    //-----
    public void init(int x, int y) {
        x1 = x;
        y1 = y;
        x2 = x1 + w;
        y2 = y1 + h;
    }
    //-----
    public void setSize(int w_, int h_) {
        w = w_;
        h = h_;
    }
    //-----
    public bool contains(int xp, int yp) {
        return (x1 <= xp) && (xp <= x2) &&
               (y1 <= yp) && (yp <= y2);
    }
  }
}
```

This allows us to just check each name when we redraw and create a selected folder instance where it is needed.

```
private void Pic_MouseMove(object sender, MouseEventArgs e) {
    string oldname = selectedName;  //save old name
    bool found = false;
    posn.reset ();
    int i = 0;
```

```
      selectedName = "";
      while (i < names.Count && ! found) {
            rect.init (posn.nextX() , posn.nextY ());
            //see if a rectangle contains the mouse
            if (rect.contains(e.X, e.Y) ){
                  selectedName = (string)names[i];
                  found = true;
            }
            posn.incr ();
            i++;
      }
      //only refresh if mouse in new rectangle
      if(  !oldname.Equals ( selectedName)) {
            Pic.Refresh();
      }
}
```

Handling the Mouse and Paint Events

In C# we intercept the paint and mouse events by adding event handlers. To do the painting of the folders, we add a paint event handler to the picture box.

```
Pic.Paint += new PaintEventHandler (picPaint);
```

The picPaint handler we add draws the folders, as we showed above. We added this code manually because we knew the signature of a paint routine.

```
private void picPaint(object sender,  PaintEventArgs e ) {
```

While the mouse move event handler is very much analogous, we might not remember its exact form. So, we use the Visual Studio IDE to generate it for us. While displaying the form in design mode, we click on the PictureBox and in the Properties window we click on the lightning bolt to display the possible events for the PictureBox, as shown in Figure 19-4.

Then we double-click on MouseMove, and it generates the correct code for the mouse move event and adds the event handler automatically. The generated empty method is as follows.

```
private void Pic_MouseMove(object sender, MouseEventArgs e) {
}
```

The code generated to add the event handler is inside the Windows Form Designer generated section. It amounts to this.

```
Pic.MouseMove += new MouseEventHandler(Pic_MouseMove);
```

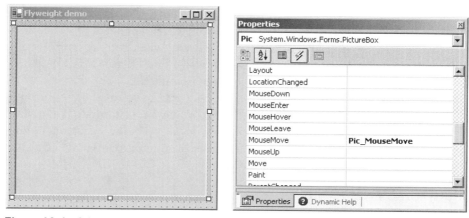

Figure 19-4   Selecting the MouseMove event from the Properties window

Flyweight Uses in C#

Flyweights are not frequently used at the application level in C#. They are more of a system resource management technique used at a lower level than C#. However, there are a number of stateless objects that get created in Internet programming that are somewhat analogous to Flyweights. It is generally useful to recognize that this technique exists so you can use it if you need it.

Some objects within the C# language could be implemented under the covers as Flyweights. For example, if there are two instances of a String constant with identical characters, they could refer to the same storage location. Similarly, it might be that two integer or float constants that contain the same value could be implemented as Flyweights, although they probably are not.

Sharable Objects

The *Smalltalk Companion* points out that sharable objects are much like Flyweights, although the purpose is somewhat different. When you have a very large object containing a lot of complex data, such as tables or bitmaps, you would want to minimize the number of instances of that object. Instead, in such cases, you'd return one instance to every part of the program that asked for it and avoid creating other instances.

A problem with such sharable objects occurs when one part of a program wants to change some data in a shared object. You then must decide whether to change the object for all users, prevent any change, or create a new instance with the changed data. If you change the object for every instance, you may have to notify them that the object has changed.

Sharable objects are also useful when you are referring to large data systems outside of C#, such as databases. The DBase class we developed previously in the Façade pattern could be a candidate for a sharable object. We might not want a number of separate connections to the database from different program modules, preferring that only one be instantiated. However, should several modules in different threads decide to make queries simultaneously, the Database class might have to queue the queries or spawn extra connections.

Copy-on-Write Objects

The Flyweight pattern uses just a few object instances to represent many different objects in a program. All of them normally have the same base properties as intrinsic data and a few properties that represent extrinsic data that vary with each manifestation of the class instance. However, it could occur that some of these instances eventually take on new intrinsic properties (such as shape or folder tab position) and require a new specific instance of the class to represent them. Rather than creating these in advance as special subclasses, it is possible to copy the class instance and change its intrinsic properties when the program flow indicates that a new separate instance is required. The class copies this itself when the change becomes inevitable, changing those intrinsic properties in the new class. We call this process "copy-on-write" and can build this into Flyweights as well as a number of other classes, such as the Proxy, which we discuss next.

Thought Question

If buttons can appear on several different tabs of a TabDialog, but each of them controls the same one or two tasks, is this an appropriate use for a Flyweight?

Program on the CD-ROM

C# Folders	\Flyweight

CHAPTER 20

The Proxy Pattern

The Proxy pattern is used when you need to represent an object that is complex or time consuming to create with a simpler one. If creating an object is expensive in time or computer resources, Proxy allows you to postpone this creation until you need the actual object. A Proxy usually has the same methods as the object it represents, and once the object is loaded, it passes on the method calls from the Proxy to the actual object.

There are several cases where a Proxy can be useful.

1. An object, such as a large image, takes a long time to load.

2. The results of a computation take a long time to complete, and you need to display intermediate results while the computation continues.

3. The object is on a remote machine, and loading it over the network may be slow, especially during peak network load periods.

4. The object has limited access rights, and the proxy can validate the access permissions for that user.

Proxies can also be used to distinguish between requesting an instance of an object and the actual need to access it. For example, program initialization may set up a number of objects that may not all be used right away. In that case, the proxy can load the real object only when it is needed.

Let's consider the case of a large image that a program must load and display. When the program starts, there must be some indication that an image is to be displayed so that the screen lays out correctly, but the actual image display can be postponed until the image is completely loaded. This is particularly important in programs such as word processors and Web browsers that lay out text around the images even before the images are available.

An image proxy can note the image and begin loading it in the background while drawing a simple rectangle or other symbol to represent the image's extent on the screen before it appears. The proxy can even delay loading the image at all until it receives a paint request and only then begin the process.

Sample Code

In this example, we create a simple program to display an image on an Image control when it is loaded. Rather than loading the image directly, we use a class we call ImageProxy to defer loading and draw a rectangle until loading is completed.

```
private void init() {
        imgProxy = new ImageProxy ();
}
//-----
public Form1() {
        InitializeComponent();
        init();
}
//-----
private void button1_Click(object sender, EventArgs e) {
        Pic.Image = imgProxy.getImage ();
}
```

Note that we create the instance of the ImageProxy just as we would have for an Image. The ImageProxy class sets up the image loading and creates an Imager object to follow the loading process. It returns a class that implements the Imager interface.

```
public interface Imager   {
    Image getImage() ;
}
```

In this simple case, the ImageProxy class just delays five seconds and then switches from the preliminary image to the final image. It does this using an instance of the Timer class. Timers are handled using a TimerCallback class that defines the method to be called when the timer ticks. This is very similar to the way we add other event handlers. And this callback method, *timerCall,* sets the done flag and turns off the timer.

```
public class ImageProxy   {
    private bool done;
    private Timer timer;
    //-----
    public ImageProxy()                    {
    //create a timer thread and start it
        timer = new Timer (
```

```
                     new TimerCallback (timerCall), this, 5000, 0);
        }
        //-----
        //called when timer completes
        private void timerCall(object obj) {
                done = true;
                timer.Dispose ();
        }
        //-----
        public Image getImage() {
                Imager img;
                if (done)
                        img = new FinalImage ();
                else
                        img = new QuickImage ();
                return img.getImage ();
        }
}
```

We implement the Imager interface in two tiny classes we called QuickImage and FinalImage. One gets a small gif image and the other a larger (and presumably slower) jpeg image. In C#, Image is an abstract class, and the Bitmap, Cursor, Icon, and Metafile classes are derived from it. So the actual class we will return is derived from Image. The QuickImage class returns a Bitmap from a gif file, and the final image a jpeg file.

```
public class QuickImage : Imager {
      public QuickImage() {}
      public Image getImage() {
              return new Bitmap ("Box.gif");
      }
}
//------------
public class FinalImage :Imager {
      public FinalImage() {}
      public Image getImage() {
              return new Bitmap("flowrtree.jpg");
      }
}
```

When you go to fetch an image, you initially get the quick image, and after five seconds, if you call the method again, you get the final image. The program's two states are illustrated in Figure 20-1.

Figure 20-1   The proxy image display on the top is shown until the image loads as shown on the bottom.

Proxies in C#

You see more proxylike behavior in C# than in other languages because it is crafted for network and Internet use. For example, the ADO.NET database connection classes are all effectively proxies.

Copy-on-Write

You can also use proxies to keep copies of large objects that may or may not change. If you create a second instance of an expensive object, a Proxy can decide there is no reason to make a copy yet. It simply uses the original object. Then if the program makes a change in the new copy, the Proxy can copy the original object and make the change in the new instance. This can be a great time and space saver when objects do not always change after they are instantiated.

Comparison with Related Patterns

Both the Adapter and the Proxy constitute a thin layer around an object. However, the Adapter provides a different interface for an object, whereas the Proxy provides the same interface for the object but interposes itself where it can postpone processing or data transmission effort.

A Decorator also has the same interface as the object it surrounds, but its purpose is to add additional (sometimes visual) function to the original object. A Proxy, by contrast, controls access to the contained class.

Thought Question

You have designed a server that connects to a database. If several clients connect to your server at once, how might Proxies be of help?

Program on the CD-ROM

Image Proxy	\Proxy

Summary of Structural Patterns

Part 3 covered the following structural patterns.

The **Adapter pattern** is used to change the interface of one class to that of another one.

The **Bridge pattern** is designed to separate a class's interface from its implementation so you can vary or replace the implementation without changing the client code.

The **Composite pattern** is a collection of objects, any one of which may be either itself a Composite or just a leaf object.

The **Decorator pattern,** a class that surrounds a given class, adds new capabilities to it, and passes all the unchanged methods to the underlying class.

The **Façade pattern** groups a complex set of objects and provides a new, simpler interface to access those data.

The **Flyweight pattern** provides a way to limit the proliferation of small, similar instances by moving some of the class data outside the class and passing it in during various execution methods.

The **Proxy pattern** provides a simple placeholder object for a more complex object that is in some way time consuming or expensive to instantiate.

PART 4

Behavioral Patterns

Behavioral patterns are mostly concerned with communication between objects. In Part 4, we examine the following.

The **Chain of Responsibility** allows a decoupling between objects by passing a request from one object to the next in a chain until the request is recognized.

The **Command pattern** utilizes simple objects to represent execution of software commands and allows you to support logging and undo operations.

The **Interpreter pattern** provides a definition of how to include language elements in a program.

The **Iterator pattern** formalizes the way we move through a list of data within a class.

The **Mediator pattern** defines how communication between objects can be simplified by using a separate object to keep all objects from having to know about each other.

The **Memento pattern** defines how you might save the contents of an instance of a class and restore it later.

The **Observer pattern** defines the way a number of objects can be notified of a change.

The **State pattern** allows an object to modify its behavior when its internal state changes.

The **Strategy pattern** encapsulates an algorithm inside a class.

The **Template Method pattern** provides an abstract definition of an algorithm.

The **Visitor pattern** adds polymorphic functions to a class noninvasively.

CHAPTER 21

Chain of Responsibility

The Chain of Responsibility pattern allows a number of classes to attempt to handle a request without any of them knowing about the capabilities of the other classes. It provides a loose coupling between these classes; the only common link is the request that is passed between them. The request is passed along until one of the classes can handle it.

One example of such a chain pattern is a help system like the one shown in Figure 21-1. This is a simple application where different kinds of help could be useful, where every screen region of an application invites you to seek help but in which there are window background areas where more generic help is the only suitable result.

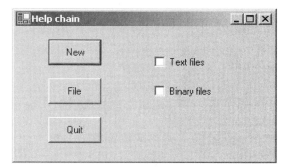

Figure 21-1   A simple application where different kinds of help could be useful

When you select an area for help, that visual control forwards its ID or name to the chain. Suppose you selected the New button. If the first module can handle the New button, it displays the help message. If not, it forwards the request to the next module. Eventually, the message is forwarded to an All buttons class that can display a general message about how buttons work. If there is no general button help, the message is forwarded to the general help module that tells you how the system works in general. If that doesn't exist, the message is lost, and no information is displayed. This is illustrated in Figure 21-2.

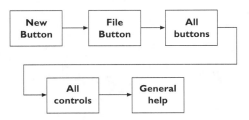

Figure 21-2   A simple Chain of Responsibility

There are two significant points we can observe from this example: First, the chain is organized from most specific to most general, and second, there is no guarantee that the request will produce a response in all cases. We will see shortly that you can use the Observer pattern to provide a way for a number of classes to be notified of a change.

Applicability

The Chain of Responsibility is a good example of a pattern that helps keep knowledge separate of what each object in a program can do. In other words, it reduces the coupling between objects so that they can act independently. This also applies to the object that constitutes the main program and contains instances of the other objects. You will find this pattern helpful in the following situations.

- Several objects with similar methods are appropriate for the action the program is requesting. However, it is more appropriate for the objects to decide which one is to carry out the action than it is for you to build this decision into the calling code.
- One of the objects may be most suitable, but you don't want to build in a series of if-else or switch statements to select a particular object.
- There might be new objects that you want to add to the possible list of processing options while the program is executing.
- There might be cases when more than one object will have to act on a request, and you don't want to build knowledge of these interactions into the calling program.

Sample Code

The help system we just described is a little involved for a first example. Instead, let's start with a simple visual command-interpreter program (Figure 21-3) that illustrates how the chain works. This program displays the results of typed-in commands. While this first case is constrained to keep the example code tractable, we'll see that this Chain of Responsibility pattern is commonly used for parsers and even compilers.

In this example, the commands can be any of the following.

- Image filenames
- General filenames
- Color names
- All other commands

In the first three cases, we can display a concrete result of the request, and in the fourth case, we can only display the request text itself.

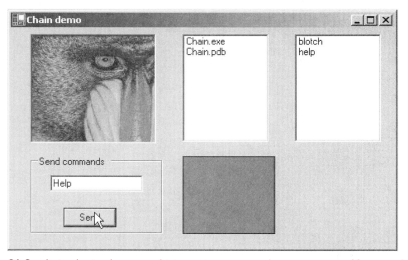

Figure 21-3 A simple visual command-interpreter program that acts on one of four panels, depending on the command typed in

In the preceding example system, we do the following.

1. We type in "Mandrill" and see a display of the image Mandrill.jpg.

2. Then we type in "File," and that filename is displayed in the center list box.

3. Next, we type in "blue," and that color is displayed in the lower center panel.

Finally, if we type in anything that is neither a filename nor a color, that text is displayed in the final, right-hand list box. This is shown in Figure 21-4.

Figure 21-4   How the command chain works for the program in Figure 21-3

To write this simple Chain of Responsibility program, we start with an abstract Chain class.

```
public abstract class Chain        {
     //describes how all chains work
     private bool hasLink;
     protected Chain chn;
     public Chain()        {
           hasLink = false;
     }
     //you must implement this in derived classes
     public abstract void sendToChain(string mesg);
     //-----
     public void addToChain(Chain c) {
     //add new element to chain
           chn = c;
           hasLink = true;        //flag existence
     }
     //-----
     public Chain getChain() {
           return chn;            //get the chain link
     }
     //-----
     public bool hasChain() {
           return hasLink;        //true if linked to another
     }
     //-----
     protected void sendChain(string mesg) {
     //send message on down the chain
           if(chn != null)
                 chn.sendToChain (mesg);
     }
}
```

The *addToChain* method adds another class to the chain of classes. The *getChain* method returns the current class to which messages are being forwarded. These two methods allow us to modify the chain dynamically and add additional classes in the middle of an existing chain. The *sendToChain* method forwards a message to the next object in the chain. And the protected sendChain method only sends the message down the chain if the next link is not null.

Our main program assembles the Chain classes and sets a reference to a control into each of them. We start with the ImageChain class, which takes the message string and looks for a .jpg file of that name. If it finds one, it displays it in the Image control, and if not, it sends the command on to the next element in the chain.

```
public class ImageChain :Chain   {
    PictureBox picBox;           //image goes here
    //-----
    public ImageChain(PictureBox pc)          {
        picBox = pc;          //save reference
    }
    //-----
    public override void sendToChain(string mesg) {
        //put image in picture box
        string fname = mesg + ".jpg";
        //assume jpg filename
        csFile fl = new csFile(fname);
        if(fl.exists())
                picBox.Image = new Bitmap(fname);
        else{
            if (hasChain()){    //send off down chain
                chn.sendToChain(mesg);
            }
        }

    }
}
```

In a similar fashion, the ColorChain class simply interprets the message as a color name and displays it if it can. This example only interprets three colors, but you could implement any number. Note how we interpret the color names by using them as keys to a Hashtable of color objects where the string names are the keys.

```
public class ColorChain : Chain {
    private Hashtable colHash; //color list kept here
    private Panel panel;                //color goes here
    //-----
    public ColorChain(Panel pnl)                {
        panel = pnl;                //save reference
        //create Hash table to correlate color names
        //with actual Color objects
        colHash = new Hashtable ();
        colHash.Add ("red", Color.Red);
        colHash.Add ("green", Color.Green);
        colHash.Add ("blue", Color.Blue);
    }
    //-----
    public override void sendToChain(string mesg) {
        mesg = mesg.ToLower ();
```

```
        try {
                Color c = (Color)colHash[mesg];
                //if this is a color, put it in the panel
                panel.BackColor =c;
        }
        catch (NullReferenceException e) {
                //send on if this doesn't work
                sendChain(mesg);
        }

    }
}
```

ListBoxes

Both the file list and the list of unrecognized commands are ListBoxes. If the message matches part of a filename, the filename is displayed in the fileList box, and if not, the message is sent on to the NoCmd Chain element.

```
public override void sendToChain( string mesg) {
    //if the string matches any part of a filename
    //put those filenames in the file list box
    string[] files;
    string fname = mesg + "*.*";
    files = Directory.GetFiles(
            Directory.GetCurrentDirectory(), fname);
    //add them all to the listbox
    if (files.Length > 0){
            for (int i = 0; i< files.Length; i++) {
                    csFile vbf = new csFile(files[i]);
                    flist.Items.Add(vbf.getRootName());
            }
    }
    else {
            if ( hasChain()) {
                    chn.sendToChain(mesg);
            }
    }
}
```

The NoCmd Chain class is very similar. It, however, has no class to which to send data.

```
public class NoCmd :Chain   {
    private ListBox lsNocmd;  //commands go here
    //-----
    public NoCmd(ListBox lb)            {
            lsNocmd = lb;                  //copy reference
    }
    //-----
    public override void sendToChain(string mesg) {
            //adds unknown commands to list box
```

```
        lsNocmd.Items.Add (mesg);
    }
}
```

Finally, we link these classes together in the Form_Load routine to create the Chain.

```
private void init() {
    //set up chains
    ColorChain clrChain = new ColorChain(pnlColor);
    FileChain flChain = new FileChain(lsFiles);
    NoCmd noChain = new NoCmd(lsNocmd);
    //create chain links
    chn = new ImageChain(picImage);
    chn.addToChain(clrChain);
    clrChain.addToChain(flChain);
    flChain.addToChain(noChain);
}
```

Finally, we kick off the Chain by clicking on the Send button, which takes the current message in the text box and sends it along the chain.

```
private void btSend_Click(object sender, EventArgs e) {
            chn.sendToChain (txCommand.Text );
}
```

You can see the relationship between these classes in the UML diagram in Figure 21-5.

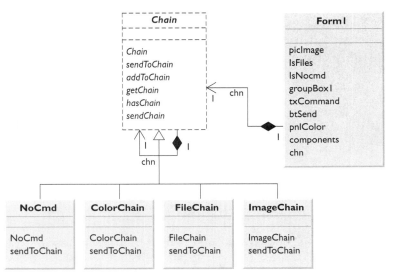

Figure 21-5   The class structure of the Chain of Responsibility program

The Sender class is the initial class that implements the Chain interface. It receives the button clicks and obtains the text from the text field. It passes the command on to the Imager class, the FileList class, the ColorImage class, and finally to the NoCmd class.

Programming a Help System

As we noted at the beginning of this discussion, help systems provide good examples of how the Chain of Responsibility pattern can be used. Now that we've outlined a way to write such chains, we'll consider a help system for a window with several controls. The program (Figure 21-6) pops up a help dialog message when the user presses the F1 (help) key. The message depends on which control is selected when the F1 key is pressed.

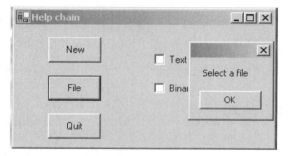

Figure 21-6   A simple help demonstration

In the preceding example, the user has selected the Quit key, which does not have a specific help message associated with it. Instead, the chain forwards the help request to a general button help object that displays the message shown on the right.

To write this help chain system, we begin with an abstract Chain class that has handled Controls instead of messages. Note that no message is passed into the sendToChain method and that the current control is stored in the class.

```
public abstract class Chain        {
      //describes how all chains work
      private bool hasLink;
      protected Control control;
      protected Chain chn;
      protected string message;

      public Chain(Control c, string mesg)    {
            hasLink = false;
            control = c;            //save the control
```

```
                message = mesg;
        }

        public abstract void sendToChain();
        //-----
        public void addToChain(Chain c) {
                //add new element to chain
                chn = c;
                hasLink = true;            //flag existence
        }
        //-----
        public Chain getChain() {
                return chn;  //get the chain link
        }
        //-----
        public bool hasChain() {
                return hasLink;            //true if linked to nother
                }
        //-----
        protected void sendChain() {
        //send message on down the chain
                if(chn != null)
                        chn.sendToChain ();
        }
}
```

Then you might create specific classes for each of the help message categories you want to produce. As we illustrated earlier, we want help messages for the following.

- The New button
- The File button
- A general button
- A general visual control (covering the check boxes)

In C#, one control will always have the focus, and thus we don't really need a case for the Window itself. However, we'll include one for completeness. However, there is little to be gained by creating separate classes for each message and assigning different controls to them. Instead, we'll create a general ControlChain class and pass in the control and the message. Then within the class it checks to see if that control has the focus, and if it does, it issues the associated help message.

```
public class ControlChain:Chain  {
        public ControlChain(Control c, string mesg):base(c, mesg){}
        public override void sendToChain() {
                //if it has the focus display the message
                if (control.Focused ) {
                        MessageBox.Show (message);
```

```
        }
        else
                //otherwise pass on down the chain
                sendChain();
    }
}
```

Finally, we need one special case: the end of Chain that will display a message regardless of whether the control has the focus. This is the EndChain class, and it is for completeness. Since one of the controls will presumably always have the focus, it is unlikely that it will ever be called.

```
public class EndChain:Chain       {
    public EndChain(Control c, string mesg):base(c, mesg){}
    //default message display class
    public override void sendToChain() {
        MessageBox.Show (message);
    }
}
```

We construct the Chain in the form initializer as follows.

```
chn = new ControlChain(btNew, "Create new files");
Chain fl =new ControlChain (btFile, "Select a file");
chn.addToChain (fl);
Chain bq = new ControlChain (btQuit, "Exit from program");
fl.addToChain (bq);
Chain cb =new ControlChain (ckBinary, "Use binary files");
bq.addToChain (cb);
Chain ct =  new ControlChain (ckText, "Use text files");
cb.addToChain (ct);
Chain ce = new EndChain (this, "General message");
ct.addToChain (ce);
```

Receiving the Help Command

Now we need to assign keyboard listeners to look for the F1 keypress. At first, you might think we need five such listeners—for the three buttons and the two check boxes. However, we can simply make a single KeyDown event listener and assign it to each of the controls.

```
KeyEventHandler keyev =  new KeyEventHandler(Form1_KeyDown);
    btNew.KeyDown += keyev;
    btFile.KeyDown += keyev;
    btQuit.KeyDown += keyev;
    ckBinary.KeyDown += keyev;
    ckText.KeyDown += keyev;
```

Then, of course, the KeyDown event launches the Chain if the F1 key is pressed.

```
private void Form1_KeyDown(object sender, KeyEventArgs e) {
    if(e.KeyCode  == Keys.F1 )
        chn.sendToChain ();
}
```

We show the complete class diagram for this help system in Figure 21-7.

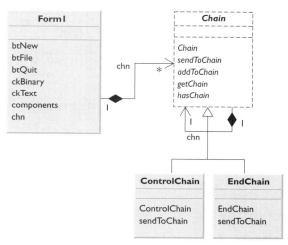

Figure 21-7   The class diagram for the help system

A Chain or a Tree?

Of course, a Chain of Responsibility does not have to be linear. The *Smalltalk Companion* suggests that it is more generally a tree structure with a number of specific entry points all pointing upward to the most general node, as shown in Figure 21-8.

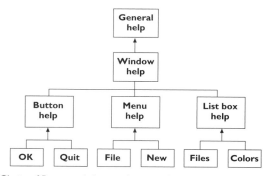

Figure 21-8   The Chain of Responsibility implemented as a tree structure

However, this sort of structure seems to imply that each button, or its handler, knows where to enter the Chain. This can complicate the design in some cases and may preclude the need for the Chain at all.

Another way of handling a treelike structure is to have a single entry point that branches to the specific button, menu, or other widget types and then "unbranches," as previously, to more general help cases. There is little reason for this complexity—you could align the classes into a single Chain, starting at the bottom, and going left to right and up a row at a time until the entire system had been traversed, as shown in Figure 21-9.

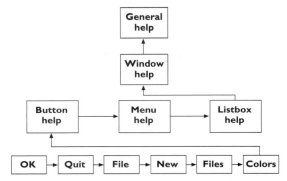

Figure 21-9   The same Chain of Responsibility implemented as a linear Chain

Kinds of Requests

The request or message passed along the Chain of Responsibility may well be a great deal more complicated than just the string or Control that we conveniently used on these examples. The information could include various data types or a complete object with a number of methods. Since various classes along the Chain may use different properties of such a request object, you might end up designing an abstract Request type and any number of derived classes with additional methods.

Examples in C#

Under the covers, C# form windows receive various events, such as Mouse-Move, and then forward them to the controls the form contains. However, only the final control ever receives the message in C#, whereas in some other languages, each containing control does as well. This is a clear implementation of the Chain of Responsibility pattern. We could also argue that, in general, the C# class inheritance structure itself exemplifies this pattern. If you call for a method to be executed in a deeply derived class, that method is passed up the inheritance Chain until the first parent class containing that method is found. The fact that further parents contain other implementations of that method does not come into play.

We will also see that the Chain of Responsibility is ideal for implementing Interpreters, and we use one in the Interpreter pattern we discuss later.

The Chain of Responsibility

The main purpose for this pattern, like many others, is to reduce coupling between objects. An object only needs to know how to forward the request to other objects.

Each C# object in the chain is self-contained. It knows nothing of the others and only need decide whether it can satisfy the request. This makes both writing each one and constructing the chain very easy.

You can decide whether the final object in the chain handles all requests it receives in some default fashion or just discards them. However, you do have to know which object will be last in the chain for this to be effective.

Finally, since C# cannot provide multiple inheritance, the basic Chain class sometimes needs to be an interface rather than an abstract class so the individual objects can inherit from another useful hierarchy, as we did here by deriving them all from Control. The disadvantage of this approach is that you often have to implement the linking, sending, and forwarding code in each module separately or, as we did here, by subclassing a concrete class that implements the Chain interface.

Thought Question

Suggest how you might use a Chain of Responsibility to implement an e-mail filter.

Programs on the CD-ROM

Program showing how a help system can be implemented	\Chain\HelpChain
Chain of file and image displays	\Chain\Chain

CHAPTER 22

The Command Pattern

The Chain of Responsibility forwards requests along a chain of classes, but the Command pattern forwards a request only to a specific object. It encloses a request for a specific action inside an object and gives it a known public interface. It lets you give the client the ability to make requests without knowing anything about the actual action that will be performed and allows you to change that action without affecting the client program in any way.

Motivation

When you build a C# user interface, you provide menu items, buttons, check boxes, and so forth to allow the user to tell the program what to do. When a user selects one of these controls, the program receives a clicked event, which it receives into a special routine in the user interface. Let's suppose we build a very simple program that allows you to select the menu items File | Open, and File | Exit, and click on a button marked Red that turns the background of the window red. This program is shown in Figure 22-1.

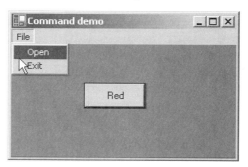

Figure 22-1   A simple program that receives events from the button and menu items

The program consists of the File Menu object with the mnuOpen, and mnuExit MenuItems added to it. It also contains one button called btnRed. During the design phase, clicking on any of these items creates a little method in the Form class that gets called when the control is clicked.

As long as there are only a few menu items and buttons, this approach works fine, but when you have dozens of menu items and several buttons, the Form module code can get pretty unwieldy. In addition, we might eventually like the red command to be carried out both from the button and a menu item.

Command Objects

One way to ensure that every object receives its own commands directly is to use the Command pattern and create individual Command objects. A Command object always has an Execute() method that is called when an action occurs on that object. Most simply, a Command object implements at least the following interface.

```
public interface Command          {
      void Execute();
}
```

One objective of using this interface is to separate the user interface code from the actions the program must carry out, as shown here.

```
private void commandClick(object sender, EventArgs e) {
     Command comd = (Command)sender;
     comd.Execute ();
}
```

This event can be connected to every single user interface element that can be clicked, and each will contain its own implementation of the Execute method by simply deriving a new class from Button and MenuItem that supports this Command interface.

Then we can provide an Execute method for each object that carries out the desired action, thus keeping the knowledge of what to do inside the object where it belongs, instead of having another part of the program make these decisions.

One important purpose of the Command pattern is to keep the program and user interface objects completely separate from the actions that they initiate. In other words, these program objects should be completely separate from each other and should not have to know how other objects work. The user interface receives a command and tells a Command object to carry out whatever duties it has been instructed to do. The UI does not and should not need to know what tasks will be executed. This decouples the UI class from the execution of specific commands, making it possible to modify or completely change the action code without changing the classes containing the user interface.

The Command object can also be used when you need to tell the program to execute the command when the resources are available rather than immediately. In such cases, you are *queuing* commands to be executed later. Finally, you can use Command objects to remember operations so you can support Undo requests.

Building Command Objects

There are several ways to go about building Command objects for a program like this, and each has some advantages. We'll start with the simplest one: creating new classes and implementing the Command interface in each. In the case of the button that turns the background red, we derive a RedButton class from Button and include an Execute method, satisfying the Command interface.

```
public class RedButton : System.Windows.Forms.Button, Command {
    //A Command button that turns the background red
    private System.ComponentModel.Container components = null;
    //-----
    public  void Execute() {
        Control c = this.Parent;
        c.BackColor =Color.Red ;
        this.BackColor =Color.LightGray  ;
    }
    public RedButton()           {
        InitializeComponent();
    }
}
```

In this implementation, we can deduce the background window by asking the button for its parent and setting that background to red. We could just as easily have passed the Form in as an argument to the constructor.

Remember, to create a class derived from Button that you can use in the IDE environment, you create a user control and change its inheritance from User-Control to Button and compile it. This adds an icon to the toolbox that you can drag onto the Form1 window.

To create a MenuItem that also implements the Command interface, you could use the MainMenu control on the toolbar and name it MenuBar. The designer is shown in Figure 22-2.

It is just as easy, however, to create the MainMenu in code as we see following. We derive the OpenMenu and ExitMenu classes from the MenuItem class.

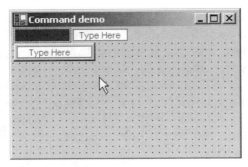

Figure 22-2   The menu designer interface

However, we have to add these in the program code, since there is no way to add them in the Form Designer.

```
private void init() {
      //create a main menu and install it
      MainMenu main = new MainMenu();
      this.Menu =main;

      //create a click-event handler
      EventHandler evh = new EventHandler (commandClick);
      btRed.Click += evh;          //add to existing red button

      //create a "File" top level entry
      MenuItem file = new MenuItem("File");

      //create File Open command
      FileOpen mnflo = new FileOpen ();
      mnflo.Click += evh;          //add same handler
      main.MenuItems.Add ( file );

      //create a File-Exit command
      FileExit fex = new FileExit(this);
      file.MenuItems.AddRange( new MenuItem[]{ mnflo, fex} );
      fex.Click += evh;            //add same handler
}
```

Here is an example of the FileExit class.

```
public class FileExit :MenuItem, Command        {
      private Form form;
      //----------
      public FileExit(Form frm) :base ("Exit") {
            form = frm;
      }
      //----------
      public void Execute() {
            form.Close ();
      }
}
```

Then the File | Exit command will call it when you call that item's Execute method. This certainly lets us simplify the user interface code, but it does require that we create and instantiate a new class for each action we want to execute.

Classes that require specific parameters to work need to have those parameters passed in the constructor or in a set method. For example, the File | Exit command requires that you pass it an instance of the Form object so the command can close it.

```
//create a File-Exit command
 FileExit fex = new FileExit(this);
```

Consequences of the Command Pattern

The main disadvantage of the Command pattern seems to be a proliferation of little classes that clutter up the program. However, even in the case where we have separate click events, we usually call little private methods to carry out the actual function. It turns out that these private methods are just about as long as our little classes, so there is frequently little difference in complexity between building the Command classes and just writing more methods. The main difference is that the Command pattern produces little classes that are much more readable.

The CommandHolder Interface

While it is advantageous to encapsulate the action in a Command object, binding that object into the element that causes the action (such as the menu item or button) is not exactly what the Command pattern is about. Instead, the Command object really ought to be separate from the invoking client so you can vary the invoking program and the details of the command action separately. Rather than having the command be part of the menu or button, we can make the menu and button classes *containers* for a Command object that exists separately. We thus make these UI elements implement a CommandHolder interface.

```
public interface CommandHolder   {
     Command getCommand();
     void setCommand(Command cmd);
}
```

This simple interface says that there is a way to put a command object into a class and a way to retrieve it to execute it. This is particularly important where we have several ways of calling the same action, such as when we have both a

Red button and a Red menu item. In such a case, you would certainly not want the same code to be executed inside both the MenuItem and the Button classes. Instead, you should fetch references to the same command object from both classes and execute that command.

Then we create CommandMenu class, which implements this interface.

```
public class CommandMenu : MenuItem, CommandHolder    {
     private Command command;
     public CommandMenu(string name):base(name)         {}
     //-----
     public void setCommand (Command comd) {
          command = comd;
     }
     //-----
     public Command getCommand () {
          return command;
     }
}
```

This actually simplifies our program. We don't have to create a separate menu class for each action we want to carry out. We just create instances of the menu and pass them different labels and Command objects.

For example, our RedCommand object takes a Form in the constructor and sets its background to red in the Execute method.

```
public class RedCommand : Command          {
     private Control window;
     //-----
     public RedCommand(Control win)               {
          window = win;
     }
     //-----
     void Command.Execute () {
          window.BackColor =Color.Red ;
     }
}
```

We can set an instance of this command into both the RedButton and the red menu item objects, as we show below.

```
private void init() {
     //create a main menu and install it
     MainMenu main = new MainMenu();
     this.Menu =main;

     //create a click-event handler
     //note: btRed was added in the IDE
     EventHandler evh = new EventHandler (commandClick);
```

```
        btRed.Click += evh;          //add to existing red button
        RedCommand cRed = new RedCommand (this);
        btRed.setCommand (cRed);
        //create a "File" top level entry
        MenuItem file = new CommandMenu("File");
        main.MenuItems.Add ( file );

        //create File Open command
        CommandMenu mnuFlo = new CommandMenu("Open");
        mnuFlo.setCommand (new OpenCommand ());
        mnuFlo.Click += evh;                 //add same handler

        //create a Red menu item, too
        CommandMenu mnuRed = new CommandMenu("Red");
        mnuRed.setCommand(cRed);
        mnuRed.Click += evh;                 //add same handler

        //create a File-Exit command
        CommandMenu mnuFex = new CommandMenu("Exit");
        mnuFex.setCommand (new ExitCommand(this));
        file.MenuItems.AddRange(
                new CommandMenu[]{ mnuFlo, mnuRed, mnuFex} );
        mnuFex.Click += evh;                 //add same handler
    }
```

In the CommandHolder approach, we still have to create separate Command objects, but they are no longer part of the user interface classes. For example, the OpenCommand class is just this.

```
public class OpenCommand :Command          {
    public OpenCommand()
    {}
    public void Execute() {
            OpenFileDialog fd = new OpenFileDialog ();
            fd.ShowDialog ();
    }
}
```

Then our click event handler method needs to obtain the actual command object from the UI object that caused the action and execute that command.

```
private void commandClick(object sender, EventArgs e) {
    Command comd = ((CommandHolder)sender).getCommand ();
    comd.Execute ();
}
```

This is only slightly more complicated than our original routine and again keeps the action separate from the user interface elements. We can see this program in action in Figure 22-3.

Figure 22-3   Menu part of Command pattern using CommandHolder interface

We can see the relations between theses classes and interfaces clearly in the UML diagram in Figure 22-4.

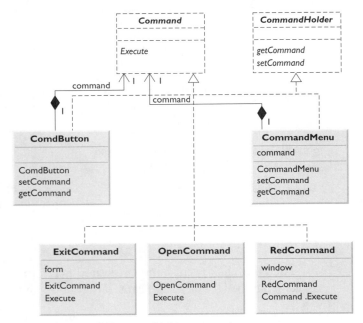

Figure 22-4   Class diagram of CommandHolder approach

Providing Undo

Another of the main reasons for using Command design patterns is that they provide a convenient way to store and execute an Undo function. Each command object can remember what it just did and restore that state when requested to do so if the computational and memory requirements are not too overwhelming. At the top level, we simply redefine the Command interface to have three methods.

```
public interface Command      {
      void Execute();
      void Undo();
      bool isUndo();
}
```

Then we have to design each command object to keep a record of what it last did so it can undo it. This can be a little more complicated than it first appears, since having a number of interleaved Commands executed and then undone can lead to some hysteresis. In addition, each command will need to store enough information about each execution of the command that it will know what specifically has to be undone.

The problem of undoing commands is actually a multipart problem. First, you must keep a list of the commands that have been executed, and second, each command has to keep a list of its executions. To illustrate how we use the Command pattern to carry out undo operations, let's consider the program shown in Figure 22-5 that draws successive red or blue lines on the screen, using two buttons to draw a new instance of each line. You can undo the last line you drew with the undo button.

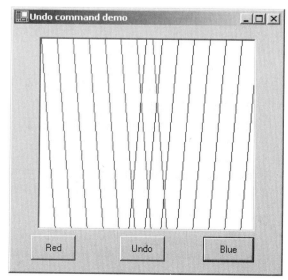

Figure 22-5   A program that draws red and blue lines each time you click the Red and Blue buttons

If you click on Undo several times, you'd expect the last several lines to disappear no matter what order the buttons were clicked in, as shown in Figure 22-6.

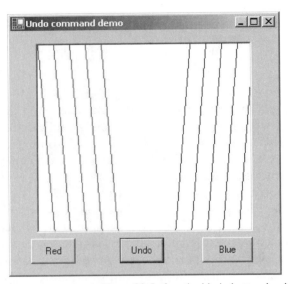

Figure 22-6   The same program as in Figure 22-5 after the Undo button has been clicked several times

Thus, any undoable program needs a single sequential list of all the commands that have been executed. Each time we click on any button, we add its corresponding command to the list.

```
private void commandClick(object sender, EventArgs e) {
     //get the command
     Command comd = ((CommandHolder)sender).getCommand ();
     undoC.add (comd);    //add to undo list
     comd.Execute ();     //and execute it
}
```

Further, the list to which we add the Command objects is maintained inside the Undo command object so it can access that list conveniently.

```
public class UndoComd:Command    {
     private ArrayList undoList;
     public UndoComd()    {
          undoList = new ArrayList ();
     }
     //-----
     public void add(Command comd) {
          if(! comd.isUndo ()) {
               undoList.Add (comd);
```

```
                }
        }
        //-----
        public bool isUndo() {
                return true;
        }
        //-----
        public void Undo() {                    }
        //-----
        public void Execute() {
                int index = undoList.Count - 1;
                if (index >= 0) {
                        Command cmd = (Command)undoList[index];
                        cmd.Undo();
                        undoList.RemoveAt(index);
                }
        }
}
```

The undoCommand object keeps a list of *Commands,* not a list of actual data. Each command object has its unDo method called to execute the actual undo operation. Note that since the undoCommand object implements the Command interface, it, too, needs to have an unDo method. However, the idea of undoing successive unDo operations is a little complex for this simple example program. Consequently, you should note that the *add* method adds all Commands to the list *except* the undoCommand itself, since we have just defined undoing an unDo command as doing nothing. For this reason, our new Command interface includes an *isUndo* method that returns false for the RedCommand and BlueCommand objects and true for the UndoCommand object.

The RedCommand and BlueCommand classes simply use different colors and start at opposite sides of the window, although both implement the revised Command interface. Each class keeps a list of lines to be drawn in a Collection as a series of *DrawData* objects containing the coordinates of each line. Undoing a line from either the red or the blue line list simply means removing the last *DrawData* object from the *drawList* collection. Then either command forces a repaint of the screen. Since they do the same thing except for the color of the line and its diagonal direction, we can create a ColorCommand base class and derive our RedCommand and BlueCommand classes from it. Here is the base ColorCommand class.

```
public class ColorCommand :Command
        {
                protected Color color;              //line color
                protected PictureBox pbox;          //box to draw in
                protected ArrayList drawList;       //list of lines
                protected int x, y, dx, dy;         //coordinates
                //------
                public ColorCommand(PictureBox pict)
```

```
        {
                pbox = pict; //copy in picture box
                drawList = new ArrayList ();      //create list
        }
        //------
        public void Execute() {
                //create a new line to draw
                DrawData dl = new DrawData(x, y, dx, dy);
                drawList.Add(dl);    //add it to the list
                x = x + dx;          //increment the positions
                y = y + dy;
                pbox.Refresh();
        }
        //-----
        public bool isUndo() {
                return false;
        }
        //-----
        public void Undo() {
                DrawData dl;
                int index = drawList.Count - 1;
                if (index >= 0) {
                        dl = (DrawData)drawList[index];
                        drawList.RemoveAt(index);
                        x = dl.getX();
                        y = dl.getY();
                }
                pbox.Refresh();
        }
        //-----
        public void draw(Graphics g) {
                Pen rpen = new Pen(color, 1);
                int h = pbox.Height;
                int w = pbox.Width;
        //draw all the lines in the list
                for (int i = 0; i < drawList.Count ; i++) {
                        DrawData dl = (DrawData)drawList[i];
                        g.DrawLine(rpen, dl.getX(), dl.getY(),
                                dl.getX() + dx, dl.getDy() + h);
                }
        }
    }
```

Note that the *draw* method in the *drawCommand* class redraws the entire list of lines the command object has stored. These two draw methods are called from the paint handler of the form.

```
public void paintHandler(object sender, PaintEventArgs e) {
      Graphics g = e.Graphics ;
      blueC.draw(g);
      redC.draw (g);
}
```

We can then derive the BlueCommand and RedCommand classes from the ColorCommand class. Here is the BlueCommand class.

```
public class BlueCommand :ColorCommand     {
    public BlueCommand(PictureBox pict):base(pict) {
        color = Color.Blue ;
        x = pbox.Width ;
        dx = -20;
        y = 0;
        dy = 0;
    }
}
```

We can create the RedCommand just as easily.

```
public class RedCommand : ColorCommand    {
    public RedCommand(PictureBox pict):base(pict){
        color = Color.Red;
        x = 0;
        dx = 20;
        y = 0;
        dy = 0;
    }
}
```

The set of classes we use in this Undo program is shown in Figure 22-7.

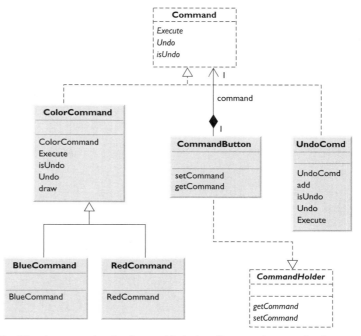

Figure 22-7   The classes used to implement Undo in a Command pattern implementation

Thought Questions

1. Mouse clicks on list box items and on radio buttons also constitute commands. Clicks on multiselect list boxes could also be represented as commands. Design a program including these features.

2. A lottery system uses a random number generator constrained to integers from 1 to 50. The selections are made at intervals selected by a random timer. Each selection must be unique. Design command patterns to choose the winning numbers each week.

Programs on the CD-ROM

Buttons and menus using Command pattern	`\Command\ButtonMenu`
C# program showing line drawing and Undo	`\Command\UndoCommand`
C# program showing CommandHolder interface	`\Command\ComdHolder`

CHAPTER 23

The Interpreter Pattern

Some programs benefit from having a language to describe operations they can perform. The Interpreter pattern generally describes defining a grammar for that language and using that grammar to interpret statements in that language.

Motivation

When a program presents a number of different but somewhat similar cases it can deal with, it can be advantageous to use a simple language to describe these cases and then have the program interpret that language. Such cases can be as simple as the sort of Macro language recording facilities a number of office suite programs provide or as complex as Visual Basic for Applications (VBA). VBA is not only included in Microsoft Office products, but it can be embedded in any number of third-party products quite simply.

One of the problems we must deal with is how to recognize when a language can be helpful. The Macro language recorder simply records menu and keystroke operations for later playback and just barely qualifies as a language; it may not actually have a written form or grammar. Languages such as VBA, on the other hand, are quite complex, but they are far beyond the capabilities of the individual application developer. Further, embedding commercial languages usually require substantial licensing fees, which makes them less attractive to all but the largest developers.

Applicability

As the *SmallTalk Companion* notes, recognizing cases where an Interpreter can be helpful is much of the problem, and programmers without formal language/

compiler training frequently overlook this approach. There are not many such cases, but there are three general places where languages are applicable.

1. *When you need a command interpreter to parse user commands.* The user can type queries of various kinds and obtain a variety of answers.

2. *When the program must parse an algebraic string.* This case is fairly obvious. The program is asked to carry out its operations based on a computation where the user enters an equation of some sort. This frequently occurs in mathematical-graphics programs where the program renders a curve or surface based on any equation it can evaluate. Programs like *Mathematica* and graph drawing packages such as *Origin* work in this way.

3. *When the program must produce varying kinds of output.* This case is a little less obvious but far more useful. Consider a program that can display columns of data in any order and sort them in various ways. These programs are frequently referred to as Report Generators, and while the underlying data may be stored in a relational database, the user interface to the report program is usually much simpler than the SQL language that the database uses. In fact, in some cases, the simple report language may be interpreted by the report program and translated into SQL.

A Simple Report Example

Let's consider a simplified report generator that can operate on five columns of data in a table and return various reports on these data. Suppose we have the following results from a swimming competition.

Amanda	McCarthy	12	WCA	29.28
Jamie	Falco	12	HNHS	29.80
Meaghan	O'Donnell	12	EDST	30.00
Greer	Gibbs	12	CDEV	30.04
Rhiannon	Jeffrey	11	WYW	30.04
Sophie	Connolly	12	WAC	30.05
Dana	Helyer	12	ARAC	30.18

The five columns are *frname, lname, age, club* and *time*. If we consider the complete race results of 51 swimmers, we realize that it might be convenient to sort these results by club, by last name, or by age. Since there are a number of useful reports we could produce from these data in which the order of the columns changes as well as the sorting, a language is one useful way to handle these reports.

We'll define a very simple nonrecursive grammar of this sort.

```
Print lname frname club time Sortby club Thenby time
```

For the purposes of this example, we define these three verbs.

```
Print
Sortby
Thenby
```

And we'll define the five column names we listed earlier.

```
Frname
Lname
Age
Club
Time
```

For convenience, we'll assume that the language is case insensitive. We'll also note that the simple grammar of this language is punctuation free and amounts in brief to the following.

Print var[var] [sortby var [thenby var]]

Finally, there is only one main verb, and while each statement is a declaration, there is no assignment statement or computational ability in this grammar.

Interpreting the Language

Interpreting the language is a three-step process.

1. Parsing the language symbols into tokens.

2. Reducing the tokens into actions.

3. Executing the actions.

We parse the language into tokens by simply scanning each statement with a StringTokenizer and then substituting a number for each word. Usually parsers push each parsed token onto a *stack,* and we will use that technique here. We implement the Stack class using an ArrayList—where we have *push, pop, top,* and *nextTop* methods to examine and manipulate the stack contents. After parsing, our stack could look like this.

Type	Token	
Var	Time	<-top of stack
Verb	Thenby	
Var	Club	
Verb	Sortby	
Var	Time	
Var	Club	
Var	Frname	
Var	Lname	
Verb	Print	

However, we quickly realize that the "verb" *Thenby* has no real meaning other than clarification, and it is more likely that we'd parse the tokens and skip the *Thenby* word altogether. Our initial stack then, looks like this.

```
Time
Club
Sortby
Time
Club
Frname
Lname
Print
```

Objects Used in Parsing

In this parsing procedure, we do not push just a numeric token onto the stack but a *ParseObject* that has both a type and a value property.

```
public class ParseObject  {
     public const int VERB=1000;
     public const int VAR=1010;
     public const int MULTVAR=1020;
     protected int value, type;
     //-----
     public ParseObject(int val, int typ)    {
          value = val;
          type = typ;
     }
     //-----
```

```
public int getValue() {
      return value;
}
//-----
public int getType() {
      return type;
}
}
```

These objects can take on the type VERB or VAR. Then we extend this object into ParseVerb and ParseVar objects, whose value fields can take on PRINT or SORT for ParseVerb and FRNAME, LNAME, and so on for Parse-Var. For later use in reducing the parse list, we then derive *Print* and *Sort* objects from ParseVerb.

This gives us the simple hierarchy shown in Figure 23-1.

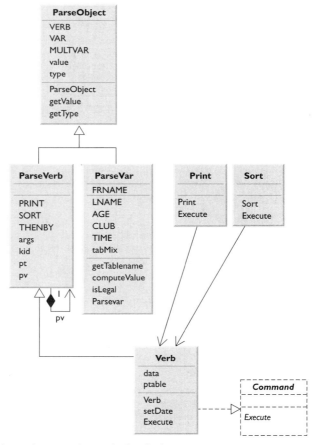

Figure 23-1   A simple parsing hierarchy for the Interpreter pattern

The parsing process is just the following simple code, using the String-Tokenizer and the parse objects. Part of the main Parser class is shown here.

```
public class Parser        {
     private Stack stk;
     private ArrayList actionList;
     private Data dat;
     private ListBox ptable;
     private Chain chn;
     //-----
     public Parser(string line, KidData kd, ListBox pt){
          stk = new Stack ();
          //list of verbs accumulates here
          actionList = new ArrayList ();
          setData(kd, pt);
          buildStack(line);    //create token stack
          buildChain();         //create chain of responsibility
     }
     //-----
     private void buildChain() {
          chn = new VarVarParse(); //start of chain
          VarMultvarParse vmvp = new VarMultvarParse();
          chn.addToChain(vmvp);
          MultVarVarParse mvvp = new MultVarVarParse();
          vmvp.addToChain(mvvp);
          VerbMultvarParse vrvp = new VerbMultvarParse();
          mvvp.addToChain(vrvp);
          VerbVarParse vvp = new VerbVarParse();
          vrvp.addToChain(vvp);
          VerbAction va = new VerbAction(actionList);
          vvp.addToChain(va);
          Nomatch nom = new Nomatch ();      //error handler
          va.addToChain (nom);
     }
     //-----
     public void setData(KidData kd, ListBox pt) {
          dat = new Data(kd.getData ());
          ptable = pt;
     }
     //-----
     private void buildStack(string s) {
          StringTokenizer tok = new StringTokenizer (s);
          while(tok.hasMoreElements () ) {
               ParseObject token = tokenize(tok.nextToken ));
                    stk.push (token);
          }
     }
     //-----
     protected ParseObject tokenize(string s) {
          ParseObject obj;
          int type;
          try {
               obj = getVerb(s);
               type = obj.getType ();
```

```
            }
            catch(NullReferenceException) {
                    obj = getVar(s);
            }
            return obj;
    }
    //-----
    protected ParseVerb getVerb(string s) {
            ParseVerb v = new ParseVerb (s, dat, ptable);
            if(v.isLegal () )
                    return v.getVerb (s);
            else
                    return null;
    }
    //-----
    protected ParseVar getVar(string s) {
            ParseVar v = new ParseVar (s);
            if( v.isLegal())
                    return v;
            else
                    return null;
    }
}
```

The ParseVerb and ParseVar classes return objects with *isLegal* set to true if they recognize the word.

```
public class ParseVerb:ParseObject      {
    protected const int PRINT = 100;
    protected const int SORT = 110;
    protected const int THENBY = 120;
    protected ArrayList args;
    protected Data kid;
    protected ListBox pt;
    protected ParseVerb pv;
    //-----
    public ParseVerb(string s, Data kd, ListBox ls):
                    base(-1, VERB) {
            args = new ArrayList ();
            kid = kd;
            pt = ls;
            if(s.ToLower().Equals ("print")) {
                    value = PRINT;
            }
            if(s.ToLower().Equals ("sortby")) {
                    value = SORT;
            }
    }
    //------
    public ParseVerb getVerb(string s) {
            pv = null;
            if(s.ToLower ().Equals ("print"))
                    pv =new Print(s,kid, pt);
```

```
            if(s.ToLower ().Equals ("sortby"))
                    pv = new Sort (s, kid, pt);
            return pv;
    }
    //-----
    public void addArgs(MultVar mv) {
            args = mv.getVector ();
    }
```

Reducing the Parsed Stack

The tokens on the stack have this form.

```
Var
Var
Verb
Var
Var
Var
Var
Verb
```

We reduce the stack a token at a time, folding successive Vars into a MultVar class until the arguments are folded into the verb objects, as shown in Figure 23-2.

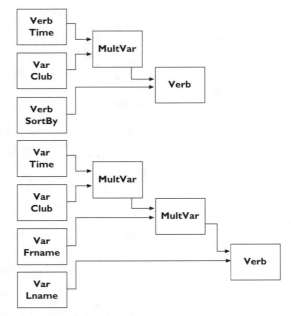

Figure 23-2 How the stack is reduced during parsing

When the stack reduces to a verb, this verb and its arguments are placed in an action list; when the stack is empty, the actions are executed.

Creating a Parser class that is a Command object and executing it when the Go button is pressed on the user interface carries out this entire process.

```
private void btCompute_Click(object sender, EventArgs e) {
    parse();
}
private void parse() {
    Parser par = new Parser (txCommand.Text, kdata, lsResults);
    par.Execute ();
}
```

The parser itself just reduces the tokens, as the preceding shows. It checks for various pairs of tokens on the stack and reduces each pair to a single one for each of five different cases.

Implementing the Interpreter Pattern

It would certainly be possible to write a parser for this simple grammar as just a series of *if* statements. For each of the six possible stack configurations, reduce the stack until only a verb remains. Then, since we have made the Print and Sort verb classes Command objects, we can just Execute them one by one as the action list is enumerated.

However, the real advantage of the Interpreter pattern is its flexibility. By making each parsing case an individual object, we can represent the parse tree as a series of connected objects that reduce the stack successively. Using this arrangement, we can easily change the parsing rules without much in the way of program changes: We just create new objects and insert them into the parse tree.

According to the Gang of Four, these are the names for the participating objects in the Interpreter pattern.

- **AbstractExpression**—declares the abstract Interpret operation.
- **TerminalExpression**—interprets expressions containing any of the terminal tokens in the grammar.
- **NonTerminalExpression**—interprets all of the nonterminal expressions in the grammar.
- **Context**—contains the global information that is part of the parser—in this case, the token stack.
- **Client**—builds the syntax tree from the preceding expression types and invokes the Interpret operation.

The Syntax Tree

The syntax tree we construct to carry out the parsing of the stack we just showed can be quite simple. We just need to look for each of the stack configurations we defined and reduce them to an executable form. In fact, the best way to implement this tree is using a Chain of Responsibility, which passes the stack configuration along between classes until one of them recognizes that configuration and acts on it. You can decide whether a successful stack reduction should end that pass or not. It is perfectly possible to have several successive chain members work on the stack in a single pass. The processing ends when the stack is empty. We see a diagram of the individual parse chain elements in Figure 23-3.

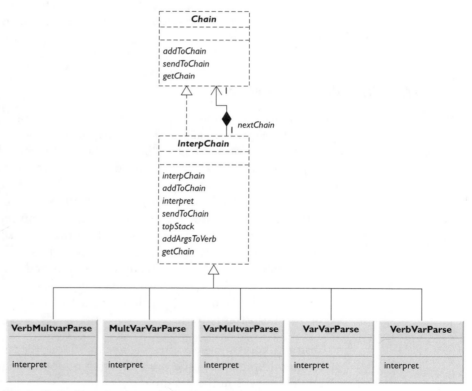

Figure 23-3   How the classes that perform the parsing interact

In this class structure, we start with the AbstractExpression interpreter class *InterpChain*.

```
public abstract class InterpChain:Chain {
      private Chain nextChain;
      protected Stack stk;
      private bool hasChain;
      //-----
      public InterpChain()        {
            stk = new Stack ();
            hasChain = false;
      }
      //-----
      public void addToChain(Chain c) {
            nextChain = c;
            hasChain = true;
      }
      //-----
      public abstract bool interpret();
      //-----
      public void sendToChain(Stack stack) {
            stk = stack;
            if(! interpret()   ) {                   //interpret stack
                  nextChain.sendToChain (stk);        //pass along
            }
      }
      //-----
      public bool topStack(int c1, int c2) {
            ParseObject p1, p2;
            p1 = stk.top ();
            p2 = stk.nextTop ();
            try{
            return (p1.getType() == c1 && p2.getType() == c2);
            }
            catch(NullReferenceException) {
                  return false;
            }
      }
      //-----
      public void addArgsToVerb() {
            ParseObject p = (ParseObject) stk.pop();
            ParseVerb v =  (ParseVerb) stk.pop();
            v.addArgs (p);
            stk.push (v);
      }
      //-----
      public Chain getChain() {
            return nextChain;
      }
```

This class also contains the methods for manipulating objects on the stack. Each of the subclasses implements the *interpret* operation differently and reduces the stack accordingly. For example, the complete VarVarParse class reduces two variables on the stack in succession to a single MultVar object.

```
public class VarVarParse : InterpChain  {
      public override bool interpret() {
            if(topStack(ParseVar.VAR , ParseVar.VAR )) {
                  //reduces VAR VAR to MULTVAR
                  ParseVar v1 = (ParseVar) stk.pop();
                  ParseVar v2 = (ParseVar) stk.pop();
                  MultVar mv = new MultVar (v2, v1);
                  stk.push (mv);
                  return true;
            }
            else
                  return false;
      }
}
```

Thus, in this implementation of the pattern, the stack constitutes the Context participant. Each of the first five subclasses of *InterpChain* are NonTerminal Expression participants, and the ActionVerb class that moves the completed verb and action objects to the actionList constitutes the TerminalExpression participant.

The client object is the Parser class that builds the stack object list from the typed-in command text and constructs the Chain of Responsibility from the various interpreter classes. We just showed most of the Parser class already. However, it also implements the Command pattern and sends the stack through the chain until it is empty and then executes the verbs that have accumulated in the action list when its Execute method is called.

```
   //executes parse and interpretation of command line
public void Execute() {
      while(stk.hasMoreElements () ) {
            chn.sendToChain (stk);
      }
      //now execute the verbs
      for(int i=0; i< actionList.Count ; i++ ) {
            Verb v = (Verb)actionList[i];
            v.setData (dat, ptable);
            v.Execute ();
      }
}
```

The final visual program is shown in Figure 23-4.

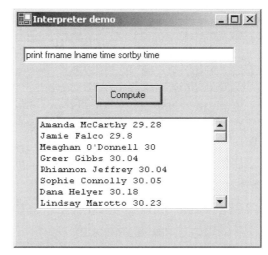

Figure 23-4   The Interpreter pattern operating on the simple command in the text field

Consequences of the Interpreter Pattern

Whenever you introduce an interpreter into a program, you need to provide a simple way for the program user to enter commands in that language. It can be as simple as the Macro record button we noted earlier, or it can be an editable text field like the one in the preceding program.

However, introducing a language and its accompanying grammar also requires fairly extensive error checking for misspelled terms or misplaced grammatical elements. This can easily consume a great deal of programming effort unless some template code is available for implementing this checking. Further, effective methods for notifying the users of these errors are not easy to design and implement.

In the preceding Interpreter example, the only error handling is that keywords that are not recognized are not converted to ParseObjects and pushed onto the stack. Thus, nothing will happen because the resulting stack sequence probably cannot be parsed successfully, or if it can, the item represented by the misspelled keyword will not be included.

You can also consider generating a language automatically from a user interface of radio and command buttons and list boxes. While it may seem that having such an interface obviates the necessity for a language at all, the same requirements of sequence and computation still apply. When you have to have a way to specify the order of sequential operations, a language is a good way to do so, even if the language is generated from the user interface.

The Interpreter pattern has the advantage that you can extend or revise the grammar fairly easily once you have built the general parsing and reduction tools. You can also add new verbs or variables easily once the foundation is constructed. However, as the syntax of the grammar becomes more complex, you run the risk of creating a hard-to-maintain program.

While interpreters are not all that common in solving general programming problems, the Iterator pattern we take up next is one of the most common ones you'll be using.

Thought Question

Design a system to compute the results of simple quadratic expressions such as

$$4x^2 + 3x - 4$$

where the user can enter x or a range of x's and can type in the equation.

Program on the CD-ROM

C# Interpreter	\Interpreter

CHAPTER 24

The Iterator Pattern

The Iterator is one of the simplest and most frequently used of the design patterns. The Iterator pattern allows you to move through a list or collection of data using a standard interface without having to know the details of the internal representations of that data. In addition, you can also define special iterators that perform some special processing and return only specified elements of the data collection.

Motivation

The Iterator is useful because it provides a defined way to move through a set of data elements without exposing what is taking place inside the class. Since the Iterator is an *interface*, you can implement it in any way that is convenient for the data you are returning. *Design Patterns* suggests that a suitable interface for an Iterator might be the following.

```
public interface Iterator   {
      object First();
      object Next();
      bool isDone();
      object currentItem();
}
```

Here you can move to the top of the list, move through the list, find out if there are more elements, and find the current list item. This interface is easy to implement, and it has certain advantages, but a number of other similar interfaces are possible. For example, when we discussed the Composite pattern, we introduced the getSubordinates method:

```
IEnumerator getSubordinates();       //get subordinates
```

to provide a way to loop through all of the subordinates any employee may have. The IEnumerator interface can be represented in C# as

```
bool MoveNext();
void Reset();
object Current {get;}
```

This also allows us to loop through a list of zero or more elements in some internal list structure without our having to know how that list is organized inside the class.

One disadvantage of this Enumeration over similar constructs in C++ and Smalltalk is the strong typing of the C# language. This prevents the *Current()* property from returning an object of the actual type of the data in the collection. Instead, you must convert the returned object type to the actual type of the data in the collection. Thus, while this IEnumerator interface is intended to be polymorphic, this is not directly possible in C#.

Sample Iterator Code

Let's reuse the list of swimmers, clubs, and times we described earlier, and add some enumeration capabilities to the KidData class. This class is essentially a collection of Kids, each with a name, club, and time, and these Kid objects are stored in an ArrayList.

```
public class KidData :IEnumerator {
     private ArrayList kids;
     private int index;
     public KidData(string filename)            {
             kids = new ArrayList ();
             csFile fl = new csFile (filename);
             fl.OpenForRead ();
             string line = fl.readLine ();
             while(line != null) {
                     Kid kd = new Kid (line);
                     kids.Add (kd);
                     line = fl.readLine ();
             }
             fl.close ();
             index = 0;
     }
```

To obtain an enumeration of all the Kids in the collection, we simply use the methods of the IEnumerator interface we just defined.

```
public bool MoveNext() {
     index++;
     return index < kids.Count ;
```

```
}
//------
public object Current {
      get {
              return kids[index];
      }
}
//------
public void Reset() {
      index = 0;
}
```

Reading in the data and displaying a list of names are quite easy. We initial-ize the Kids class with the filename and have it build the collection of Kid objects. Then we treat the Kids class as an instance of IEnumerator and move through it to get out the kids and display their names.

```
private void init() {
  kids = new KidData("50free.txt");
  while (kids.MoveNext () ) {
      Kid kd = (Kid)kids.Current ;
      lsKids.Items.Add (kd.getFrname()+ " "+ kd.getLname ());
  }
}
```

Fetching an Iterator

Another slightly more flexible way to handle iterators in a class is to provide the class with a getIterator method that returns instances of an iterator for that class's data. This is somewhat more flexible because you can have any number of iterators active simultaneously on the same data. Our KidIterator class can then be the one that implements our Iterator interface.

```
public class KidIterator : IEnumerator  {
      private ArrayList kids;
      private int index;
      public KidIterator(ArrayList kidz)          {
              kids = kidz;
              index = 0;
      }
      //------
      public bool MoveNext() {
              index++;
              return index < kids.Count ;
      }
      //------
      public object Current {
              get {
                      return kids[index];
```

```
                      }
              }
              //------
              public void Reset() {
                      index = 0;
              }
      }
```

We can fetch iterators from the main KidList class by creating them as needed.

```
public KidIterator getIterator() {
        return new KidIterator (kids);
}
```

Filtered Iterators

While having a clearly defined method of moving through a collection is helpful, you can also define filtered Iterators that perform some computation on the data before returning it. For example, you could return the data ordered in some particular way or only those objects that match a particular criterion. Then rather than have a lot of very similar interfaces for these filtered iterators, you simply provide a method that returns each type of enumeration with each one of these enumerations having the same methods.

The Filtered Iterator

Suppose, however, that we wanted to enumerate only those kids who belonged to a certain club. This necessitates a special Iterator class that has access to the data in the KidData class. This is very simple because the methods we just defined give us that access. Then we only need to write an Iterator that only returns kids belonging to a specified club.

```
public class FilteredIterator : IEnumerator   {
        private ArrayList kids;
        private int index;
        private string club;
        public FilteredIterator(ArrayList kidz, string club)  {
                kids = kidz;
                index = 0;
                this.club = club;
        }
        //------
        public bool MoveNext() {
                bool more = index < kids.Count-1 ;
                if(more) {
```

```
                        Kid kd = (Kid)kids[++index];
                        more = index < kids.Count;
                        while(more && ! kd.getClub().Equals (club)) {
                                kd = (Kid)kids[index++];
                                more = index < kids.Count ;
                        }
                }
                return more;
        }
        //------
        public object Current {
                get {
                        return kids[index];
                }
        }
        //------
        public void Reset() {
                index = 0;
        }
}
```

All of the work is done in the *MoveNext()* method, which scans through the collection for another kid belonging to the club specified in the constructor. Then it returns either true or false.

Finally, we need to add a method to KidData to return this new filtered Enumeration.

```
public FilteredIterator getFilteredIterator(string club) {
        return new FilteredIterator (kids, club);
}
```

This simple method passes the collection to the new Iterator class FilteredIterator along with the club initials. A simple program is shown in Figure 24-1 that displays all of the kids on the left side. It fills a combo box with a list of the clubs and then allows the user to select a club and fills the right-hand list box with those belonging to a single club. The class diagram is shown in Figure 24-2. Note that the *elements* method in KidData supplies an Enumeration, and the kidClub class is in fact itself an Enumeration class.

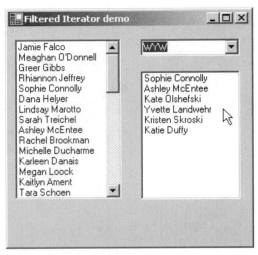

Figure 24-1   A simple program illustrating filtered Enumeration

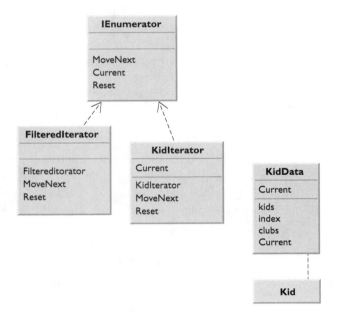

Figure 24-2   The classes used in the filtered Enumeration

Keeping Track of the Clubs

We need to obtain a unique list of the clubs with which to load the combo box in Figure 24-1. As we read in each kid, we can do this by putting the clubs in a Hashtable.

```
while(line != null) {
      Kid kd = new Kid (line);
      string club = kd.getClub ();
      if(! clubs.Contains (club ) ) {
            clubs.Add (club, club);
      }
      kids.Add (kd);
      line = fl.readLine ();
}
```

Then when we want to get the list of clubs, we can ask the Hashtable for an iterator of its contents. The Hashtable class has a method, getEnumerator, that should return this information. However, this method returns an IdictionaryEnumerator, which is slightly different. While it is derived from IEnumerator, it uses a Value method to return the contents of the Hashtable. Thus, we load the combo box with the following code.

```
IDictionaryEnumerator clubiter = kdata.getClubs ();
while(clubiter.MoveNext ()) {
      cbClubs.Items.Add ((string)clubiter.Value );
}
```

When we click on the combo box, it gets the selected club to generate a filtered iterator and load the kidclub list box.

```
private void cbClubs_SelectedIndexChanged(object sender,
                          EventArgs e) {
      string club = (String)cbClubs.SelectedItem ;
      FilteredIterator iter = kdata.getFilteredIterator ( club);
      lsClubKids.Items.Clear ();
      while(iter.MoveNext() ) {
        Kid kd = (Kid) iter.Current;
        lsClubKids.Items.Add (kd.getFrname() +" "+
            kd.getLname ());
      }
}
```

Consequences of the Iterator Pattern

1. *Data modification.* The most significant question iterators may raise is the question of iterating through data while it is being changed. If your code is wide ranging and only occasionally moves to the next element, it is possible that an element might be added or deleted from the underlying collection while you are moving through it. It is also possible that another thread could change the collection. There are no simple answers to this problem. If you want to move through a loop using an Enumeration and delete certain items, you must be careful of the consequences. Deleting or adding an

element might mean that a particular element is skipped or accessed twice, depending on the storage mechanism you are using.

2. *Privileged access.* Enumeration classes may need to have some sort of privileged access to the underlying data structures of the original container class so they can move through the data. If the data is stored in an ArrayList or Hashtable, this is pretty easy to accomplish, but if it is in some other collection structure contained in a class, you probably have to make that structure available through a *get* operation. Alternatively, you could make the Iterator a derived class of the containment class and access the data directly.

3. *External versus Internal Iterators.* The *Design Patterns* text describes two types of iterators: external and internal. Thus far we have only described external iterators. Internal iterators are methods that move through the entire collection, performing some operation on each element directly without any specific requests from the user. These are less common in C#, but you could imagine methods that normalized a collection of data values to lie between 0 and 1 or converted all of the strings to a particular case. In general, external iterators give you more control because the calling program accesses each element directly and can decide whether to perform an operation on it.

Programs on the CD-ROM

Kid list using Iterator	\Iterator\SimpleIterator
Filtered iterator by team name	\Iterator\FilteredIterator

CHAPTER 25

The Mediator Pattern

When a program is made up of a number of classes, the logic and computation is divided logically among these classes. However, as more of these isolated classes are developed in a program, the problem of communication between these classes becomes more complex. The more each class needs to know about the methods of another class, the more tangled the class structure can become. This makes the program harder to read and harder to maintain. Further, it can become difficult to change the program, since any change may affect code in several other classes. The Mediator pattern addresses this problem by promoting looser coupling between these classes. Mediators accomplish this by being the only class that has detailed knowledge of the methods of other classes. Classes inform the Mediator when changes occur, and the Mediator passes on the changes to any other classes that need to be informed.

An Example System

Let's consider a program that has two buttons, two list boxes, and a text entry field, as shown in Figure 25-1.

When the program starts, the Copy and Clear buttons are disabled.

1. When you select one of the names in the left-hand list box, it is copied into the text field for editing, and the *Copy* button is enabled.

2. When you click on *Copy,* that text is added to the right-hand list box, and the *Clear* button is enabled, as we see in Figure 25-2.

3. If you click on the *Clear* button, the right-hand list box and the text field are cleared, the list box is deselected, and the two buttons are again disabled.

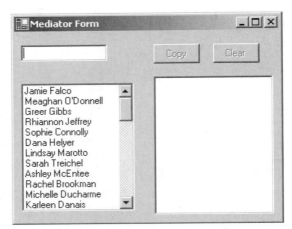

Figure 25-1   A simple program with two lists, two buttons, and a text field that will interact

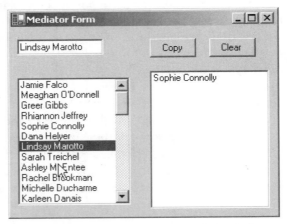

Figure 25-2   When you select a name, the buttons are enabled, and when you click
on Copy, the name is copied to the right list box.

User interfaces such as this one are commonly used to select lists of people or
products from longer lists. Further, they are usually even more complicated than
this one, involving insert, delete, and undo operations as well.

Interactions between Controls

The interactions between the visual controls are pretty complex, even in this
simple example. Each visual object needs to know about two or more others,
leading to quite a tangled relationship diagram, as shown in Figure 25-3.

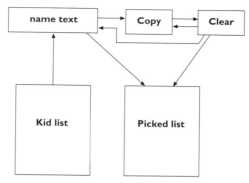

Figure 25-3 A tangled web of interactions between classes in the simple visual interface
we presented in Figures 25-1 and 25-2

The Mediator pattern simplifies this system by being the only class that is aware of the other classes in the system. Each of the controls with which the Mediator communicates is called a Colleague. Each Colleague informs the Mediator when it has received a user event, and the Mediator decides which other classes should be informed of this event. This simpler interaction scheme is illustrated in Figure 25-4.

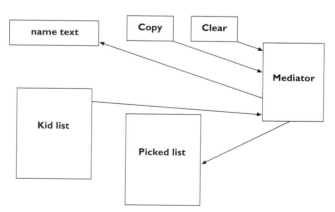

Figure 25-4 A Mediator class simplifies the interactions between classes.

The advantage of the Mediator is clear: It is the only class that is aware of the other classes and thus the only one that would need to be changed if one of the other classes changes or if other interface control classes are added.

Sample Code

Let's consider this program in detail and decide how each control is constructed. The main difference in writing a program using a Mediator class is that each class needs to be aware of the existence of the Mediator. You start by creating an instance of your Mediator class and then pass the instance of the Mediator to each class in its constructor.

```
med = new Mediator (btCopy, btClear, lsKids, lsSelected);
btCopy.setMediator (med);   //set mediator ref in each control
btClear.setMediator (med);
lsKids.setMediator (med);
med.setText (txName);        //tell mediator about text box
```

We derive our two button classes from the Button class, so they can also implement the Command interface. These buttons are passed to the Mediator in its constructor. Here is the CpyButton class.

```
public class CpyButton : System.Windows.Forms.Button, Command {
      private Container components = null;
      private Mediator med;
      //-----
      public CpyButton()          {
            InitializeComponent();
      }
      //-----
      public void setMediator(Mediator md) {
            med = md;
      }
      //-----
      public void Execute() {
            med.copyClicked ();
      }
}
```

Its Execute method simply tells the Mediator class that it has been clicked, and it lets the Mediator decide what to do when this happens. The Clear button is exactly analogous.

We derive the KidList class from the ListBox class and have it loaded with names within the Mediator's constructor.

```
public Mediator(CpyButton cp, ClrButton clr, KidList kl,
                          ListBox pk)          {
      cpButton = cp;                         //copy in buttons
      clrButton = clr;
      klist = kl;                            //copy in list boxes
      pkList = pk;
      kds = new KidData ("50free.txt"); //create data list class
      clearClicked();                        //clear all controls
      KidIterator kiter = kds.getIterator ();
```

```
        while(kiter.MoveNext () ) {                 //load list box
            Kid kd = (Kid) kiter.Current ;
            klist.Items .Add (kd.getFrname() +" "+
                        kd.getLname ());
        }
    }
```

We don't have to do anything special to the text field, since all its activity takes place within the Mediator. We just pass it to the Mediator using the setText method as we just illustrated.

The only other important part of our initialization is creating a single event handler for the two buttons and the list box. Rather than letting the development environment generate these click events for us, we create a single event and add it to the click handlers for the two buttons and the list box's Select-IndexChanged event. The intriguing thing about this event handler is that all it needs to do is call each control's Execute method and let the Mediator methods called by those Execute methods do all the real work.

The event handler for these click events is simply as follows.

```
//each control is a command object
public void clickHandler(object obj, EventArgs e) {
    Command comd = (Command)obj;        //get command object
    comd.Execute ();                    //and execute command
}
```

We show the complete Form initialization method that creates this event connections below.

```
private void init() {
    //set up mediator and pass in referencs to controls
    med = new Mediator (btCopy, btClear, lsKids, lsSelected);
    btCopy.setMediator (med);  // mediator ref in each control
    btClear.setMediator (med);
    lsKids.setMediator (med);
    med.setText (txName);       //tell mediator about text box

    //create event handler for all command objects
    EventHandler evh = new EventHandler (clickHandler);
    btClear.Click += evh;
    btCopy.Click += evh;
    lsKids.SelectedIndexChanged += evh;
}
```

The general point of all these classes is that each knows about the Mediator and tells the Mediator of its existence so the Mediator can send commands to it when appropriate.

The Mediator itself is very simple. It supports the Copy, Clear, and Select methods and has a register method for the TextBox. The two buttons and the

ListBox are passed in the Mediator's constructor. Note that there is no real reason to choose setXxx methods over constructor arguments for passing in references to these controls. We simply illustrate both approaches in this example.

```
public class Mediator    {
      private CpyButton cpButton;         //buttons
      private ClrButton clrButton;
      private TextBox txKids;             //text box
      private ListBox pkList;             //list boxes
      private KidList klist;
      private KidData kds;                //list of data from file

      public Mediator(CpyButton cp, ClrButton clr,
            KidList kl, ListBox pk)            {
            cpButton = cp;              //copy in buttons
            clrButton = clr;
            klist = kl;                //copy in list boxes
            pkList = pk;
            kds = new KidData ("50free.txt"); //create data list
            clearClicked();            //clear all controls
            KidIterator kiter = kds.getIterator ();
            while(kiter.MoveNext () ) {    //load list box
                  Kid kd = (Kid) kiter.Current ;
                  klist.Items .Add (kd.getFrname() +
                        " "+kd.getLname ());
            }
      }
      //-----
      //get text box reference
            public void setText(TextBox tx) {
                  txKids = tx;
            }
      //-----
      //clear lists and set buttons to disabled
      public void clearClicked() {
            //disable buttons and clear list
            cpButton.Enabled = false;
            clrButton.Enabled = false;
            pkList.Items.Clear();
      }
      //-----
      //copy data from text box to list box
      public void copyClicked() {
            //copy name to picked list
            pkList.Items.Add(txKids.Text);
            //clear button enabled
            clrButton.Enabled = true;
            klist.SelectedIndex = -1;
      }
      //-----
      //copy selected kid to text box
      //enable copy button
```

```
public void kidPicked() {
        //copy text from list to textbox
        txK    ids.Text = klist.Text;
        //copy button enabled
        cpButton.Enabled = true;
    }
}
```

Initialization of the System

One further operation that is best delegated to the Mediator is the initialization of all the controls to the desired state. When we launch the program, each control must be in a known, default state, and since these states may change as the program evolves, we simply carry out this initialization in the Mediator's constructor, which sets all the controls to the desired state. In this case, that state is the same as the one achieved by the Clear button, and we simply call that method the following.

```
clearClicked();            //clear all controls
```

Mediators and Command Objects

The two buttons in this program use command objects. Just as we noted earlier, this makes processing of the button click events quite simple.

In either case, however, this represents the solution to one of the problems we noted in the Command pattern chapter: Each button needed knowledge of many of the other user interface classes in order to execute its command. Here, we delegate that knowledge to the Mediator, so the Command buttons do not need any knowledge of the methods of the other visual objects. The class diagram for this program is shown in Figure 25-5, illustrating both the Mediator pattern and the use of the Command pattern.

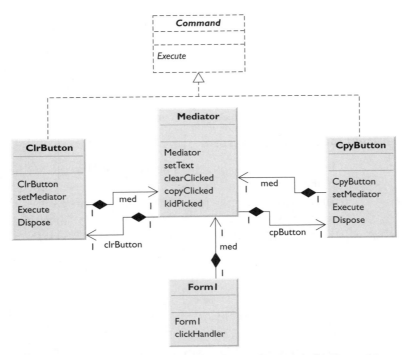

Figure 25-5   The interactions between the Command objects and the Mediator object

Consequences of the Mediator Pattern

1. The Mediator pattern keeps classes from becoming entangled when actions in one class need to be reflected in the state of another class.

2. Using a Mediator makes it easy to change a program's behavior. For many kinds of changes, you can merely change or subclass the Mediator, leaving the rest of the program unchanged.

3. You can add new controls or other classes without changing anything except the Mediator.

4. The Mediator solves the problem of each Command object needing to know too much about the objects and methods in the rest of a user interface.

5. The Mediator can become a "god class," having too much knowledge of the rest of the program. This can make it hard to change and maintain. Sometimes you can improve this situation by putting more of the function into the individual classes and less into the Mediator. Each object should carry out its own tasks, and the Mediator should only manage the interaction between objects.

6. Each Mediator is a custom-written class that has methods for each Colleague to call and knows what methods each Colleague has available. This makes it difficult to reuse Mediator code in different projects. On the other hand, most Mediators are quite simple, and writing this code is far easier than managing the complex object interactions any other way.

Single Interface Mediators

The Mediator pattern described here acts as a kind of Observer pattern, observing changes in each of the Colleague elements, with each element having a custom interface to the Mediator. Another approach is to have a single interface to your Mediator and pass to that method various objects that tell the Mediator which operations to perform.

In this approach, we avoid registering the active components and create a single action method with different polymorphic arguments for each of the action elements.

```
public void action(MoveButton mv);
public void action(clrButton clr);
public void action(KidList klist);
```

Thus, we need not register the action objects, such as the buttons and source list boxes, since we can pass them as part of generic *action* methods.

In the same fashion, you can have a single Colleague interface that each Colleague implements, and each Colleague then decides what operation it is to carry out.

Implementation Issues

Mediators are not limited to use in visual interface programs, but it is their most common application. You can use them whenever you are faced with the problem of complex intercommunication between a number of objects.

Program on the CD-ROM

Mediator	\Mediator

CHAPTER 26

The Memento Pattern

In this chapter, we discuss how to use the Memento pattern to save data about an object so you can restore it later. For example, you might like to save the color, size, pattern, or shape of objects in a drafting or painting program. Ideally, it should be possible to save and restore this state without making each object take care of this task and without violating encapsulation. This is the purpose of the Memento pattern.

Motivation

Objects normally shouldn't expose much of their internal state using public methods, but you would still like to be able to save the entire state of an object because you might need to restore it later. In some cases, you could obtain enough information from the public interfaces (such as the drawing position of graphical objects) to save and restore that data. In other cases, the color, shading, angle, and connection relationships to other graphical objects need to be saved, and this information is not readily available. This sort of information saving and restoration is common in systems that need to support Undo commands.

If all of the information describing an object is available in public variables, it is not that difficult to save them in some external store. However, making these data public makes the entire system vulnerable to change by external program code, when we usually expect data inside an object to be private and encapsulated from the outside world.

The Memento pattern attempts to solve this problem in some languages by having privileged access to the state of the object you want to save. Other objects have only a more restricted access to the object, thus preserving their encapsulation. In C#, however, there is only a limited notion of privileged access, but we will use it in this example.

This pattern defines three roles for objects.

1. The **Originator** is the object whose state we want to save.

2. The **Memento** is another object that saves the state of the Originator.

3. The **Caretaker** manages the timing of the saving of the state, saves the Memento, and, if needed, uses the Memento to restore the state of the Originator.

Implementation

Saving the state of an object without making all of its variables publicly available is tricky and can be done with varying degrees of success in various languages. *Design Patterns* suggests using the C++ *friend* construction to achieve this access, and the *Smalltalk Companion* notes that it is not directly possible in Smalltalk. In Java, this privileged access is possible using the package protected mode. The *internal* keyword is available in C#, but all that means is that any class method labeled as *internal* will only be accessible within the project. If you make a library from such classes, the methods marked as internal will not be exported and available. Instead, we will define a property to fetch and store the important internal values and make use of no other properties for any purpose in that class. For consistency, we'll use the internal keyword on these properties, but remember that this linguistic use of *internal* is not very restrictive.

Sample Code

Let's consider a simple prototype of a graphics drawing program that creates rectangles and allows you to select them and move them around by dragging them with the mouse. This program has a toolbar containing three buttons—Rectangle, Undo, and Clear—as we see in Figure 26-1.

The Rectangle button is a toolbar ToggleButton that stays selected until you click the mouse to draw a new rectangle. Once you have drawn the rectangle, you can click in any rectangle to select it, as we see in Figure 26-2.

Once it is selected, you can drag that rectangle to a new position, using the mouse, as shown in Figure 26-3.

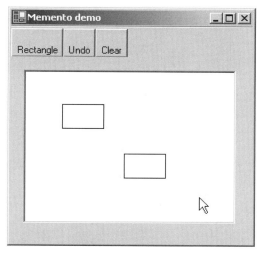

Figure 26-1 A simple graphics drawing program that allows you to draw rectangles, undo their drawing, and clear the screen

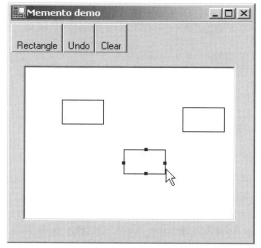

Figure 26-2 Selecting a rectangle causes "handles" to appear, indicating that it is selected and can be moved.

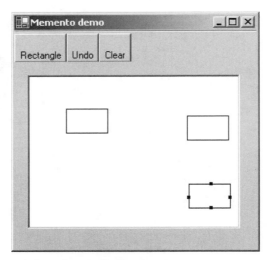

Figure 26-3   The same selected rectangle after dragging

The Undo button can undo a succession of operations. Specifically, it can undo moving a rectangle, and it can undo the creation of each rectangle. There are five actions to which we must respond in this program.

1. Rectangle button click

2. Undo button click

3. Clear button click

4. Mouse click

5. Mouse drag

The three buttons can be constructed as Command objects, and the mouse click and drag can be treated as commands as well. Since we have a number of visual objects that control the display of screen objects, this suggests an opportunity to use the Mediator pattern, and that is, in fact, the way this program is constructed.

We will create a Caretaker class to manage the Undo action list. It can keep a list of the last *n* operations so they can be undone. The Mediator maintains the list of drawing objects and communicates with the Caretaker object as well. In fact, since there could be any number of actions to save and undo in such a program, a Mediator is virtually required so there is a single place to send these commands to the Undo list in the Caretaker.

In this program, we save and undo only two actions: creating new rectangles and changing the position of rectangles. Let's start with our VisRectangle class, which actually draws each instance of the rectangles.

```
public class VisRectangle   {
      private int x, y, w, h;
      private const int SIZE=30;
      private CsharpPats.Rectangle rect;
      private bool selected;
      private Pen bPen;
      private SolidBrush bBrush;
      //-----
      public VisRectangle(int xp, int yp)                    {
            x = xp;                     y = yp;
            w = SIZE;                   h = SIZE;
            saveAsRect();
            bPen = new Pen(Color.Black);
            bBrush = new SolidBrush(Color.Black);
      }
      //-----
      //used by Memento for saving and restoring state
      internal CsharpPats.Rectangle rects {
            get {
                  return rect;
            }
            set {
                  x=value.x;
                  y=value.y;
                  w=value.w;
                  h=value.h;
                  saveAsRect();
            }
      }
      //------
      public void setSelected(bool b) {
            selected = b;
      }
      //-----
      //move to new position
      public void move(int xp, int yp) {
            x = xp;
            y = yp;
            saveAsRect();
      }
      //-----
      public void draw(Graphics g) {
            //draw rectangle
            g.DrawRectangle(bPen, x, y, w, h);

      if (selected) {    //draw handles
      g.FillRectangle(bBrush, x + w / 2, y - 2, , 4);
      g.FillRectangle(bBrush, x - 2, y + h / 2, 4, 4);
      g.FillRectangle(bBrush, x + (w / 2), y + h - 2, 4, );
      g.FillRectangle(bBrush, x + (w - 2),
                              y + (h / 2), 4, 4);
      }
      }
```

```
//-----
//return whether point is inside rectangle
public bool contains(int x, int y) {
      return rect.contains (x, y);
}
//------
//create Rectangle object from new position
private void saveAsRect() {
      rect = new CsharpPats.Rectangle (x,y,w,h);
}
```

We also use the same Rectangle class that we developed before that contains Get and Set properties for the x, y, w, and h values and a *contains* method.

Drawing the rectangle is pretty straightforward. Now, let's look at our simple Memento class that we use to store the state of a rectangle.

```
public class Memento        {
      private int x, y, w, h;
      private CsharpPats.Rectangle rect;
      private VisRectangle visRect;
      //------
      public Memento(VisRectangle vrect)                          {
            visRect = vrect;
            rect = visRect.rects ;
            x = rect.x ;
            y = rect.y;
            w = rect.w;
            h = rect.h;
      }
      //------
      public void restore() {
            rect.x = x;
            rect.y = y;
            rect.h = h;
            rect.w = w;
            visRect.rects = rect;
      }
}
```

When we create an instance of the Memento class, we pass it the VisRectangle instance we want to save, using the init method. It copies the size and position parameters and saves a copy of the instance of the VisRectangle itself. Later, when we want to restore these parameters, the Memento knows which instance to which it must restore them, and it can do it directly, as we see in the *restore()* method.

The rest of the activity takes place in the Mediator class, where we save the previous state of the list of drawings as an integer on the undo list.

```
public void createRect(int x, int y) {
      unpick();              //make sure none is selected
```

```
                    if (startRect) {  //if rect button is depressed
                          int count = drawings.Count;
                          caretakr.Add(count);  //Save list size
                          //create a rectangle
                          VisRectangle v = new VisRectangle(x, y);
                                drawings.Add(v);//add element to list
                          startRect = false;    //done with rectangle
                          rect.setSelected(false);    //unclick button
                          canvas.Refresh();
                    }
                    else
                          //if not pressed look for rect to select
                          pickRect(x, y);

                    }
        }
```

On the other hand, if you click on the panel when the Rectangle button has not been selected, you are trying to select an existing rectangle. This is tested here.

```
public void pickRect(int x, int y) {
        //save current selected rectangle
        //to avoid double save of undo
        int lastPick = -1;
        if (selectedIndex >= 0) {
                lastPick = selectedIndex;
        }
        unpick();  //undo any selection
        //see if one is being selected
        for (int i = 0; i< drawings.Count; i++) {
                VisRectangle v = (VisRectangle)drawings[i];
                if (v.contains(x, y)) {
                        //did click inside a rectangle
                        selectedIndex = i;     //save it
                        rectSelected = true;
                        if (selectedIndex != lastPick) {
                                //but don't save twice
                                caretakr.rememberPosition(v);
                        }
                        v.setSelected(true);     //turn on handles
                        repaint();            //and redraw
                }
        }
}
```

The Caretaker class remembers the previous position of the rectangle in a Memento object and adds it to the undo list.

```
public void rememberPosition(VisRectangle vr) {
        Memento mem = new Memento (vr);
        undoList.Add (mem);
}
```

The Caretaker class manages the undo list. This list is a Collection of integers and Memento objects. If the value is an integer, it represents the number of drawings to be drawn at that instant. If it is a Memento, it represents the previous state of a VisRectangle that is to be restored. In other words, the undo list can undo the adding of new rectangles and the movement of existing rectangles.

Our undo method simply decides whether to reduce the drawing list by one or to invoke the *restore* method of a Memento. Since the undo list contains both integer objects and Memento objects, we cast the list element to a Memento type, and if this fails, we catch the cast exception and recognize that it will be a drawing list element to be removed.

```
public void undo() {
      if(undoList.Count > 0) {
            int last = undoList.Count -1;
            object obj = undoList[last];
            try{
                  Memento mem = (Memento)obj;
                  remove(mem);
            }
            catch (Exception) {
                  removeDrawing();
            }
            undoList.RemoveAt (last);
      }
}
```

The two remove methods either reduce the number of drawings or restore the position of a rectangle.

```
public void removeDrawing() {
      drawings.RemoveAt (drawings.Count -1);
}
public void remove(Memento mem) {
      mem.restore ();
}
```

A Cautionary Note

While it is helpful in this example to call out the differences between a Memento of a rectangle position and an integer specifying the addition of a new drawing, this is in general an absolutely terrible example of OO programming. You should *never* need to check the type of an object to decide what to do with it. Instead, you should be able to call the correct method on that object and have it do the right thing.

A better way to have written this example would be to have both the drawing element and the Memento class have their own restore methods and have them both be members of a general Memento class (or interface). We take this approach in the State example pattern in Chapter 28.

Command Objects in the User Interface

We can also use the Command pattern to help simplify the code in the user interface. You can build a toolbar and create ToolbarButtons in C# using the IDE, but if you do, it is difficult to subclass them to make them into command objects. There are two possible solutions: First, you can keep a parallel array of Command objects for the RectButton, the UndoButton, and the Clear button and call them in the toolbar click routine.

You should note, however, that the toolbar buttons do not have an Index property, and you cannot just ask which one has been clicked by its index and relate it to the command array. Instead, we can use the GetHashCode property of each tool button to get a unique identifier for that button and keep the corresponding command objects in a Hashtable keyed off these button hash codes. We construct the Hashtable as follows.

```
private void init() {
        med = new Mediator(pic);       //create Mediator
        commands = new Hashtable();  //and Hash table
        //create the command objectsb
        RectButton rbutn = new RectButton(med, tbar.Buttons[0]);
        UndoButton ubutn = new UndoButton(med, tbar.Buttons[1]);
        ClrButton clrbutn = new ClrButton(med);
        med.registerRectButton (rbutn);
        //add them to the hashtable using the button hash values
        commands.Add(btRect.GetHashCode(), rbutn);
        commands.Add(btUndo.GetHashCode(), ubutn);
        commands.Add(btClear.GetHashCode(), clrbutn);
        pic.Paint += new PaintEventHandler (paintHandler);
}
```

Then the command interpretation devolves to just a few lines of code, since all the buttons call the same click event already. We can use these hash codes to get the right command object when the buttons are clicked.

```
private void tbar_ButtonClick(object sender,
                    ToolBarButtonClickEventArgs e) {
        ToolBarButton tbutn = e.Button ;
        Command comd = (Command)commands[tbutn.GetHashCode ()];
        comd.Execute ();
}
```

Alternatively, you could create the toolbar under IDE control but add the tool buttons to the collection programmatically and use derived buttons with a Command interface instead. We illustrate this approach in the State pattern.

The RectButton command class is where most of the activity takes place.

```
public class RectButton :  Command      {
     private ToolBarButton bt;
     private Mediator med;
     //------
     public RectButton(Mediator md, ToolBarButton tb)      {
          med = md;
          bt = tb;
     }
     //------
     public void setSelected(bool sel) {
          bt.Pushed  = sel;
     }
     //------
     public void Execute() {
          if(bt.Pushed  )
               med.startRectangle ();
     }
}
```

Handling Mouse and Paint Events

We also must catch the mouse down, up, and move events and pass them on to the Mediator to handle.

```
private void pic_MouseDown(object sender, MouseEventArgs e) {
     mouse_down = true;
     med.createRect (e.X, e.Y);
}
//------
private void pic_MouseUp(object sender, MouseEventArgs e) {
     mouse_down = false;
}
//------
private void pic_MouseMove(object sender, MouseEventArgs e) {
     if(mouse_down)
          med.drag(e.X , e.Y);
}
```

Whenever the Mediator makes a change, it calls for a refresh of the picture box, which in turn calls the Paint event. We then pass this back to the Mediator to draw the rectangles in their new positions.

```
private void paintHandler(object sender, PaintEventArgs e ) {
     Graphics g =  e.Graphics ;
     med.reDraw (g);
}
```

The complete class structure is diagrammed in Figure 26-4.

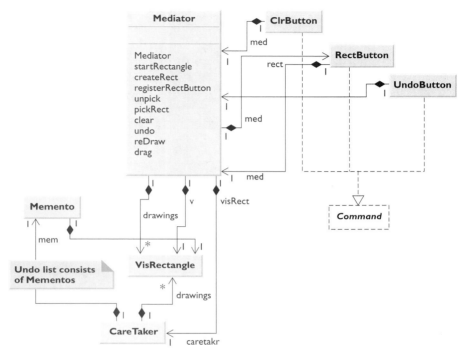

Figure 26-4   The UML diagram for the drawing program using a Memento

Consequences of the Memento

The Memento provides a way to preserve the state of an object while preserving encapsulation in languages where this is possible. Thus, data to which only the Originator class should have access effectively remain private. It also preserves the simplicity of the Originator class by delegating the saving and restoring of information to the Memento class.

On the other hand, the amount of information that a Memento has to save might be quite large, thus taking up fair amounts of storage. This further has an effect on the Caretaker class that may have to design strategies to limit the number of objects for which it saves state. In our simple example, we impose no such limits. In cases where objects change in a predictable manner, each Memento may be able to get by with saving only incremental changes of an object's state.

In our example code in this chapter, we have to use not only the Memento but the Command and Mediator patterns as well. This clustering of several patterns is very common, and the more you see of good OO programs, the more you will see these pattern groupings.

Thought Question

Mementos can also be used to restore the state of an object when a process fails. If a database update fails because of a dropped network connection, you should be able to restore the data in your cached data to their previous state. Rewrite the Database class in the Façade chapter to allow for such failures.

Program on the CD-ROM

| Memento Example | \Memento |

CHAPTER 27

The Observer Pattern

In this chapter we discuss how you can use the Observer pattern to present data in several forms at once. In our new, more sophisticated windowing world, we often would like to display data in more than one form at the same time and have all of the displays reflect any changes in that data. For example, you might represent stock price changes both as a graph and as a table or list box. Each time the price changes, we'd expect both representations to change at once without any action on our part.

We expect this sort of behavior because there are any number of Windows applications, like Excel, where we see that behavior. Now there is nothing inherent in Windows to allow this activity, and as you may know, programming directly in Windows in C or C++ is pretty complicated. In C#, however, we can easily use the Observer design pattern to make our program behave this way.

The Observer pattern assumes that the object containing the data is separate from the objects that display the data and that these display objects *observe* changes in that data. This is simple to illustrate, as we see in Figure 27-1.

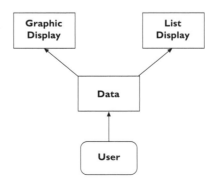

Figure 27-1 Data are displayed as a list and in some graphical mode.

313

When we implement the Observer pattern, we usually refer to the data as the Subject and each of the displays as an Observer. Each of these observers registers its interest in the data by calling a public method in the Subject. Then each observer has a known interface that the subject calls when the data change. We could define these interfaces as follows.

```
public interface Observer {
     void sendNotify(string message);
//-----
public interface Subject  {
     void registerInterest(Observer obs);
}
```

The advantages of defining these abstract interfaces are (1) you can write any sort of class objects you want as long as they implement these interfaces, and (2) you can declare these objects to be of type Subject and Observer no matter what else they do.

Watching Colors Change

Let's write a simple program to illustrate how we can use this powerful concept. Our program shows a display form containing three radio buttons named Red, Blue, and Green, as shown in Figure 27-2.

Figure 27-2   A simple control panel to create red, green, or blue "data"

Now our main form class implements the Subject interface. That means it must provide a public method for registering interest in the data in this class. This method is the *registerInterest* method, which just adds Observer objects to an ArrayList.

```
public void registerInterest(Observer obs ) {
     observers.Add (obs);
}
```

Now we create two observers: one that displays the color (and its name) and one that adds the current color to a list box. Each of these is actually a Windows form that also implements the Observer interface. When we create instances of these forms, we pass to them the base or startup form as an argument. Since this startup form is actually the Subject, they can register their interest in its events. So the main form's initialization creates these instances and passes them a reference to itself.

```
ListObs lobs = new ListObs (this);
lobs.Show ();
ColObserver colObs = new ColObserver (this);
colObs.Show();
```

Then when we create our ListObs window, we register our interest in the data in the main program.

```
public ListObs(Subject subj)                    {
     InitializeComponent();
     init(subj);
}
//------
public void init(Subject subj) {
     subj.registerInterest (this);
}
```

When it receives a sendNotify message from the main subject program, all it has to do is add the color name to the list.

```
public void sendNotify(string message){
     lsColors.Items.Add(message);
}
```

Our color window is also an observer, and it has to change the background color of the picture box and paint the color name using a brush. Note that we change the picture box's background color in the sendNotify event and change the text in a paint event. The entire class is shown here.

```
public class ColObserver : Form, Observer{
     private Container components = null;
     private Brush bBrush;
     private System.Windows.Forms.PictureBox pic;
     private Font fnt;
     private Hashtable colors;
```

```
            private string colName;
            //-----
            public ColObserver(Subject subj)            {
                    InitializeComponent();
                    init(subj);
            }
            //-----
            private void init(Subject subj) {
                    subj.registerInterest (this);
                    fnt = new Font("arial", 18, FontStyle.Bold);
                    bBrush = new SolidBrush(Color.Black);
                    pic.Paint+= new PaintEventHandler (paintHandler);
                    //make Hashtable for converting color strings
                    colors = new Hashtable ();
                    colors.Add("red", Color.Red );
                    colors.Add ("blue", Color.Blue );
                    colors.Add ("green", Color.Green );
                    colName = "";
            }
            //-----
            public void sendNotify(string message) {
                    colName = message;
                    message = message.ToLower ();
                    //convert color string to color object
                    Color col = (Color)colors[message];
                    pic.BackColor = col;
            }
            //-----
            private void paintHandler(object sender,
                        PaintEventArgs e) {
                    Graphics g = e.Graphics ;
                    g.DrawString(colName, fnt, bBrush, 20, 40)
            }
```

Note that our sendNotify event receives a string representing the color name and that we use a Hashtable to convert these strings to actual Color objects.

Meanwhile, in our main program, every time someone clicks on one of the radio buttons, it calls the *sendNotify* method of each Observer who has registered interest in these changes by simply running through the objects in the Observer's Collection.

```
private void opButton_Click(object sender, EventArgs e) {
    RadioButton but = (RadioButton)sender;
    for(int i=0; i< observers.Count ; i++ ) {
            Observer obs = (Observer)observers[i];
            obs.sendNotify (but.Text );
    }
}
```

In the case of the ColorForm observer, the sendNotify method changes the background color and the text string in the form Picturebox. In the case of the

ListForm observer, however, it just adds the name of the new color to the list box. We see the final program running in Figure 27-3 and a UML representation of the interfaces as in Figure 27-4.

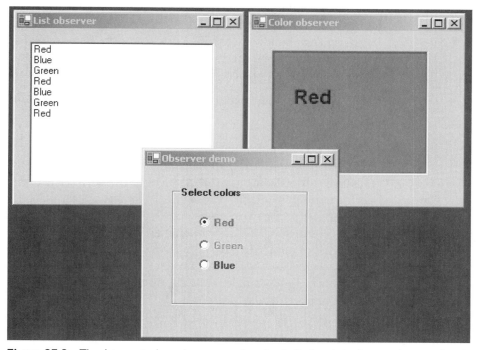

Figure 27-3 The data control panel generates data that is displayed simultaneously as a colored panel and as a list box. This is a candidate for an Observer pattern.

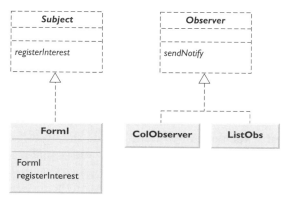

Figure 27-4 The observer interface and subject interface implementation of the Observer pattern

The Message to the Media

What kind of notification should a subject send to its observers? In this carefully circumscribed example, the notification message is the string representing the color itself. When we click on one of the radio buttons, we can get the caption for that button and send it to the observers. This, of course, assumes that all the observers can handle that string representation. In more realistic situations, this might not always be the case, especially if the observers could also be used to observe other data objects. Here we undertake two simple data conversions.

1. We get the label from the radio button and send it to the observers.

2. We convert the label to an actual color in the ColObserver.

In more complicated systems, we might have observers that demand specific, but different, kinds of data. Rather than have each observer convert the message to the right data type, we could use an intermediate Adapter class to perform this conversion.

Another problem observers may have to deal with is the case where the data of the central subject class can change in several ways. We could delete points from a list of data, edit their values, or change the scale of the data we are viewing. In these cases we either need to send different change messages to the observers or send a single message and then have the observer ask which sort of change has occurred.

Consequences of the Observer Pattern

Observers promote abstract coupling to subjects. A subject doesn't know the details of any of its observers. However, this has the potential disadvantage of successive or repeated updates to the observers when there are a series of incremental changes to the data. If the cost of these updates is high, it may be necessary to introduce some sort of change management so the observers are not notified too soon or too frequently.

When one client makes a change in the underlying data, you need to decide which object will initiate the notification of the change to the other observers. If the subject notifies all the observers when it is changed, each client is not responsible for remembering to initiate the notification. On the other hand, this can result in a number of small successive updates being triggered. If the clients tell the subject when to notify the other clients, this cascading notification can be avoided, but the clients are left with the responsibility of telling the subject when to send the notifications. If one client "forgets," the program simply won't work properly.

Finally, you can specify the kind of notification you choose to send by defining a number of update methods for the observers to receive, depending on the type or scope of change. In some cases, the clients will thus be able to ignore some of these notifications.

Program on the CD-ROM

Observer Example	\Observer

CHAPTER 28

The State Pattern

The State pattern is used when you want to have an object represent the state of your application and switch application states by switching objects. For example, you could have an enclosing class switch between a number of related contained classes and pass method calls on to the current contained class. *Design Patterns* suggests that the State pattern switches between internal classes in such a way that the enclosing object appears to change its class. In C#, at least, this is a bit of an exaggeration, but the actual purpose to which the classes are applied can change significantly.

Many programmers have had the experience of creating a class that performs slightly different computations or displays different information based on the arguments passed into the class. This frequently leads to some types of *select case* or *if-else* statements inside the class that determine which behavior to carry out. It is this inelegance that the State pattern seeks to replace.

Sample Code

Let's consider the case of a drawing program similar to the one we developed for the Memento class. Our program will have toolbar buttons for Select, Rectangle, Circle, Fill, Undo, and Clear. We show this program in Figure 28-1.

Each one of the tool buttons does something rather different when it is selected, and you click or drag your mouse across the screen. Thus, the *state* of the graphical editor affects the behavior the program should exhibit. This suggests some sort of design using the State pattern.

Initially we might design our program like this, with a Mediator managing the actions of five command buttons, as shown in Figure 28-2.

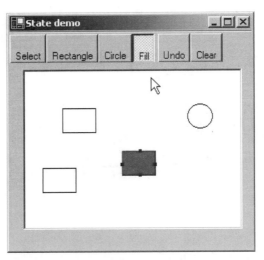

Figure 28-1   A simple drawing program for illustrating the State pattern

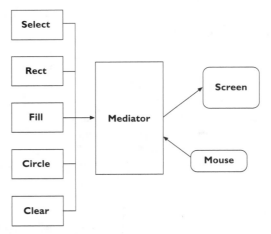

Figure 28-2   One possible interaction between the classes needed to support the
simple drawing program

However, this initial design puts the entire burden of maintaining the
state of the program on the Mediator, and we know that the main purpose of a
Mediator is to coordinate activities between various controls, such as the buttons. Keeping the state of the buttons and the desired mouse activity inside the
Mediator can make it unduly complicated, as well as result in a set of *If* or *Select*
tests that can make the program difficult to read and maintain.

Further, this set of large, monolithic conditional statements might have
to be repeated for each action the Mediator interprets, such as mouseUp,

mouseDrag, rightClick, and so forth. This makes the program very hard to read and maintain.

Instead, let's analyze the expected behavior for each of the buttons.

1. If the Select button is selected, clicking inside a drawing element should cause it to be highlighted or appear with "handles." If the mouse is dragged and a drawing element is already selected, the element should move on the screen.

2. If the Rect button is selected, clicking on the screen should cause a new rectangle drawing element to be created.

3. If the Fill button is selected and a drawing element is already selected, that element should be filled with the current color. If no drawing is selected, then clicking inside a drawing should fill it with the current color.

4. If the Circle button is selected, clicking on the screen should cause a new circle drawing element to be created.

5. If the Clear button is selected, all the drawing elements are removed.

There are some common threads among several of these actions that we should explore. Four of them use the mouse click event to cause actions. One uses the mouse drag event to cause an action. Thus, we really want to create a system that can help us redirect these events based on which button is currently selected.

Let's consider creating a State object that handles mouse activities.

```
public class State    {
     //keeps state of each button
     protected Mediator med;
     public State(Mediator md) {
          med = md;    //save reference to mediator
     }
     public virtual void mouseDown(int x, int y) {}
     public virtual void mouseUp(int x, int y) {    }
     public virtual void mouseDrag(int x, int y) {}
}
```

Note that we are creating an actual class here with empty methods rather than an interface. This allows us to derive new State objects from this class and only have to fill in the mouse actions that actually do anything for that case. Then we'll create four derived State classes for Pick, Rect, Circle, and Fill and put instances of all of them inside a StateManager class that sets the current state and executes methods on that state object. In *Design Patterns*, this State-Manager class is referred to as a *Context*. This object is illustrated in Figure 28-3.

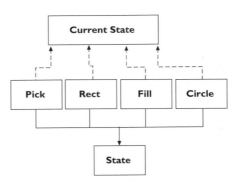

Figure 28-3   A StateManager class that keeps track of the current state

A typical State object simply overrides those event methods that it must handle specially. For example, this is the complete Rectangle state object. Note that since it only needs to respond to the mouseDown event, we don't have to write any code at all for the other events.

```
public class RectState :State    {
    public RectState(Mediator md) :base (md) {}
    //-----
    public override void mouseDown(int x, int y) {
        VisRectangle vr = new VisRectangle(x, y);
        med.addDrawing (vr);
    }
}
```

The RectState object simply tells the Mediator to add a rectangle drawing to the drawing list. Similarly, the Circle state object tells the Mediator to add a circle to the drawing list.

```
public class CircleState : State {
    public CircleState(Mediator md) :base (md){ }
    //-----
    public override void mouseDown(int x, int y) {
        VisCircle c = new VisCircle(x, y);
        med.addDrawing (c);
    }
}
```

The only tricky button is the Fill button because we have defined two actions for it.

1. If an object is already selected, fill it.

2. If the mouse is clicked inside an object, fill that one.

In order to carry out these tasks, we need to add the *selectOne* method to our base State interface. This method is called when each tool button is selected.

```
public class State    {
     //keeps state of each button
     protected Mediator med;
     public State(Mediator md) {
          med = md;      //save reference to mediator
     }
     public virtual void mouseDown(int x, int y) {}
     public virtual void mouseUp(int x, int y) {}
     public virtual void mouseDrag(int x, int y) {}
     public virtual void selectOne(Drawing d) {}
}
```

The Drawing argument is either the currently selected Drawing or null if
none is selected. In this simple program, we have arbitrarily set the fill color to
red, so our Fill state class becomes the following.

```
public class FillState : State   {
     public FillState(Mediator md): base(md) { }
     //-----
     public override void mouseDown(int x, int y) {
          //Fill drawing if you click inside one
          int i = med.findDrawing(x, y);
          if (i >= 0) {
               Drawing d = med.getDrawing(i);
               d.setFill(true);  //fill drawing
          }
     }
     //-----
     public override void selectOne(Drawing d) {
          //fill drawing if selected
          d.setFill (true);
     }
}
```

Switching between States

Now that we have defined how each state behaves when mouse events are sent
to it, we need to examine how the StateManager switches between states. We
create an instance of each state, and then we simply set the currentState variable
to the state indicated by the button that is selected.

```
public class StateManager {
     private State currentState;
     private RectState rState;
     private ArrowState aState;
     private CircleState cState;
     private FillState fState;

     public StateManager(Mediator med)                            {
          //create an instance of each state
          rState = new RectState(med);
```

```
          cState = new CircleState(med);
          aState = new ArrowState(med);
          fState = new FillState(med);
          //and initialize them
          //set default state
          currentState = aState;
     }
```

Note that in this version of the StateManager, we create an instance of each state during the constructor and copy the correct one into the state variable when the set methods are called. It would also be possible to create these states on demand. This might be advisable if there are a large number of states that each consume a fair number of resources.

The remainder of the StateManager code simply calls the methods of whichever state object is current. This is the critical piece—there is no conditional testing. Instead, the correct state is already in place, and its methods are ready to be called.

```
    public void mouseDown(int x, int y) {
          currentState.mouseDown (x, y);
    }
    public void mouseUp(int x, int y) {
          currentState.mouseUp (x, y);
    }
    public void mouseDrag(int x, int y) {
          currentState.mouseDrag (x, y);
    }
    public void selectOne(Drawing d) {
          currentState.selectOne (d);
    }
```

How the Mediator Interacts with the StateManager

We mentioned that it is clearer to separate the state management from the Mediator's button and mouse event management. The Mediator is the critical class, however, since it tells the StateManager when the current program state changes. The beginning part of the Mediator illustrates how this state change takes place. Note that each button click calls one of these methods and changes the state of the application. The remaining statements in each method simply turn off the other toggle buttons so only one button at a time can be depressed.

```
public class Mediator         {
     private bool startRect;
     private int selectedIndex;
     private RectButton rectb;
     private bool dSelected;
     private ArrayList drawings;
```

```
            private ArrayList undoList;
            private RectButton rButton;
            private FillButton filButton;
            private CircleButton circButton;
            private PickButton arrowButton;
            private PictureBox canvas;
            private int selectedDrawing;
            private StateManager stMgr;
            //-----
            public Mediator(PictureBox pic)                   {
                    startRect = false;
                    dSelected = false;
                    drawings = new ArrayList();
                    undoList = new ArrayList();
                    stMgr = new StateManager(this);
                    canvas = pic;
                    selectedDrawing = -1;
            }
            //-----
            public void startRectangle() {
                    stMgr.setRect();
                    arrowButton.setSelected(false);
                    circButton.setSelected(false);
                    filButton.setSelected(false);
            }
            //-----
            public void startCircle() {
                    stMgr.setCircle();
                    rectb.setSelected(false);
                    arrowButton.setSelected(false);
                    filButton.setSelected(false);
            }
```

The ComdToolBarButton

In the discussion of the Memento pattern, we created a series of button Command objects paralleling the toolbar buttons and keep them in a Hashtable to be called when the toolbar button click event occurs. However, a powerful alternative is to create a ComdToolBarButton class that implements the Command interface as well as being a ToolBarButton. Then, each button can have an Execute method that defines its purpose. Here is the base class.

```
public class ComdToolBarButton : ToolBarButton , Command     {
      private System.ComponentModel.Container components = null;
      protected Mediator med;
      protected  bool selected;
      public ComdToolBarButton(string caption, Mediator md)
      {
              InitializeComponent();
              med = md;
```

```
            this.Text =caption;
    }
    //------
    public void setSelected(bool b) {
            selected = b;
            if(!selected)
                    this.Pushed =false;
    }
    //-----
    public virtual void Execute() {
    }
```

Note that the Execute method is empty in this base class, but it is virtual, so we can override it in each derived class. In this case, we cannot use the IDE to create the toolbar but can simply add the buttons to the toolbar programmatically.

```
private void init() {
            //create a Mediator
            med = new Mediator(pic);
            //create the buttons
            rctButton = new RectButton(med);
            arowButton = new PickButton(med);
            circButton = new CircleButton(med);
            flButton = new FillButton(med);
            undoB = new UndoButton(med);
            clrb = new ClearButton(med);
            //add the buttons into the toolbar
            tBar.Buttons.Add(arowButton);
            tBar.Buttons.Add(rctButton);
            tBar.Buttons.Add(circButton);
            tBar.Buttons.Add(flButton);
            //include a separator
            ToolBarButton sep =new ToolBarButton();
            sep.Style = ToolBarButtonStyle.Separator;
            tBar.Buttons.Add(sep);
            tBar.Buttons.Add(undoB);
            tBar.Buttons.Add(clrb);
    }
```

Then we can catch all the toolbar button click events in a single method and call each button's Execute method.

```
private void tBar_ButtonClick(object sender,
            ToolBarButtonClickEventArgs e) {
    Command comd = (Command)e.Button ;
    comd.Execute ();
}
```

The class diagram for this program illustrating the State pattern in this application is illustrated in two parts. The State section is shown in Figure 28-4.

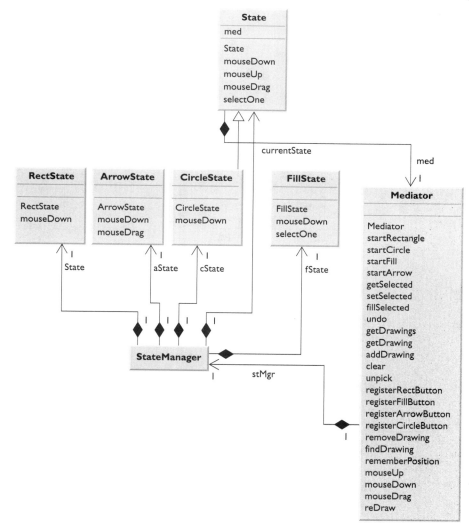

Figure 28-4 The StateManager and the Mediator

The connection of the Mediator to the buttons is shown in Figure 28-5.

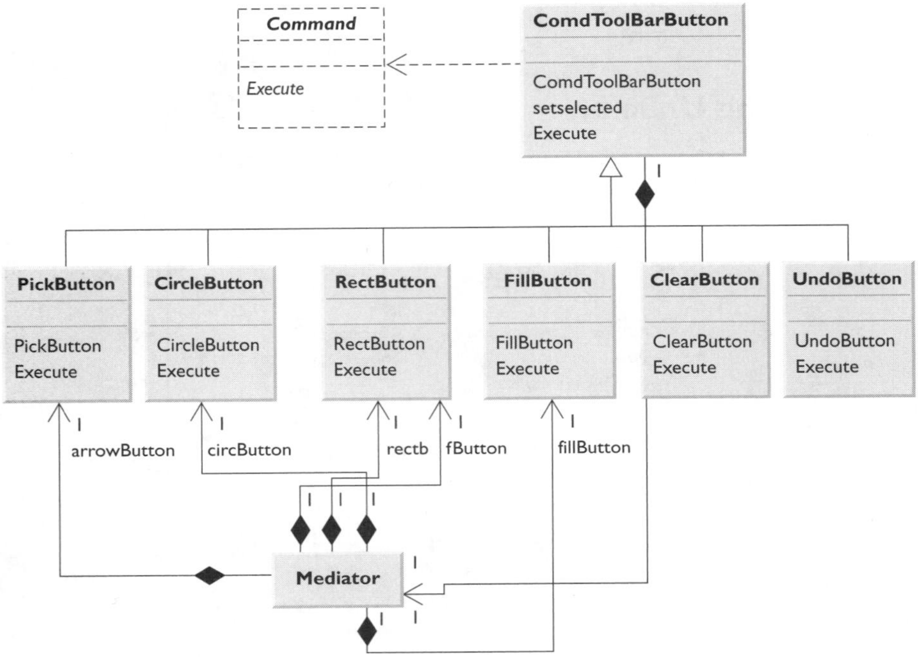

Figure 28-5   Interaction between the buttons and the Mediator

Handling the Fill State

The Fill State object is only slightly more complex because we have to handle two cases. The program will fill the currently selected object if one exists or fill the next one that you click on. This means there are two State methods we have to fill in for these two cases, as we see here.

```
public class FillState : State   {
    public FillState(Mediator md): base(md) { }
    //-----
    public override void mouseDown(int x, int y) {
        //Fill drawing if you click inside one
        int i = med.findDrawing(x, y);
        if (i >= 0) {
            Drawing d = med.getDrawing(i);
            d.setFill(true);  //fill drawing
        }
    }
    //-----
    public override void selectOne(Drawing d) {
```

```
                    //fill drawing if selected
                    d.setFill (true);
           }
       }
```

Handling the Undo List

Now we should be able to undo each of the actions we carry out in this drawing program, and this means that we keep them in an undo list of some kind. These are the actions we can carry out and undo.

1. Creating a rectangle

2. Creating a circle

3. Moving a rectangle or circle

4. Filling a rectangle or circle

In our discussion of the Memento pattern, we indicated that we would use a Memento object to store the state of the rectangle object and restore its position from that Memento as needed. This is generally true for both rectangles and circles, since we need to save and restore the same kind of position information. However, the addition of rectangles or circles and the filling of various figures are also activities we want to be able to undo. And, as we indicated in our previous Memento discussion, the idea of checking for the type of object in the undo list and performing the correct undo operation is a really terrible idea.

```
//really terrible programming approach
    object obj = undoList[last];
    try{
            Memento mem = (Memento)obj;
            remove(mem);
    }
    catch (Exception) {
            removeDrawing();
    }
```

Instead, let's define the Memento as an interface.

```
public interface Memento    {
      void restore();
}
```

Then all of the objects we add into the undo list will implement the Memento interface and will have a restore method that performs some operation. Some kinds of Mementos will save and restore the coordinates of drawings, and others will simply remove drawings or undo fill states.

First, we will have both our circle and rectangle objects implement the Drawing interface.

```
public interface Drawing  {
     void setSelected(bool b);
     void draw(Graphics g);
     void move(int xpt, int ypt );
     bool contains(int x,int y);
     void setFill(bool b);
     CsharpPats.Rectangle getRects();
     void setRects(CsharpPats.Rectangle rect);
}
```

The Memento we will use for saving the state of a Drawing will be similar to the one we used in the Memento chapter, except that we specifically make it implement the Memento interface.

```
public class DrawMemento : Memento      {
     private int x, y, w, h;
     private Rectangle  rect;
     private Drawing visDraw;
     //------
     public DrawMemento(Drawing d)     {
            visDraw = d;
            rect = visDraw.getRects ();
            x = rect.x;
            y = rect.y ;
            w = rect.w;
            h = rect.h;
     }
     //-----
     public void restore() {
            //restore the state of a drawing object
            rect.x = x;
            rect.y = y;
            rect.h = h;
            rect.w = w;
            visDraw.setRects( rect);
     }
     }
```

Now for the case where we just want to remove a drawing from the list to be redrawn, we create a class to remember that index of that drawing and remove it when its *restore* method is called.

```
public class DrawInstance :Memento {
     private int intg;
     private Mediator med;
     //-----
     public DrawInstance(int intg, Mediator md)      {
            this.intg = intg;
            med = md;
```

```
        }
        //-----
        public int integ {
                get { return intg;                            }
        }
        //-----
        public void restore() {
                med.removeDrawing(intg);
        }
}
```

We handle the FillMemento in just the same way, except that its restore method
turns off the fill flag for that drawing element.

```
public class FillMemento : Memento      {
        private int index;
        private Mediator med;
        //-----
        public FillMemento(int dindex, Mediator md) {
                index = dindex;
                med = md;
        }
        //-----
        public void restore() {
                Drawing d = med.getDrawing(index);
                d.setFill(false);
        }
}
```

The VisRectangle and VisCircle Classes

We can take some useful advantage of inheritance in designing our VisRectangle
and VisCircle classes. We make VisRectangle *implement* the Drawing interface and then have VisCircle *inherit* from VisRectangle. This allows us to reuse
the setSelected, setFill, and move methods and the rects properties. In addition,
we can split off the drawHandle method and use it in both classes. Our new
VisRectangle class looks like this.

```
public class VisRectangle : Drawing      {
        protected int x, y, w, h;
        private const int SIZE=30;
        private CsharpPats.Rectangle rect;
        protected bool selected;
        protected bool filled;
        protected Pen bPen;
        protected SolidBrush bBrush, rBrush;
        //-----
        public VisRectangle(int xp, int yp)                  {
                x = xp;                      y = yp;
                w = SIZE;                    h = SIZE;
```

```
            saveAsRect();
            bPen = new Pen(Color.Black);
            bBrush = new SolidBrush(Color.Black);
            rBrush = new SolidBrush (Color.Red );
      }
      //-----
      //used by Memento for saving and restoring state
      public CsharpPats.Rectangle getRects() {
            return rect;
      }
      //-----
      public void setRects(CsharpPats.Rectangle value) {
                  x=value.x;                y=value.y;
                  w=value.w;                h=value.h;
                  saveAsRect();
      }
      //------
      public void setSelected(bool b) {
            selected = b;
      }
      //-----
      //move to new position
      public void move(int xp, int yp) {
            x = xp;        y = yp;
            saveAsRect();
      }
      //-----
      public virtual void draw(Graphics g) {
            //draw rectangle
            g.DrawRectangle(bPen, x, y, w, h);
            if(filled)
                  g.FillRectangle (rBrush, x,y,w,h);
            drawHandles(g);
      }
      //-----
      public void drawHandles(Graphics g) {
      if (selected) {    //draw handles
            g.FillRectangle(bBrush, x + w / 2, y - 2, 4, );
            g.FillRectangle(bBrush, x - 2, y + h / 2, 4, );
            g.FillRectangle(bBrush, x + (w / 2),
                  y + h - 2, 4, 4);
            g.FillRectangle(bBrush, x + (w - 2),
            y + (h / 2), 4, 4);
      }
      }
      //-----
      //return whether point is inside rectangle
      public bool contains(int x, int y) {
            return rect.contains (x, y);
      }
      //------
      //create Rectangle object from new position
      protected void saveAsRect() {
            rect = new CsharpPats.Rectangle (x,y,w,h);
      }
```

```
public void setFill(bool b) {
       filled = b;
}
```

However, our VisCircle class only needs to override the draw method and have a slightly different constructor.

```
public class VisCircle : VisRectangle   {
      private int r;
      public VisCircle(int x, int y):base(x, y)                    {
            r = 15; w = 30; h = 30;
            saveAsRect();
      }
      //-----
      public override void draw(Graphics g) {
            if (filled) {
                    g.FillEllipse(rBrush, x, y, w, h);
            }
      g.DrawEllipse(bPen, x, y, w, h);
      if (selected ){
            drawHandles(g);
            }
      }
}
```

Note that since we have made the x, y, and filled variables protected, we can refer to them in the derived VisCircle class without declaring them at all.

Mediators and the God Class

One big problem with programs when this many objects are interacting is putting too much knowledge of the system into the Mediator so it becomes a "god class." In the preceding example, the Mediator communicates with the six buttons, the drawing list, and the StateManager. We could write this program another way so that the button Command objects communicate with the State-Manager and the Mediator only deals with the buttons and the drawing list. Here, each button creates an instance of the required state and sends it to the StateManager. This we will leave as an exercise for the reader.

Consequences of the State Pattern

1. The State pattern creates a subclass of a basic State object for each state an application can have and switches between them as the application changes between states.

2. You don't need to have a long set of conditional *if* or *switch* statements associated with the various states, since each is encapsulated in a class.

3. Since there is no variable anywhere that specifies which state a program is in, this approach reduces errors caused by programmers forgetting to test this state variable.

4. You could share state objects between several parts of an application, such as separate windows, as long as none of the state objects have specific instance variables. In this example, only the FillState class has an instance variable, and this could be easily rewritten to be an argument passed in each time.

5. This approach generates a number of small class objects but in the process simplifies and clarifies the program.

6. In C#, all of the States must implement a common interface, and they must thus all have common methods, although some of those methods can be empty. In other languages, the states can be implemented by function pointers with much less type checking and, of course, greater chance of error.

State Transitions

The transition between states can be specified internally or externally. In our example, the Mediator tells the StateManager when to switch between states. However, it is also possible that each state can decide automatically what each successor state will be. For example, when a rectangle or circle drawing object is created, the program could automatically switch back to the Arrow-object State.

Thought Questions

1. Rewrite the StateManager to use a Factory pattern to produce the states on demand.

2. While visual graphics programs provide obvious examples of State patterns, server programs can benefit from this approach. Outline a simple server that uses a State pattern.

Program on the CD-ROM

State Drawing Program	\State

CHAPTER 29

The Strategy Pattern

The Strategy pattern is much like the State pattern in outline but a little different in intent. The Strategy pattern consists of a number of related algorithms encapsulated in a driver class called the Context. Your client program can select one of these differing algorithms, or in some cases, the Context might select the best one for you. The intent is to make these algorithms interchangeable and provide a way to choose the most appropriate one. The difference between State and Strategy is that the user generally chooses which of several strategies to apply and that only one strategy at a time is likely to be instantiated and active within the Context class. By contrast, as we have seen, it is possible that all of the different States will be active at once, and switching may occur frequently between them. In addition, Strategy encapsulates several algorithms that do more or less the same thing, whereas State encapsulates related classes that each do something somewhat differently. Finally, the concept of transition between different States is completely missing in the Strategy pattern.

Motivation

A program that requires a particular service or function and that has several ways of carrying out that function is a candidate for the Strategy pattern. Programs choose between these algorithms based on computational efficiency or user choice. There can be any number of strategies, more can be added, and any of them can be changed at any time.

There are a number of cases in programs where we'd like to do the same thing in several different ways. Some of these are listed in the *Smalltalk Companion*.

- Save files in different formats
- Compress files using different algorithms

- Capture video data using different compression schemes
- Use different line-breaking strategies to display text data
- Plot the same data in different formats: line graph, bar chart, or pie chart

In each case we could imagine the client program telling a driver module (Context) which of these strategies to use and then asking it to carry out the operation.

The idea behind Strategy is to encapsulate the various strategies in a single module and provide a simple interface to allow choice between these strategies. Each of them should have the same programming interface, although they need not all be members of the same class hierarchy. However, they do have to implement the same programming interface.

Sample Code

Let's consider a simplified graphing program that can present data as a line graph or a bar chart. We'll start with an abstract PlotStrategy class and derive the two plotting classes from it, as illustrated in Figure 29-1.

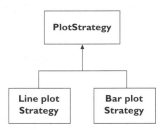

Figure 29-1   Two instances of a PlotStrategy class

Our base PlotStrategy class is an abstract class containing the plot routine to be filled in in the derived strategy classes. It also contains the max and min computation code, which we will use in the derived classes by containing an instance of this class.

```
public abstract class PlotStrategy     {
     public abstract void plot( float[] x, float[] y);
}
```

Then one of the derived classes must implement a method called *plot* with two float arrays as arguments. Each of these classes can do any kind of plot that is appropriate.

The Context

The Context class is the traffic cop that decides which strategy is to be called. The decision is usually based on a request from the client program, and all that the Context needs to do is set a variable to refer to one concrete strategy or another.

```
public class Context        {
    float[] x, y;
    PlotStrategy plts;  //strategy selected goes here
    //-----
    public void plot() {
        readFile();          //read in data
        plts.plot (x, y);
    }
    //-----
    //select bar plot
    public void setBarPlot() {
        plts = new BarPlotStrategy ();
    }
    //-----
    //select line plot
    public void setLinePlot() {
        plts = new LinePlotStrategy();
    }
    //-----
    public void readFile()           {
    //reads data in from data file
    }
}
```

The Context class is also responsible for handling the data. Either it obtains the data from a file or database or it is passed in when the Context is created. Depending on the magnitude of the data, it can either be passed on to the plot strategies or the Context can pass an instance of itself into the plot strategies and provide a public method to fetch the data.

The Program Commands

This simple program (Figure 29-2) is just a panel with two buttons that call the two plots. Each of the buttons is a derived Button class that implements the Command interface. It selects the correct strategy and then calls the Context's plot routine. For example, here is the complete Line graph command Button class.

```
public class LineButton : System.Windows.Forms.Button, Command
{
    private System.ComponentModel.Container components = null;
    private Context contxt;
```

```
public LineButton()    {
        InitializeComponent();
        this.Text = "Line plot";
}
public void setContext(Context ctx) {
        contxt = ctx;
}
public void Execute() {
        contxt.setLinePlot();
        contxt.plot();
}
```

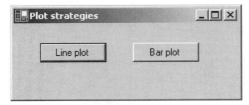

Figure 29-2   A simple panel to call two different plots

The Line and Bar Graph Strategies

The two Strategy classes are pretty much the same: They set up the window size for plotting and call a plot method specific for that display panel. Here is the LinePlotStrategy.

```
public class LinePlotStrategy : PlotStrategy   {
    public override void plot(float[] x, float[] y) {
            LinePlot lplt = new LinePlot();
            lplt.Show ();
            lplt.plot (x, y);
    }
}
```

The BarPlotStrategy is more or less identical.

The plotting amounts to copying in a reference to the x and y arrays, calling the scaling routine, and then causing the Picturebox control to be refreshed, which will then call the paint routine to paint the bars.

```
public void plot(float[] xp, float[] yp) {
    x = xp;
    y = yp;
    setPlotBounds();        //compute scaling factors
    hasData = true;
    pic.Refresh();
}
```

Drawing Plots in C#

Note that both the LinePlot and the BarPlot window have plot methods that are called by the plot methods of the LinePlotStrategy and BarPlotStrategy classes. Both plot windows have a setBounds method that computes the scaling between the window coordinates and the x-y coordinate scheme. Since they can use the same scaling function, we write it once in the BarPlot window and derive the LinePlot window from it to use the same methods.

```
public virtual void setPlotBounds() {
     findBounds();
     //compute scaling factors
     h = pic.Height;
     w = pic.Width;
     xfactor = 0.8F * w / (xmax - xmin);
     xpmin = 0.05F * w;
     xpmax = w - xpmin;
     yfactor = 0.9F * h / (ymax - ymin);
     ypmin = 0.05F * h;
     ypmax = h - ypmin;
     //create array of colors for bars
     colors = new ArrayList();
     colors.Add(new SolidBrush(Color.Red));
     colors.Add(new SolidBrush(Color.Green));
     colors.Add(new SolidBrush(Color.Blue));
     colors.Add(new SolidBrush(Color.Magenta));
     colors.Add(new SolidBrush(Color.Yellow));
}
//-----
public int calcx(float xp) {
     int ix = (int)((xp - xmin) * xfactor + xpmin);
     return ix;
}
//-----
public int calcy(float yp) {
     yp = ((yp - ymin) * yfactor);
     int iy = h - (int)(ypmax - yp);
     return iy;
}
```

Making Bar Plots

The actual bar plot is drawn in a Paint routine that is called when a paint event occurs.

```
protected virtual void pic_Paint(object sender, PaintEventArgs e)
{
     Graphics g = e.Graphics;
     if (hasData) {
```

```
            for (int i = 0; i< x.Length; i++){
                    int ix = calcx(x[i]);
                    int iy = calcy(y[i]);
                    Brush br = (Brush)colors[i];
                    g.FillRectangle(br, ix, h - iy, 20, iy);
            }
        }
    }
```

Making Line Plots

The LinePlot class is very simple, since we derive it from the BarPlot class, and we need only write a new Paint method.

```
public class LinePlot :BarPlot {
        public LinePlot() {
                bPen = new Pen(Color.Black);
                this.Text = "Line Plot";
        }
        protected override void pic_Paint(object sender,
                        PaintEventArgs e) {
                Graphics g= e.Graphics;
                if (hasData) {
                        for (int i = 1; i< x.Length; i++) {
                                int ix = calcx(x[i - 1]);
                                int iy = calcy(y[i - 1]);
                                int ix1 = calcx(x[i]);
                                int iy1 = calcy(y[i]);
                                g.DrawLine(bPen, ix, iy, ix1, iy1);
                        }
                }
        }
}
```

The UML diagram of these class relations is shown in Figure 29-3. The final two plots are shown in Figure 29-4.

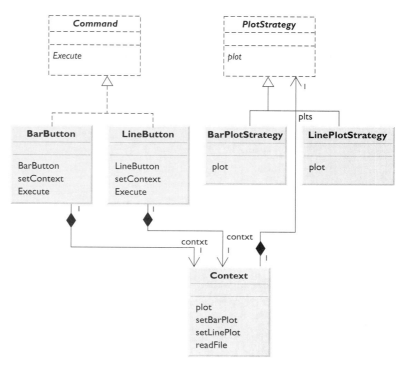

Figure 29-3 The UML diagram of the Strategy pattern

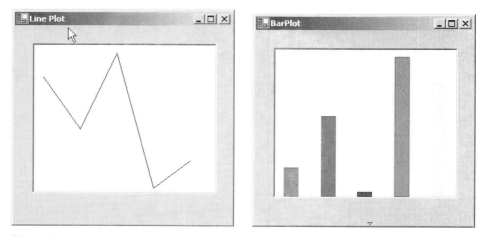

Figure 29-4 The line graph (left) and the bar graph (right)

Consequences of the Strategy Pattern

Strategy allows you to select one of several algorithms dynamically. These algorithms can be related in an inheritance hierarchy, or they can be unrelated as long as they implement a common interface. Since the Context switches between strategies at your request, you have more flexibility than if you simply called the desired derived class. This approach also avoids the sort of condition statements that can make code hard to read and maintain.

On the other hand, strategies don't hide everything. The client code is usually aware that there are a number of alternative strategies, and it has some criteria for choosing among them. This shifts an algorithmic decision to the client programmer or the user.

Since there are a number of different parameters that you might pass to different algorithms, you have to develop a Context interface and strategy methods that are broad enough to allow for passing in parameters that are not used by that particular algorithm. For example, the *setPenColor* method in our Plot-Strategy is actually only used by the LineGraph strategy. It is ignored by the BarGraph strategy, since it sets up its own list of colors for the successive bars it draws.

Program on the CD-ROM

Plot Strategy	\Strategy

CHAPTER 30

The Template Method Pattern

The Template Method pattern is a very simple pattern that you will find yourself using frequently. Whenever you write a parent class where you leave one or more of the methods to be implemented by derived classes, you are in essence using the Template pattern. The Template pattern formalizes the idea of defining an algorithm in a class but leaving some of the details to be implemented in subclasses. In other words, if your base class is an abstract class, as often happens in these design patterns, you are using a simple form of the Template pattern.

Motivation

Templates are so fundamental, you have probably used them dozens of times without even thinking about it. The idea behind the Template pattern is that some parts of an algorithm are well defined and can be implemented in the base class, whereas other parts may have several implementations and are best left to derived classes. Another main theme is recognizing that there are some basic parts of a class that can be factored out and put in a base class so they do not need to be repeated in several subclasses.

For example, in developing the BarPlot and LinePlot classes we used in the Strategy pattern examples in the previous chapter, we discovered that in plotting both line graphs and bar charts we needed similar code to scale the data and compute the x and y pixel positions.

```
public abstract class PlotWindow : Form {
    protected float ymin, ymax, xfactor, yfactor;
    protected float xpmin, xpmax, ypmin, ypmax, xp, yp;
    private float xmin, xmax;
    protected int w, h;
    protected float[] x, y;
```

```
protected Pen bPen;
protected bool hasData;
protected const float max = 1.0e38f;
protected PictureBox pic;
//-----
protected virtual void init() {
      pic.Paint += new PaintEventHandler (pic_Paint);
}
//-----
public void setPenColor(Color c){
      bPen = new Pen(c);
}
//-----
public void plot(float[] xp, float[] yp) {
      x = xp;
      y = yp;
      setPlotBounds();      //compute scaling factors
      hasData = true;
}
//-----
public void findBounds() {
      xmin = max;
      xmax = -max;
      ymin = max;
      ymax = -max;
      for (int i = 0; i<  x.Length ; i++) {
              if (x[i] > xmax) xmax = x[i];
              if (x[i] < xmin) xmin = x[i];
              if (y[i] > ymax) ymax = y[i];
              if (y[i] < ymin) ymin = y[i];
      }
}
//-----
public virtual void setPlotBounds() {
      findBounds();
      //compute scaling factors
      h = pic.Height;
      w = pic.Width;
      xfactor = 0.8F * w / (xmax - xmin);
      xpmin = 0.05F * w;
      xpmax = w - xpmin;
      yfactor = 0.9F * h / (ymax - ymin);
      ypmin = 0.05F * h;
      ypmax = h - ypmin;
}
//-----
public int calcx(float xp) {
      int ix = (int)((xp - xmin) * xfactor + xpmin);
      return ix;
}
//-----
public int calcy(float yp) {
      yp = ((yp - ymin) * yfactor);
      int iy = h - (int)(ypmax - yp);
```

```
            return iy;
    }
    //-----
    public abstract void repaint(Graphics g) ;
    //-----
    protected virtual void pic_Paint(object sender,
                        PaintEvntArgs e) {
        Graphics g = e.Graphics;
        repaint(g);
    }
}
```

Thus, these methods all belong in a base PlotPanel class without any actual plotting capabilities. Note that the pic_Paint event handler just calls the abstract *repaint* method. The actual repaint method is deferred to the derived classes. It is exactly this sort of extension to derived classes that exemplifies the Template Method pattern.

Kinds of Methods in a Template Class

As discussed in *Design Patterns*, the Template Method pattern has four kinds of methods that you can use in derived classes.

1. Complete methods that carry out some basic function that all the subclasses will want to use, such as *calcx* and *calcy* in the preceding example. These are called *concrete* methods.

2. Methods that are not filled in at all and must be implemented in derived classes. In C#, you would declare these as *virtual* methods.

3. Methods that contain a default implementation of some operations but that may be overridden in derived classes. These are called *hook* methods. Of course, this is somewhat arbitrary because in C# you can override any public or protected method in the derived class but hook methods, however, are intended to be overridden, whereas concrete methods are not.

4. Finally, a Template class may contain methods that themselves call any combination of abstract, hook, and concrete methods. These methods are not intended to be overridden but describe an algorithm without actually implementing its details. *Design Patterns* refers to these as Template methods.

Sample Code

Let's consider a simple program for drawing triangles on a screen. We'll start with an abstract Triangle class and then derive some special triangle types from it, as we see in Figure 30-1.

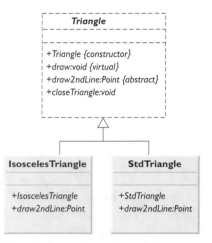

Figure 30-1   The abstract Triangle class and two of its subclasses

Our abstract Triangle class illustrates the Template pattern.

```
public abstract class Triangle     {
      private Point p1, p2, p3;
      protected Pen pen;
      //-----
      public Triangle(Point a, Point b, Point c) {
            p1 = a;
            p2 =  b;
            p3 = c;
            pen = new Pen(Color.Black , 1);
      }
      //-----
      public virtual void draw(Graphics g) {
            g.DrawLine (pen, p1, p2);
            Point c = draw2ndLine(g, p2, p3);
            closeTriangle(g, c);
      }
      //-----
      public abstract Point draw2ndLine(Graphics g,
                          Point a, Point b);
      //-----
      public void closeTriangle(Graphics g, Point c) {
            g.DrawLine (pen, c, p1);
      }
}
```

This Triangle class saves the coordinates of three lines, but the *draw* routine draws only the first and the last lines. The all-important *draw2ndLine* method that draws a line to the third point is left as an abstract method. That way the derived class can move the third point to create the kind of rectangle you wish to draw.

This is a general example of a class using the Template pattern. The *draw* method calls two concrete base class methods and one abstract method that must be overridden in any concrete class derived from Triangle.

Another very similar way to implement the Triangle class is to include default code for the *draw2ndLine* method.

```
public virtual void draw2ndLine(Graphics g,
                Point a, Point b) {
    g.drawLine(a, b);
}
```

In this case, the *draw2ndLine* method becomes a Hook method that can be overridden for other classes.

Drawing a Standard Triangle

To draw a general triangle with no restrictions on its shape, we simply implement the *draw2ndLine* method in a derived *stdTriangle* class.

```
public class StdTriangle :Triangle          {
    public StdTriangle(Point a, Point b, Point c)
                  : base(a, b, c) {}
    //------
    public override Point draw2ndLine(Graphics g,
                Point a, Point b) {
        g.DrawLine (pen, a, b);
        return b;
    }
}
```

Drawing an Isosceles Triangle

This class computes a new third data point that will make the two sides equal in length and saves that new point inside the class.

```
public class IsoscelesTriangle : Triangle       {
    private Point newc;
    private int newcx, newcy;
    //-----
    public IsoscelesTriangle(Point a, Point b, Point c) :
                base(a, b, c) {
        float dx1, dy1, dx2, dy2, side1, side2;
        float slope, intercept;
        int incr;
        dx1 = b.X - a.X;
        dy1 = b.Y - a.Y;
        dx2 = c.X  - b.X;
        dy2 = c.Y - b.Y;
```

```
                    side1 = calcSide(dx1, dy1);
                    side2 = calcSide(dx2, dy2);

                    if (side2 < side1)
                            incr = -1;
                    else
                            incr = 1;
                    slope = dy2 / dx2;
                    intercept = c.Y - slope * c.X;

                    //move point c so that this is an isosceles triangle
                    newcx = c.X;
                    newcy = c.Y;
                    while (Math.Abs (side1 - side2) > 1) {
                            //iterate a pixel at a time until close
                            newcx = newcx + incr;
                            newcy = (int)(slope * newcx + intercept);
                            dx2 = newcx - b.X;
                            dy2 = newcy - b.Y;
                            side2 = calcSide(dx2, dy2);
                    }
                    newc = new Point(newcx, newcy);
            }
            //-----
            private float calcSide(float a, float b) {
                    return (float)Math.Sqrt (a*a +  b*b);
            }
    }
```

When the Triangle class calls the *draw* method, it calls this new version of
draw2ndLine and draws a line to the new third point. Further, it returns that new
point to the *draw* method so it will draw the closing side of the triangle correctly.

```
public override Point draw2ndLine(Graphics g,
                    Point b, Point  c) {
            g.DrawLine (pen, b, newc);
            return newc;
    }
```

The Triangle Drawing Program

The main program simply creates instances of the triangles you want to draw.
Then it adds them to an ArrayList in the TriangleForm class.

```
private void init() {
        triangles = new ArrayList();
        StdTriangle t1 = new StdTriangle(new Point(10, 10),
            new Point(150, 50),
            new Point(100, 75));
        IsoscelesTriangle t2 = new IsoscelesTriangle(
            new Point(150, 100), new Point(240, 40),
```

```
              new Point(175, 150));
        triangles.Add(t1);
        triangles.Add(t2);
        Pic.Paint+= new PaintEventHandler (TPaint);
}
```

It is the *TPaint* method in this class that actually draws the triangles by calling each Triangle's *draw* method.

```
private void TPaint (object sender,
          System.Windows.Forms.PaintEventArgs e) {
      Graphics g = e.Graphics;
      for (int i = 0; i<  triangles.Count ; i++) {
            Triangle t = (Triangle)triangles[i];
            t.draw(g);
      }
}
```

A standard triangle and an isosceles triangle are shown in Figure 30-2.

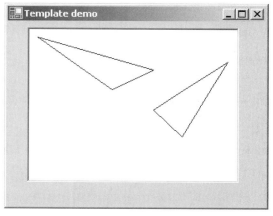

Figure 30-2 A standard triangle and an isosceles triangle

Templates and Callbacks

Design Patterns points out that Templates can exemplify the "Hollywood Principle," or "Don't call us, we'll call you." The idea here is that methods in the base class seem to call methods in the derived classes. The operative word here is *seem*. If we consider the *draw* code in our base Triangle class, we see that there are three method calls.

```
      g.DrawLine (pen, p1, p2);
      Point c = draw2ndLine(g, p2, p3);
      closeTriangle(g, c);
```

Now *drawLine* and *closeTriangle* are implemented in the base class. However, as we have seen, the *draw2ndLine* method is not implemented at all in the base class, and various derived classes can implement it differently. Since the actual methods that are being called are in the derived classes, it appears as though they are being called from the base class.

If this idea makes you uncomfortable, you will probably take solace in recognizing that *all* the method calls originate from the derived class and that these calls move up the inheritance chain until they find the first class that implements them. If this class is the base class—fine. If not, it could be any other class in between. Now when you call the *draw* method, the derived class moves up the inheritance tree until it finds an implementation of draw. Likewise, for each method called from within draw, the derived class starts at the current class and moves up the tree to find each method. When it gets to the *draw2ndLine* method, it finds it immediately in the current class. So it isn't "really" called from the base class, but it does seem that way.

Summary and Consequences

Template patterns occur all the time in OO software and are neither complex nor obscure in intent. They are a normal part of OO programming, and you shouldn't try to make them into more than they actually are.

The first significant point is that your base class may only define some of the methods it will be using, leaving the rest to be implemented in the derived classes. The second major point is that there may be methods in the base class that call a sequence of methods, some implemented in the base class and some implemented in the derived class. This Template method defines a general algorithm, although the details may not be worked out completely in the base class.

Template classes will frequently have some abstract methods that you must override in the derived classes, and they may also have some classes with a simple "placeholder" implementation that you are free to override where this is appropriate. If these placeholder classes are called from another method in the base class, then we call these overridable methods "hook" methods.

Programs on the CD-ROM

Plot strategy using Template method pattern	\Template\Stragegy
Plot of triangles	\Template\Template

CHAPTER 31

The Visitor Pattern

The Visitor pattern turns the tables on our object-oriented model and creates an external class to act on data in other classes. This is useful when you have a polymorphic operation that cannot reside in the class hierarchy for some reason—for example, because the operation wasn't considered when the hierarchy was designed or it would clutter the interface of the classes unnecessarily.

Motivation

While at first it may seem "unclean" to put operations inside one class that should be in another, there are good reasons for doing so. Suppose each of a number of drawing object classes has similar code for drawing itself. The drawing methods may be different, but they probably all use underlying utility functions that we might have to duplicate in each class. Further, a set of closely related functions is scattered throughout a number of different classes, as shown in Figure 31-1.

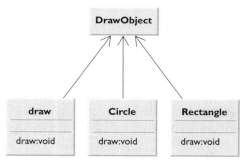

Figure 31-1   A DrawObject and three of its subclasses

Instead, we write a Visitor class that contains all the related *draw* methods and have it visit each of the objects in succession (Figure 31-2).

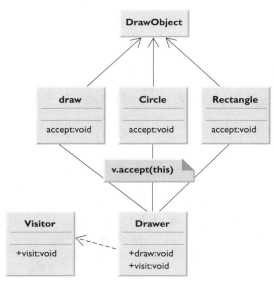

Figure 31-2   A Visitor class (Drawer) that visits each of three triangle classes

The first question that most people ask about this pattern is "What does *visiting* mean?" There is only one way that an outside class can gain access to another class, and that is by calling its public methods. In the Visitor case, visiting each class means that you are calling a method already installed for this purpose, called *accept*. The *accept* method has one argument: the instance of the visitor. In return, it calls the *visit* method of the Visitor, passing itself as an argument, as shown in Figure 31-3.

Figure 31-3   How the *visit* and *accept* methods interact

Putting it in simple code terms, every object that you want to visit must have the following method.

```
public virtual void accept(Visitor v) {
            v.visit(this);
}
```

In this way, the Visitor object receives a reference to each of the instances, one by one, and can then call its public methods to obtain data, perform calculations, generate reports, or just draw the object on the screen. Of course, if the class does not have an *accept* method, you can subclass it and add one.

When to Use the Visitor Pattern

You should consider using a Visitor pattern when you want to perform an operation on the data contained in a number of objects that have different interfaces. Visitors are also valuable if you have to perform a number of unrelated operations on these classes. Visitors are a useful way to add function to class libraries or frameworks for which you either do not have the source or cannot change the source for other technical (or political) reasons. In these latter cases, you simply subclass the classes of the framework and add the *accept* method to each subclass.

On the other hand, as we will see, Visitors are a good choice only when you do not expect many new classes to be added to your program.

Sample Code

Let's consider a simple subset of the Employee problem we discussed in the Composite pattern. We have a simple Employee object that maintains a record of the employee's name, salary, vacation taken, and number of sick days taken. The following is a simple version of this class.

```
public class Employee     {
     int sickDays, vacDays;
     float salary;
     string name;
     public Employee(string name, float salary,
          int vDays, int sDays) {
     this.name = name;
     this.salary = salary;
     sickDays = sDays;
     vacDays = vDays;
}
//-----
public string getName() {
     return name;
}
public int getSickDays() {
     return sickDays;
}
public int getVacDays() {
     return vacDays;
```

```
}
public float getSalary() {
     return salary;
}
public virtual void accept(Visitor v) {
     v.visit(this);
}
}
```

Note that we have included the *accept* method in this class. Now let's suppose that we want to prepare a report on the number of vacation days that all employees have taken so far this year. We could just write some code in the client to sum the results of calls to each Employee's *getVacDays* function, or we could put this function into a Visitor.

Since C# is a strongly typed language, our base Visitor class needs to have a suitable abstract *visit* method for each kind of class in your program. In this first simple example, we only have Employees, so our basic abstract Visitor class is just the following.

```
public abstract class Visitor    {
            public abstract void visit(Employee emp);
            public abstract void visit(Boss bos);
}
```

Notice that there is no indication what the Visitor does with each class in either the client classes or the abstract Visitor class. We can, in fact, write a whole lot of visitors that do different things to the classes in our program. The Visitor we are going to write first just sums the vacation data for all our employees.

```
public class VacationVisitor : Visitor   {
     private int totalDays;
     //-----
     public VacationVisitor()    {
            totalDays = 0;
     }
     //-----
     public int getTotalDays() {
            return totalDays;
     }
     //-----
     public override void visit(Employee emp){
            totalDays += emp.getVacDays ();
     }
     //-----
     public override void visit(Boss bos){
            totalDays += bos.getVacDays ();
     }
}
```

Visiting the Classes

Now all we have to do to compute the total vacation days taken is go through a list of the employees, visit each of them, and ask the Visitor for the total.

```
for (int i = 0;  i< empls.Length; i++) {
            empls[i].accept(vac);       //get the employee
}
lsVac.Items.Add("Total vacation days=" +
        vac.getTotalDays().ToString());
```

Let's reiterate what happens for each visit.

1. We move through a loop of all the Employees.

2. The Visitor calls each Employee's *accept* method.

3. That instance of Employee calls the Visitor's *visit* method.

4. The Visitor fetches the vacation days and adds them into the total.

5. The main program prints out the total when the loop is complete.

Visiting Several Classes

The Visitor becomes more useful when there are a number of different classes with different interfaces and we want to encapsulate how we get data from these classes. Let's extend our vacation days model by introducing a new Employee type called Boss. Let's further suppose that at this company, Bosses are rewarded with bonus vacation days (instead of money). So the Boss class has a couple of extra methods to set and obtain the bonus vacation day information.

```
public class Boss : Employee       {
     private int bonusDays;
     public Boss(string name, float salary,
          int vdays, int sdays):
                  base(name, salary, vdays, sdays) { }
     public void setBonusDays(int bdays) {
          bonusDays = bdays;
     }
     public int getBonusDays() {
          return bonusDays;
     }
     public override void accept(Visitor v ) {
          v.visit(this);
     }
}
```

When we add a class to our program, we have to add it to our Visitor as well, so that the abstract template for the Visitor is now the following.

```
public abstract class Visitor    {
     public abstract void visit(Employee emp);
     public abstract void visit(Boss bos);
}
```

This says that any concrete Visitor classes we write must provide polymorphic *visit* methods for both the Employee class and the Boss class. In the case of our vacation day counter, we need to ask the Bosses for both regular and bonus days taken, so the visits are now different. We'll write a new bVacationVisitor class that takes this difference into account.

```
public class bVacationVisitor :Visitor   {
     private int totalDays;
     public bVacationVisitor()   {
          totalDays = 0;
     }
     //-----
     public override void visit(Employee emp) {
          totalDays += emp.getVacDays();
          try {
               Manager mgr = (Manager)emp;
               totalDays += mgr.getBonusDays();
          }
          catch(Exception ){}
     }
     //-----
     public override void visit(Boss bos) {
          totalDays += bos.getVacDays();
          totalDays += bos.getBonusDays();
     }
     //-----
     public int getTotalDays() {
          return totalDays;
     }
}
```

Note that while in this case Boss is derived from Employee, it need not be related at all as long as it has an *accept* method for the Visitor class. It is quite important, however, that you implement a *visit* method in the Visitor for *every class* you will be visiting and not count on inheriting this behavior, since the *visit* method from the parent class is an Employee rather than a Boss *visit* method. Likewise, each of your derived classes (Boss, Employee, etc.) must have its own *accept* method rather than calling one in its parent class. This is illustrated in the class diagram in Figure 31-4.

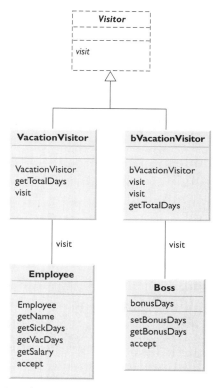

Figure 31-4   The two visitor classes visiting the Boss and Employee classes

Bosses Are Employees, Too

Figure 31-5 shows a simple application that carries out both Employee visits and Boss visits on the collection of Employees and Bosses. The original Vacation-Visitor will just treat Bosses as Employees and get only their ordinary vacation data. The bVacationVisitor will get both.

```
for (int i = 0;  i< empls.Length; i++) {
     empls[i].accept(vac);        //get the employee
     empls[i].accept(bvac);
}
lsVac.Items.Add("Total vacation days=" +
          vac.getTotalDays().ToString());
lsVac.Items.Add("Total boss vacation days=" +
          bvac.getTotalDays().ToString());
```

The two lines of displayed data represent the two sums that are computed when the user clicks on the Vacations button.

Figure 31-5   A simple application that performs the vacation visits described

Catch-All Operations with Visitors

In the preceding cases, the Visitor class has a *visit* method for each visiting class, such as the following.

```
public abstract void visit(Employee emp);
public abstract void visit(Boss bos);
```

However, if you start subclassing your visitor classes and adding new classes that might visit, you should recognize that some *visit* methods might not be satisfied by the methods in the derived class. These might instead "fall through" to methods in one of the parent classes where that object type is recognized. This provides a way of specifying default visitor behavior.

Now every class must override *accept(v)* with its own implementation so the return call *v.visit(this)* returns an object *this* of the correct type and not of the superclass's type.

Let's suppose that we introduce another layer of management into our company: the Manager. Managers are subclasses of Employees, and now they have the privileges formerly reserved for Bosses of extra vacation days. Bosses now have an additional reward—stock options. Now if we run the same program to compute vacation days but do not revise our Visitor to look for Managers, it will recognize them as mere Employees and count only their regular vacation and not their extra vacation days. However, the catch-all parent class is a good thing if subclasses may be added to the application from time to time and you want the visitor operations to continue to run without modification.

There are three ways to integrate the new Manager class into the visitor system. You could define a ManagerVisitor or use the BossVisitor to handle both. However, there could be conditions when continually modifying the Visitor structure is not desirable. In that case, you could simply test for this special case in the EmployeeVisitor class.

```
public override void visit(Employee emp) {
    totalDays += emp.getVacDays();
    try {
        Manager mgr = (Manager)emp;
        totalDays += mgr.getBonusDays();
    }
    catch(Exception ){}
}
```

While this seems "unclean" at first compared to defining classes properly, it can provide a method of catching special cases in derived classes without writing whole new visitor program hierarchies. This "catch-all" approach is discussed in some detail in the book *Pattern Hatching* (Vlissides 1998).

Double Dispatching

No discussion on the Visitor pattern is complete without mentioning that you are really dispatching a method twice for the Visitor to work. The Visitor calls the polymorphic *accept* method of a given object, and the *accept* method calls the polymorphic *visit* method of the Visitor. It is this bidirectional calling that allows you to add more operations on any class that has an *accept* method, since each new Visitor class we write can carry out whatever operations we might think of using the data available in these classes.

Why Are We Doing This?

You may be asking yourself, "Why we are jumping through these hoops when we could call the getVacationDays methods directly?" By using this "callback" approach, we are implementing "double dispatching." There is no requirement that the objects we visit be of the same or even of related types. Further, using this callback approach, you can have a different visit method called in the Visitor, depending on the actual type of class. This is harder to implement directly.

Further, if the list of objects to be visited in an ArrayList is a collection of different types, having different versions of the visit methods in the actual Visitor is the only way to handle the problem without specifically checking the type of each class.

Traversing a Series of Classes

The calling program that passes the class instances to the Visitor must know about all the existing instances of classes to be visited and must keep them in a simple structure such as an array or collection. Another possibility would be to create an Enumeration of these classes and pass it to the Visitor. Finally, the Visitor itself could keep the list of objects that it is to visit. In our simple example program, we used an array of objects, but any of the other methods would work equally well.

Consequences of the Visitor Pattern

The Visitor pattern is useful when you want to encapsulate fetching data from a number of instances of several classes. *Design Patterns* suggests that the Visitor can provide additional functionality to a class without changing it. We prefer to say that a Visitor can add functionality to a collection of classes and encapsulate the methods it uses.

The Visitor is not magic, however, and cannot obtain private data from classes. It is limited to the data available from public methods. This might force you to provide public methods that you would otherwise not have provided. However, it can obtain data from a disparate collection of unrelated classes and utilize it to present the results of a global calculation to the user program.

It is easy to add new operations to a program using Visitors, since the Visitor contains the code instead of each of the individual classes. Further, Visitors can gather related operations into a single class rather than forcing you to change or derive classes to add these operations. This can make the program simpler to write and maintain.

Visitors are less helpful during a program's growth stage, since each time you add new classes that must be visited, you have to add an abstract *visit* operation to the abstract Visitor class, and you must add an implementation for that class to each concrete Visitor you have written. Visitors can be powerful additions when the program reaches the point where many new classes are unlikely.

Visitors can be used very effectively in Composite systems, and the boss-employee system we just illustrated could well be a Composite like the one we used in the Composite chapter.

Thought Question

An investment firm's customer records consist of an object for each stock or other financial instrument each investor owns. The object contains a history of the purchase, sale, and dividend activities for that stock. Design a Visitor pattern to report on net end-of-year profit or loss on stocks sold during the year.

Program on the CD-ROM

Visitor Example	\Visitor\

BIBLIOGRAPHY

Alexander, C., Ishikawa, S., Silverstein, M., Jacobson, M., Fiksdahtking, L., and Angel, S. *A Pattern Language,* Oxford University Press, New York, 1977.

Alpert, S. R., Brown, K., and Woolf, B. *The Design Patterns Smalltalk Companion,* Addison-Wesley, Reading, MA, 1998.

Arnold, K., and Gosling, J. *The Java Programming Language,* Addison-Wesley, Reading, MA, 1996.

Booch, G., Jacobson, I., and Rumbaugh, J. *The Unified Modeling Language User Guide,* Addison-Wesley, Reading, MA, 1999.

Buschmann, F., Meunier, R., Rohnert, H., Sommerlad, P., and Stal, M. *A System of Patterns,* John Wiley and Sons, New York, 1996.

Cooper, J. W. *Java Design Patterns: A Tutorial,* Addison-Wesley, Boston, MA, 2000.

————. *Principles of Object-Oriented Programming in Java 1.1,* Coriolis (Ventana), 1997.

————. *Visual Basic Design Patterns: VB6 and VB.NET,* Addison-Wesley, Boston, MA, 2002.

Coplien, J. O. *Advanced C++ Programming Styles and Idioms,* Addison-Wesley, Reading, MA, 1992.

Coplien, J. O., and Schmidt, D. C. *Pattern Languages of Program Design,* Addison-Wesley, Reading, MA, 1995.

Fowler, M., with K. Scott. *UML Distilled,* Addison-Wesley, Reading, MA,1997.

Gamma, E. *Object-Oriented Software Development Based on BT+: Design Patterns, ClassLibrary, Tools* (in German), Springer-Verlag, Berlin, 1992.

Gamma, E., Helm, T., Johnson, R., and Vlissides, J. *Design Patterns: Abstraction and Reuse of Object Oriented Design.* Proceedings of ECOOP '93, 405–431.

————. *Design Patterns. Elements of Reusable Software,* Addison-Wesley, Reading, MA, 1995.

Grand, M. *Patterns in Java,* Volume 1, John Wiley & Sons, New York, 1998.

Krasner, G. E., and Pope, S. T. "A cookbook for using the Model-View-Controller user interface paradigm in Smalltalk-80." *Journal of Object-Oriented Programming* I(3), 1988.

Kurata, D. "Programming with objects." *Visual Basic Programmer's Journal,* June 1998.

Pree, W. *Design Patterns for Object-Oriented Software Development,* Addison-Wesley, 1995.

Riel, A. J. *Object-Oriented Design Heuristics,* Addison-Wesley, Reading, MA, 1996.

Vlissides, J. *Pattern Hatching: Design Patterns Applied,* Addison-Wesley, Reading, MA. 1998.

INDEX

Note: *Italicized* page locators refer to figures/tables.

Also Available from Addison-Wesley

Visual Basic Design Patterns

VB 6.0 and VB.NET

By James W. Cooper

0-201-70265-7
512 pages with CD-ROM
© 2002

A practical guide to writing Visual Basic (VB6 and VB.NET) programs using some of the most common design patterns, *Visual Basic Design Patterns* is a tutorial for people who want to learn about design patterns and how to use them in their work. This book also provides a convenient way for VB6 programmers to migrate to VB.NET and use its more powerful object-oriented features.

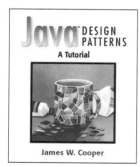

Java™ Design Patterns

A Tutorial

By James W. Cooper

0-201-48539-7
352 pages with CD-ROM
© 2000

This book presents the 23 patterns cataloged in the flagship book *Design Patterns* by Gamma, Helm, Johnson, and Vlissides. In *Java™ Design Patterns*, each of these patterns is illustrated by at least one complete visual Java program. This practical approach makes design pattern concepts more concrete and easier to grasp, brings Java programmers up to speed quickly, and enables you to take practical advantage of the power of design patterns.

CD-ROM Warranty

Addison-Wesley warrants the enclosed disc to be free of defects in materials and faulty work-manship under normal use for a period of ninety days after purchase. If a defect is discovered in the disc during this warranty period, a replacement disc can be obtained at no charge by sending the defective disc, postage prepaid, with proof of purchase to:

Editorial Department
Addison-Wesley Professional
Pearson Technology Group
75 Arlington Street, Suite 300
Boston, MA 02116
Email: AWPro@awl.com

Addison-Wesley makes no warranty or representation, either expressed or implied, with respect to this software, its quality, performance, merchantability, or fitness for a particular purpose. In no event will Addison-Wesley, its distributors, or dealers be liable for direct, indirect, special, incidental, or consequential damages arising out of the use or inability to use the software. The exclusion of implied royalties is not permitted in some states. Therefore, the above exclusion may not apply to you. This warranty provides you with specific legal rights. There may be other rights that you may have that vary from state to state. The contents of this CD-ROM are intend-ed for personal use only.

More information and updates are available at:
http://www.awprofessional.com/